TAX PLANNING
FOR YOU AND YOUR FAMILY
1998

D1104964

Prepared by

Editors-in-Chief	*Contributing KPMG Editors*
S. Brian Fisher, CA Waterloo	Joanne Ivanski, LL.B., CA Montréal
Wayne L. Tunney, FCA Toronto	Benita Loughlin, CA Burnaby/New Westminster
Editor	Michael C. Morgan, LL.M. Toronto
Joseph Petrie, BA Toronto	Judy A. Rothwell, CGA Vancouver
	Dereka Thibault, CA Calgary
	Mark Worrall, CA

Canadian Cataloguing in Publication Data

The National Library of Canada has catalogued this publication as follows:

Main entry under title:
Tax planning for you and your family

Annual.
1997 -
Continues: Personal tax planning guide (Scarborough, Ont.).
ISSN 1207-5957
ISBN 0-459-57596-1 (1998)

1. Tax planning - Canada - Popular works - Periodicals.
2. Income tax - Canada - Popular works - Periodicals.
I. KPMG (Firm).

KE5759.Y43   343.7105'2'05   C96-900735-3
KF6499.ZA2Y43

Printed in Canada.

CARSWELL
Thomson Professional Publishing

One Corporate Plaza
2075 Kennedy Road
Scarborough, Ontario
M1T 3V4

Customer Service:
Toronto: 1-416-609-3800
Elsewhere in Canada/U.S.: 1-800-387-5164
Fax: 1-416-298-5094

This book has been printed on text paper which meets Environmental Canada's and the Canadian Standards Association's "Environmental Choice Program" guidelines for recycled fibre content and environmentally safe manufacturing processes.

Overview

Table of Contents

Introduction

Many Canadians don't give much thought to how they can reduce their taxes until it's time to file their tax returns each Spring. By then, many tax saving opportunities may be lost. Filing your tax return is essentially a once-a-year accounting to the government to settle up your taxes owing or refund due for the previous year. It's the tax planning steps that you take throughout each year that will save the most money at tax time and in the years to come.

In this book we set out the most common rules and tax planning techniques that are currently available to individuals, but our emphasis is on tax planning aimed at minimizing your family's overall tax bill. Although many of the tax rules are designed in contemplation of the traditional family model, our advice is equally relevant to modern households of all types — whether you are part of a dual-income couple with children, a single or divorced parent, a common-law couple, a student or a retiree, you'll find that a few hours invested in reading this book can pay off substantially in tax savings and in the organization of your financial affairs.

Tax planning should comprise only one aspect of your family's overall financial plan. Chapter 1 discusses how tax planning can serve to facilitate the achievement of your financial goals. Your answers to the quiz in Chapter 1 will provide you with a quick check up on your financial health. The rest of this chapter provides an important overview of the financial planning framework in which your tax planning should take place, including tips for securing your family's financial future, buying a home, saving for your children's education and growing your retirement fund.

The balance of this book offers plain-language explanations of Canada's personal income tax system, along with a wealth of tax saving ideas. Key tax planning points are listed at the beginning of each chapter and highlighted in the body of the chapter itself — if you wish, you can skip directly to the planning techniques that will benefit you most.

At the end of most chapters we include references to publications that are available from Revenue Canada. These publications are a good source of more detailed information on the topics discussed.

What exactly is tax planning?

Tax planning is a perfectly legitimate activity. There is nothing shady about it. You are entitled to arrange your affairs, within the limits of the law, so that you pay a minimum amount of tax.

Tax evasion is a different story. Evasion is illegal. You are evading tax if you fail to report income or if you misstate facts so as to claim deductions or credits to which you are not entitled. If you evade tax, you will be subject to interest, penalties, fines and possibly imprisonment as well as being required to pay the tax owing.

Tax avoidance is the somewhat nebulous activity of using the tax system in a way in which it was not intended. The *Income Tax Act* contains a general anti-avoidance rule (GAAR), which can apply to avoidance activities. If you misuse or abuse the provisions of the Act, you may run into GAAR. The line between tax planning and tax avoidance is not always clear.

Note that Revenue Canada does not make the law. The *Income Tax Act* is enacted and amended by Parliament. Revenue Canada's role is to administer and enforce the Act. In this book we will occasionally refer to "Revenue Canada's position" on a particular matter, to indicate that this is an administrative position rather than a matter of law.

If you disagree with Revenue Canada's interpretation of a particular rule, and you have a good legal basis for doing so, you can object to an assessment or reassessment by filing a Notice of Objection, and, if you wish, appealing the case to the Tax Court of Canada.

This book cannot replace your tax advisor.

This book deals only in general terms. The Canadian tax system is horrendously complex, far more than the book makes it appear. The details fill shelves, not a thin book. Even if your affairs are relatively simple, you should consult a qualified tax professional (not just tax return preparer). You will likely find the savings far outweigh the fees.

The book does not go very far in dealing with the tax treatment of businesses, whether incorporated or unincorporated. Only brief treatment is given to this topic in Chapters 8 and 9. If you carry on your own business, or manage a corporation, you will benefit greatly from personalized tax advice.

The income tax system has undergone massive and rapid change over the past few years, and the process continues. If you thought you knew the rules a couple of years ago, you may find they have changed. We also cannot predict what changes are in store for the future. This book is current to July 25, 1997, and reflects the law and publicly-announced proposals for changes as of that date.

For current tax information and other KPMG tax publications — including KPMG's Canadian Tax Tip of the Day — visit our World Wide Web site at **www.kpmg.ca**.

KPMG
Chartered Accountants

Tips for achieving your financial goals

■ Define your short- and long-term financial planning goals (1.1.2)

■ Track your net worth and cash flow, and set an annual growth target (1.1.3 and 1.1.4)

■ Repay your consumer debts—the interest on these debts is likely more than your after-tax return on your investments (1.1.3)

■ Save systematically by "paying yourself first" (1.1.4)

■ Make sure you have adequate insurance (1.2.2)

■ Think about implementing an "asset allocation" plan to optimize your investment mix (1.2.5)

■ Save for your child's education with an RESP or growth mutual funds (1.3.1)

■ Encourage your children to invest the money they earn (1.3.1)

■ Think about using RRSP funds for a down payment on your first home under the Home Buyers' Plan (1.3.2)

■ Consider GST and provincial sales tax when buying a home (1.3.2)

■ Increase the frequency of your mortgage payments to reduce your mortgage interest (1.3.2)

■ Plan to minimize capital gains tax on dispositions of vacation homes (1.3.3)

■ Consider topping up your RRSP and using the tax refund to pay down your mortgage (1.3.4)

■ Shop around when choosing your financial advisors (1.4)

In this chapter we offer a primer on financial planning with emphasis on the impact of taxes on your ability to meet your family's financial goals. We also point out tax planning ideas elsewhere in this book that may help you to achieve these goals.

1.1 Developing your financial plan

For many Canadians at all stages in life, the very idea of financial planning is fraught with anxiety. It shouldn't be. Saving for retirement, financing your child's education or buying a house are within the reach of most of us—the purpose of financial planning is to clarify your objectives, set a realistic timetable for meeting them, and marshal your financial resources to support your plan. Of course, the process may require lowering your expectations, paring down your current lifestyle or other compromises. But having a sound financial plan will likely ease your financial stress by giving you a realistic picture of your family's finances and a clear path for satisfying your goals.

Since taxes are one of the biggest expenses for most of us, tax planning to minimize your family's overall tax bill should be an integral part of your family's financial plan. The balance of this book is full of ideas about how to save taxes; the rest of this chapter is an overview of the financial planning framework in which your tax planning should take place.

1.1.1 Are you financially fit?

How secure is your financial future? Take the following quiz to find out. Depending on how high you score, you may wish to simply scan the ideas in the rest of this chapter and go straight to Chapter 2. But if you score less than 16 points, you probably stand to benefit from a more thorough reading of the financial planning overview in this chapter before you move on.

	Yes	No
1. Have you sat down to determine your lifestyle goals, in the past two years?	❏	❏
2. Have you determined if your financial resources can meet those goals?	❏	❏
3. Are you satisfied with the amount of money you are saving?	❏	❏
4. Have you reviewed and updated these documents, in the past two years:		
■ Your will?	❏	❏
■ Your net worth statement?	❏	❏
■ Your disability income insurance policies?	❏	❏
■ Your excess liability (umbrella) insurance policy?	❏	❏
5. Do you have a power of attorney?	❏	❏
6. Do you have sufficient insurance coverage?	❏	❏
7. Do you contribute the maximum to an RRSP each year?	❏	❏
8. Do you make your maximum RRSP contribution within the first three months of the year?	❏	❏
9. Are you satisfied with the performance of your investments, both inside and outside your RRSP?	❏	❏
10. Have you determined your short- and long-term investment strategies?	❏	❏
11. If you have children, have you established a university/ college fund for them?	❏	❏

	Yes	No
12. Have you established an emergency fund or personal line of credit?	❏	❏
13. Do you take advantage of all tax deductions available to you?	❏	❏
14. Is the interest on your loans tax deductible?	❏	❏
15. Have you done all you can to shelter your income from taxes?	❏	❏
16. Have you used your $500,000 capital gains exemption?	❏	❏
17. If not, have you taken all possible steps to crystallize the exemption?	❏	❏
18. If you have a future tax liability, are you able to fund that obligation?	❏	❏
19. Do you know your projected income tax before the year ends?	❏	❏
20. Are you a member of a company pension plan?	❏	❏
21. Are you aware of all the benefits available through the company pension plan?	❏	❏
22. Are you maintaining a retirement fund outside of your company pension plan?	❏	❏
23. Have you determined how much income you can expect on retirement?	❏	❏
24. Do you know if your expected retirement income will meet your lifestyle needs?	❏	❏
25. Do you feel in control of your financial future?	❏	❏

Now total your points—if you answered "yes" to . . .

- **17 to 25 questions:** Congratulations, you're in great shape.
- **9 to 16 questions:** You're on your way but there is still room for improvement. Consider talking to a qualified financial counsellor, who can give good advice on putting your affairs in a better state.
- **0 to 8 questions:** You need to do some serious work. Start by reading through the rest of this chapter. Once you know the basics, consider meeting with a qualified financial advisor to develop a plan for getting into shape.

1.1.2 Defining your financial goals

Putting your dreams on paper is the first step toward realizing them. Start by setting down what you want and when you want it. If you have a spouse or domestic partner, compile your list together, compromising where necessary to make sure that you are both committed to the same objectives. You might also include your children and have them develop their own plan as a teaching exercise.

While your list should take into account your family's well-being and future financial security, be sure to include lifestyle-enhancing items like vacation homes, major renovations, luxury cars or swimming pools. If you want to take a sabbatical from work to spend time with your children or eventually start your own business, write it down. As part of this exercise, consider the discussion of important financial safeguards in 1.2 and common financial goals in 1.3.

When you have completed your list, divide it into short-, medium- and long-term goals and rank them in order of priority within each section. Set down a timeframe for meeting each goal. Then do a bit of research and cost out your goals, making sure to account for inflation. Don't let the numbers overwhelm you—over time the effects of compound growth can provide significant returns on your investments. Nevertheless, you may need to revise your list by allowing more time to achieve a certain goal or by dropping items that are beyond your means.

As time goes by, your list will serve as a guide for directing your savings and investments and as an indicator of your progress. Since your personal and financial circumstances and goals are bound to change, revisit your list once or twice a year and revise it to reflect new priorities.

1.1.3 Tracking your net worth

Now that you have a better idea of where you want to go, the next step is to figure out your starting point—your net worth. Calculating your net worth is simply a matter of adding up your total assets (what you own) and total liabilities (what you owe), and then subtracting your liabilities from your assets. The resulting figure is the springboard for most aspects of financial management and planning.

It's also a good idea to separate your assets by ownership—whether your assets are owned by you, your spouse or jointly can help in determining potential strategies for income splitting (see Chapter 4) and estate planning (see Chapter 13).

A close look at your assets will show you whether most of your assets are personal items, such as your home or your car, or investment assets, such as savings and shares. It should show you how liquid your assets are and help you determine if your investments are spread appropriately to balance expected rates of return with the degree of risk you are prepared to take (see 1.2.5).

Repay your consumer debts—the interest on the debt is likely to cost more than the after-tax return you make on your investments.

Similarly, a close look at your liabilities will show you whether your insurance coverage is adequate (see 1.2.2) and how your debts are affecting your bottom line. As we'll see in 6.2.3, interest on credit card balances, consumer loans and mortgages is not deductible for tax purposes, while interest on loans taken out to purchase income-generating investments is deductible. As a result, the interest on your consumer debts may cost you more than you make on your investments. Where possible, you should try to pay down your consumer debts and make sure that all loans you take out are for a tax deductible purpose.

Set an annual target for increasing your net worth.

Updating your net worth calculation once or twice a year is a good way to track your financial health. If you are able to increase your net worth by 15% each year, your net worth will double every five years. Ways to increase your net worth include:

- improving the rate of return on your investments;
- investing more of your income by spending less on discretionary items and minimizing taxes; and
- reducing your debt by paying off your credit card balances and accelerating your mortgage and other debt payments.

One simple rule of thumb for determining how quickly your assets will grow is to use the "Rule of 72". By taking the number 72 and dividing it by the average growth rate of your assets, you can calculate the number of years it will take to double your assets. For example, if your annual growth rate is 8%, then your assets will double in value every 9 years ($72 \div 8\% = 9$).

1.1.4 Budget to control your spending and saving

The formula for accruing the necessary funds to achieve your financial goals is no secret. Unless you expect to inherit money or win a lottery, the way to start building wealth is to save and invest a regular portion of your income. Through the mathematical "miracle" of compounding, your investment assets will grow exponentially. So the more savings you have to invest and the longer they are invested, the higher your worth will be.

As noted above, reducing your taxes through tax planning measures is one way to increase your net worth. Another way is to gain better control over your savings and expenses with a personal or family budget. Listing the amounts of money you expect to receive and pay out monthly (or over another period) for necessities and discretionary items allows you to realistically assess your cash flow and spend your money where you need and want to.

Without making lifestyle changes, there is little you can do about your mortgage payments, car payments and other fixed expenses. However, the exercise of preparing—and sticking to—a budget will probably reveal opportunities to easily reduce your variable expenses such as groceries, entertainment and gifts. There are plenty of excellent software packages available that can help you create and monitor your family budget.

Save systematically by "paying yourself first".

When preparing your budget, do not simply plan to save the amount left over at the end of each month—chances are there won't be as much left as you intended. Instead, get into the practice of saving a fixed amount of at least 10% of your income at the beginning of each month (or some other period) and using the balance for your expenses. Commonly known as the "pay yourself first" plan, this technique helps you to save systematically and to be less prone to making impulsive or needlessly expensive purchases. Although it may take you a few months to get used to having less cash readily available, you will probably be surprised at how quickly you will adjust. Consider having your financial institution automatically transfer your savings amount to a separate bank account or registered retirement savings plan ("RRSP") (see Chapter 3) on a monthly or other regular basis.

1.2 Preserving your family's financial security

The achievement of your financial goals can be delayed or derailed by unexpected changes of circumstance. Your family's financial plan should include measures to protect your family's financial security.

1.2.1 Do you have a line of credit and/or an emergency fund?

In today's economic and business environment you can no longer count on having a job for life. Job loss can also affect your company-funded benefits and pension plan. Generally speaking, you should have an emergency fund large enough to handle the loss of a job for six months to one year. Canada Savings Bonds, money market funds and cashable guaranteed investment certificates are good places to park emergency reserves.

Another way to provide an emergency fund is to establish a line of credit with your financial institution. Be careful to only use it when necessary, because the interest you'll incur will be non-deductible.

1.2.2 Do you have enough insurance?

Review your insurance needs with your financial advisors to determine the appropriate amount and form of your insurance coverage in various areas, including property loss, death, disability, sickness, personal liability and liquidity crisis.

Make sure you have adequate insurance.

A review should consider your need for life insurance. In the event of your death, life insurance may be critical for providing replacement income for your dependants and for funding your estate's tax liability. Life insurance plays many other important roles in estate planning. Some tax planning and other issues involving life insurance are discussed in 13.6.

One of your most valuable assets is your ability to earn income through employment or self-employment. Review your need for disability insurance—if you become disabled, the financial consequences can be devastating. Most disability insurance policies do not provide a level of income over and above what you need for basic ongoing living expenses. In the long-term, this could leave you without enough funds set aside for your retirement since disability income usually stops at age 65.

Make sure you have sufficient insurance to protect you from significant financial loss due to damage or destruction to your home, automobile or other personal assets. Without adequate coverage, the emotional trauma of such losses could be compounded by irreversible damage to your family's finances. Depending on your occupation or circumstances, you should also assess your need for other forms of insurance such as health and professional or director's liability coverage.

1.2.3 Is your will up-to-date?

Have you and your family members reviewed your will within the past five years, or since there has been a change in your family circumstances? Are your wills effectively tax-structured? Remember that if you die intestate (without a will) your assets will be distributed according to provincial law, possibly differently from what you would have wished. This may be particularly true for those in relationships not covered by provincial law, such as same-sex couples. Be sure to seek advice of a lawyer (or a notary in Québec) to ensure your will is legally valid and accurately reflects your wishes. You should also consult a tax advisor for assistance in reducing your estate's tax liability, including probate fees, income tax, and U.S. estate tax.

For a more detailed discussion of the role of your will in planning for the orderly distribution of your estate and the minimization of taxes on death, see 13.2.

1.2.4 Do you have a power of attorney?

A power of attorney allows you to designate a person who will take control of your financial affairs if you become incapacitated due to illness or injury. If this happens and you do not have a power of attorney, control will yield to a provincial public trustee which may hamstring your family's ability to access your financial resources.

Powers of attorney are usually limited to decisions regarding your finances. In some provinces (including Ontario and Québec), you can empower a different person to make decisions about your health care and medical treatment.

Like your will, your power of attorney should be prepared with professional advice—consider having both drawn up at the same time.

Note that a power of attorney operates only while you are alive. Once you die your will takes over.

1.2.5 **Do you have an appropriate investment strategy?**

Today's economic realities are forcing Canadians to take care of their own financial health. Even with professional advisors, most investors still take an active interest in their investment activities. But the average investor spends 90% of his or her time picking individual stocks and GICs, a practice that generally adds little to a portfolio's incremental return.

Think about implementing an "asset allocation" plan to optimize your investment mix.

Modern investment wisdom says that it's not what you select but where you select it from. Known as "asset allocation", this process works as well for $100,000 as it does for $1 million. Simply put, asset allocation is the process of deciding how to invest a pool of resources among a broad array of assets. It is considered the single most important part of managing a portfolio. According to Ibbotsen Associates of Chicago, Illinois, over 90% of a portfolio's investment return is derived from the appropriate asset allocation mix. The actual securities selection contributes only 5% - 10% of the overall return.

Asset allocation has three levels. The first level entails selecting between asset classes: cash, fixed income, and equities.

After that, a second level decision includes determining market exposure—in many cases, you would be wise to diversify your investments geographically. Most Canadians are satisfied with owning some U.S. stocks, but this usually doesn't allow enough diversification because the North American markets strongly influence each other. As we'll see in 3.1.6, there is a 20% foreign content limit for registered retirement savings plans. One way to beat the cap is to look for Canadian companies that conduct most of their business offshore.

The third level of asset allocation is deciding the currency exposure, commonly known as "hedging." This was recently illustrated by the 25% rebound in the Japanese stock market as the yen dropped by the same value against the U.S. dollar. A North American investor would be no further ahead unless he or she was hedged.

Along with these three levels, asset allocation comes in two forms: strategic and tactical. Strategic asset allocation is a long-term scheme that divides a portfolio among several asset classes according to the inherent risks and reward of each asset. Tactical allocation consists of short-term market predictions that could last an hour or a day. This type of allocation proves difficult because variables used in selecting an asset mix continually change and the portfolio must be adjusted to keep up with market movements. Other disadvantages include higher fees, lack of liquidity in esoteric markets like precious metals, and the potential to misread economic signals.

While there is no perfect asset allocation for any one person, there are definitely wrong ones. The following are some tips for getting the right mix.

Determine your objectives and risk tolerance—Before you make any investment decisions, determine your objectives and risk tolerance and then do an asset allocation. Risk tolerance is determined by your age and your family situation. For example, a 55-year-old newlywed with two young child is in a dramatically different situation than an empty-nester or single person of the same age.

Risk tolerance should also reflect your ability to replace losses. For a partner in a major law firm earning $500,000 who owns a house and has thousands of dollars in RRSPs, a loss of $50,000 in the market is replaceable. But for someone with no employment income, such a loss would be devastating. Asset allocation has to be a function of your own profile and risk tolerance. If it's right you should be able to sleep well in any market environment.

Don't separate registered from non-registered investments—Most investors make a classic mistake at the outset by separating registered from non-registered investments. As a result, whether the money is in an RRSP or not is irrelevant to the asset allocation decision. All of your assets should be amalgamated so that the right proportion of assets can be determined. Once the asset allocation is done, then you can decide, from a tax perspective, which investments are more effective to hold inside an RRSP.

Plan for a long horizon and stay on course—Once you have determined your asset allocation, let your investments grow over at least five to seven years, long enough to go through a full market cycle. Average investors often make the mistake of buying what's hot because they think it's a great time to be in the market, then panic and sell as soon as the stock goes down. A disciplined approach to long-term asset allocation will serve you better in the long run.

Pay attention to fees—Be wary of management fees. A saving in fees of 1% per annum on a $100,000 investment earning a 10% annual return for 10 years could save you well over $20,000. You can't control the market, but you can control the fees you'll eventually pay.

Don't forget inflation—Inflation is another factor you can't control. Don't make the mistake of thinking of money in nominal terms instead of its real value. If your money isn't growing, you're losing it. Consider a $1,000 investment earning an average rate of return of 10% per year. After 10 years, the investment will be worth $2,594, but inflation will have eroded its real value. Assuming an annual inflation rate of 3%, this erosion will amount to $627 by the end of the tenth year, bringing the investment's real value down at that time to $1,967.

Rebalance annually—One of the most powerful tools you can use in managing your investments is a regular discipline of portfolio rebalancing. This allows you to manage your investments for profit, by selling low and buying high.

For example, you may have decided originally that an investment mix of 40% in stocks and 60% in bonds met your objectives. However, due to a properous period in the economy, you find that the stock component of your portfolio grows to 55% while bonds now represent only 45% by value. In this case, the discipline of strategic asset allocation should force you to take profits and rebalance your original mix so that when the economy reverses—as it always does—you will be positioned to take advantage of the change.

Don't try to outsmart the market—Focus your attention on getting the asset allocation right and then, within each asset class, try to keep your costs at a minimum. Make sure you are well diversified. Be consistent in your investment style. Don't think that what happened in the past will happen in the future. In the financial market, history rarely repeats.

1.3 Some common financial goals

1.3.1 Planning your children's education

Although post-secondary education may not be the route your child chooses, having a college degree or university diploma can greatly expand their range of occupational choices and will probably enhance their future earning power. But with government support for post-secondary institutions falling and tuition fees on the rise, putting a child through college or university is becoming increasingly costly—depending where your child attends school, the cost is currently about $10,000 per year in Canada when you factor in tuition, books and living expenses. If your child decides to study outside Canada, the cost will increase exponentially. Most of us would be hard-pressed to finance these costs out of current income, so planning ahead is crucial.

Like any financial planning endeavour, decisions about funding your child's education should be made with an eye toward the effects of taxation. Below are a few common techniques for reducing your family's overall tax burden so that more funds will be available to finance your child's education.

Think about starting a "registered education savings plan".

Registered education savings plans ("RESPs") are discussed at 3.6. Unlike RRSPs, contributions to RESPs aren't tax-deductible but the income in the

RESP grows tax-free, so RESPs enjoy the effect of tax-free compounding of interest. When your child goes to college or university, the RESP provides an income to help cover the child's expenses. The income will be taxable to the child, who normally won't have much other income and so will pay little or no tax. Among other changes to make RESPs more attractive, the 1997 federal and Québec budgets raised maximum RESP contributions for 1997 and later years to $4,000 per year (up from $2,000). You can contribute up to $42,000 over your lifetime in respect of any one beneficiary. Start early to maximize the tax-free growth. See 3.6 for more details.

Invest in growth mutual funds.

As an alternative to an RESP, you could invest in growth mutual funds in your child's name. Any income from these funds is normally taxed under the preferential rules for capital gains (see Chapter 5) or dividends (see Chapter 6). In addition, any capital gains distributed by the fund or on the sale of the fund will be taxable in your child's hands at your child's lower tax rate (or not taxed at all if his or her income is low enough). Until your child turns 18, the dividends and interest will be taxed in your hands due to the attribution rules discussed in 4.2.3; however, this will usually amount to a small proportion of the fund's overall return. A mutual fund provides more investment control and flexibility. Unlike RESPs, if your child decides not to pursue further education after graduating from high school, there are no restrictions on the use of the funds, and there is no limit on the amount that can be deposited annually.

Bank your Child Tax Benefit payments.

If you receive Child Tax Benefit payments (see 2.3.1), think about depositing them to an account in your child's name. As with RESP funds, these deposits may add up to a significant investment over time and, since the anti-income splitting rules discussed in Chapter 4 don't apply, any investment income earned on the funds will be taxed in your child's hands. You may wish to withdraw the balance from the account annually and purchase higher-yielding bonds and term deposits on your child's behalf.

Have your children file tax returns to build RRSP contribution room.

If you have a child who works part-time (e.g., summer employment, paper route, etc.) with an income below the basic amount of $6,456 that can be earned tax-free (see 2.2), you might consider filing a tax return for him or her to report the earned income for RRSP purposes and allow the build up of an unused contribution limit, which may be of use in a later year when he or she becomes taxable (see 3.1.3). This can be especially useful when your child is in the teenage years and can expect to earn much more income in the future, since the unused deduction room can be carried forward indefinitely.

Also, instead of giving your child money which is easily spent, consider having him or her start an RRSP. The amount you can contribute may seem minimal—only 18% of the child's earned income from a summer or part-time job, plus the $2,000 lifetime overcontribution if the child turned 18 in the prior year (see 3.3.4). But the funds in the RRSP will enjoy tax-free compounding, which will accumulate significantly over time. For example, assuming an 8% rate of return, $1,000 a year invested in an RRSP at the end of each year beginning at age 16 will grow to $7,336 by the beginning of the year in which the child turns 22; at age 30, the RRSP will grow to $24,215, and if the annual contribution is made until the child retires at 65, the RRSP will be $530,000.

Encourage your children to invest the money they earn.

To top up your child's earnings and help finance his or her education (or other pursuits), consider lending your child, interest-free, an amount equal to what he or she earns over the year and would otherwise spend. Your child can use the loaned funds to pay for expenses such as tuition fees and invest his or her own income to earn investment income. That way, the anti-income splitting rules discussed in Chapter 4 will not attribute the investment income back to you and it will be taxed at your child's lower tax rate (or not taxed at all if his or her income is low enough). Later on, perhaps after graduating, your child can pay you back out of the invested funds, or keep the funds as "seed money" for their early working years. (This strategy is discussed in more detail in 4.3.11.)

Look into other income splitting techniques.

Chapter 4 discusses a number of techniques for splitting income with children. These strategies can significantly lower your family's overall tax burden, and the savings are bound to come in handy whether or not your child ultimately pursues a post-secondary education.

1.3.2 Buying a home

If you are renting living accommodations, instead of buying, you're missing out on one of the best investment opportunities around. A home can be a reliable hedge against inflation, a great retirement savings vehicle and a tax shelter—as we'll see in 5.5.2. If you own a home and sell it for a gain, the gain is usually tax-free as long as it has been your principal residence.

So if you can afford to buy a home, don't rent. If you are renting while you are saving for a home, consider moving to less expensive rental accommodations and saving more toward your down payment. The sooner you start putting your money in a mortgage instead of your landlord's pocket, the better off you will be. Below are a few tax planning and other issues for prospective home buyers to consider.

Make sure you can cover all the extras.

Most first-time home buyers quickly find out that the price of a new home and the interest cost in financing a mortgage are just the beginning. New home owners also need to cover substantial ongoing costs that were previously included in their rent, such as repairs, utilities, insurance and property taxes. There will also be a number of one-time costs associated with the purchase, including legal fees, moving expenses, and land transfer taxes in certain provinces. Depending on the home you buy, you should also be prepared to bear the costs of decorating a new home, or redecorating or substantially remodelling an existing house.

Look into the Home Buyers' Plan.

If you qualify, the Home Buyers' Plan can be a possible source of cash for financing your down payment. If you are saving to buy your first home, think about using your RRSP as your savings vehicle; under the Home Buyers' Plan discussed at 3.3.6, if you qualify, you can generally withdraw up to $20,000 as a loan from your RRSP to buy or build a home, without counting the withdrawal as income. You must then repay the loan, without interest, over the next 16 years.

If you do plan to withdraw RRSP funds under the Home Buyers' Plan, consider making your RRSP contribution for the year at least 90 days before you make the withdrawal to preserve your ability to deduct the contribution amount. If you are depending on your RRSP for retirement income, you will want to forecast the decline in income that will result from the loss of the tax-free compounding when you withdraw a large chunk of RRSP funds now and pay it back over the next 16 years. See 3.3.6 for a more detailed discussion of the Home Buyers' Plan.

Consider GST and provincial sales tax when buying a new home.

Since no sales tax applies to used houses, a resale home may be cheaper than a new home. Sales of new homes in Nova Scotia, New Brunswick and Newfoundland attract Harmonized Sales Tax ("HST"—see 8.2.5) at a 15% rate (the combined 7% federal and 8% provincial rates). In Québec, new home sales attract the 7% Goods and Services Tax ("GST") and Québec Sales Tax at 6.5% of the sale price including GST. New home sales in the rest of Canada attract GST at the regular 7% rate. However, if you buy a new home as your principal place of residence (or the principal residence of someone related to you), you may be entitled to a partial sales tax rebate.

Buyers of qualifying new homes priced under $450,000 can claim a partial rebate of the GST payable on the purchase (including the 7% portion of the HST in the above Atlantic provinces). The rebate is available either from Revenue Canada or directly from the vendor—in the latter case, you will pay the vendor less than the full 7% GST. For homes priced under $347,222 (before GST), the rebate is 2.52% of the purchase price and from that point to $350,000 it is capped at $8,750. For homes from $350,000 to $450,000, calculate the rebate as follows: subtract $350,000 from the purchase price, multiply by 0.0875, and subtract the result from $8,750. Once the price hits $450,000, there is no rebate and you pay the full 7% tax. Similar rebates of QST and the 8% provincial portion of the HST are also available for qualifying new homes, although the rebate rates and calculations are quite different.

Accelerate your mortgage payments.

Once you have a mortgage, consider making extra payments to reduce your interest costs. Based on a 25-year amortization period, your mortgage will be paid off at the same time whether you pay monthly or weekly and making extra payments can greatly reduce the amount of interest you'll pay over the life of your mortgage.

Accelerating your mortgage payment schedule doesn't necessarily mean that you will be shelling out any more than you do now. Here's the trick: figure out how much you can or want to pay each month and multiply that amount by 12. This is your annual payment. Then divide this number by 52 to determine the amount to pay weekly. Over the course of a year, your total mortgage payments will be identical, but more frequent payments will reduce your principal more quickly and reduce your overall interest cost.

Another way to save on mortgage interest is to maintain your original payment level when your mortgage comes up for renewal, even if interest rates have fallen. Also, each time you renew, consider increasing your payment by whatever you can commit—even an extra $5 or $10 will save you money in the long run.

1.3.3 Vacation properties

Buying a cottage, ski chalet or condo in Florida can provide years of enjoyment for your family. For a variety of reasons, a recreation property can also be a sound investment. You will probably save on your family's vacation costs. You will generally find it easy to make up some of the property's costs by renting it out when your family is not using it. Any improvements you make may significantly enhance the property's resale value. Market demand for desirable vacation properties (especially waterfront properties) within a reasonable drive from Canadian urban centres will probably remain steady, and, if historical trends continue, your vacation home could appreciate significantly during the time you own it.

Plan to minimize capital gains tax on dispositions of vacation homes.

Whether you plan to keep the property in the family or sell it for future gain, bear in mind that the capital gains tax (see 5.2) may apply on the difference between the property's cost when you bought it and its fair market value when you sell it or at the time of your death (or your spouse's death). The longer you own your cottage, the bigger the gain is likely to be.

To avoid leaving your survivors with a tax bill which they may have to fund by selling the property, consider purchasing enough life insurance to fund the taxes that will arise on your death. You may be able to shelter some of the gain on the property's sale or on your death (or your spouse's) through the principal residence exemption (see 5.5). You may be able to protect future gains from tax by transferring the property to one of your children or to a family trust (see 4.3.7). Consider also our more general discussion of estate planning in Chapter 13.

If your vacation property is situated in the U.S. and you are a Canadian resident, the double hit of U.S. estate tax and Canadian income tax arising on death can carry a potentially high tax burden. The Canada-U.S. tax treaty may ease the potential for double taxation, but, as discussed at 17.4, some rather complex tax planning may be required and you should probably seek professional tax advice.

1.3.4 Planning for your retirement

Most people can live comfortably in retirement on 70 to 80% of their pre-retirement income (adjusted for inflation). To meet this target requires dedicated long-term planning. If you are a member of a company pension plan, this should be considered as one source of retirement income, not your total retirement fund. Nor should you plan to rely too heavily on Old Age Security and Canada and Québec Pension Plans, since benefits are shrinking and the sustainability of these programs is in doubt.

Beyond these types of income, you'll have to develop resources on your own through other savings and investment strategies. If you don't start at least 15 years before you plan to retire, you'll probably find yourself working longer than you had intended and/or unable to afford the retirement lifestyle you expect.

By your mid- to late-forties, you should find it easier to put larger amounts of funds toward your nest egg: you will be entering your peak income-earning years, your children will be nearing independence, and most of your major lifestyle acquisitions (except maybe your home) will probably be bought and paid for. But don't wait until then—due to the exponential growth of your retirement investments through compounding, the earlier you can start saving for retirement, the better off you will be.

Your RRSP is one of the best possible retirement savings vehicles since it allows you to set aside money and defer the taxes you pay on it. You should try to contribute as much as possible, and do it early in the year so you have the whole year of tax-sheltered income. The tax rules governing RRSPs and a number of strategies for maximizing your RRSP's growth are covered in Chapter 3.

Consider topping up your RRSP and using the tax refund to pay down your mortgage.

Building equity in your home and building up funds in your RRSP will probably be two key components of your retirement savings plan. A commonly asked question is whether you would be further ahead in the long run to maximize your RRSP contributions or to put the same funds toward paying down your mortgage (see 1.3.2). The answer will depend on a variety of factors, including your mortgage's interest rate and remaining amortization period, your RRSP balances and the number of income-earning years you have left until you plan to retire, and the availability of other pension plans. To hedge your bets, consider taking advantage of both strategies by making maximum annual RRSP contributions and using the resulting tax refund to make a lump-sum mortgage payment.

Borrowing funds for RRSP contributions— does it make sense?

Another common question is whether it makes sense to borrow funds for your RRSP contribution. Generally, if you can repay the borrowed funds within, say, a year or if your income for the current year falls into a higher tax bracket than usual, borrowing funds for your RRSP contribution might make sense. But otherwise, the non-deductible interest that you'll pay on the loan may negate the tax benefits of your contribution. Instead, consider making regular "catch-up" payments later when you have the funds to contribute.

1.4 Selecting your professional advisors

For some financial decisions, it will be worth the expense to invest in professional advice, whether from a lawyer, tax advisor, insurance broker, investment counsellor, or a personal financial advisor. And in some financial planning endeavours, such as estate planning, professional legal and tax advice is a must.

Shop around when choosing your financial advisors.

Given what's at stake—your family's finances—you should take the time to "shop around" for advisors who are knowledgeable in their fields and with whom you feel comfortable. When interviewing prospective advisors of any profession, be sure to cover the following topics:

- Ask for client references, preferably from three or four people in circumstances similar to your own.
- Inquire into the professional's educational background, qualifications and level of experience, particularly in fields like financial planning which is only regulated in Québec.
- Ask whether the advisor belongs to any professional networks and associations to determine what sorts of resources are available to him or her.
- Make sure that you understand the fee arrangement.
- Be cautious of advisors whose sole objective may be trying to sell you investments, tax shelters, insurance or anything other than independent advice.

The level of your need for advisors will depend primarily on the complexity of your affairs, but to some extent on your own knowledge of financial matters. You will get better value for your fees to advisors if you spend some time up front educating yourself. Bookstores and libraries are full of excellent, easy-to-read books on retirement and investment planning and the business sections of newspapers are packed with investment, tax, and retirement planning tips. Various organizations also offer frequent, free retirement and investment planning seminars.

If you have a spouse, be sure that he or she is acquainted with your advisors, since your spouse will need to deal with them in the event of your death or disability. It is also a good idea to keep an up-to-date list of your advisors' names and phone numbers in one place, perhaps in the same place as your will.

Tips for your tax return

- The higher-income spouse should claim credits to reduce high-income surtax (2.1.3)
- If you're unmarried and support a family member, don't miss out on the "equivalent-to-married" credit (2.2.1)
- Working parents, single parents attending school and two-parent/student families—claim your child care expenses (2.3.2)
- Seniors—aim for at least $1,000 of pension income for both spouses (2.5.2)
- If Revenue Canada challenges your disability claim, consider objecting (2.6.1)
- Disabled persons—weigh the benefits of deducting the costs of an attendant or claiming the costs for purposes of the medical expense credit (2.6.2)
- If you're separating, co-operate to minimize your joint tax bill (2.7)
- Divorced or separated couples—aim to preserve pre-May 1997 child support arrangements where practical (2.7.3)
- Take advantage of the increased charitable donations limits (2.8.1)
- Combine two or more years of charitable donations into one year (2.8.1)
- If you're married, combine your charitable donations and claim them on the higher-income spouse's return (2.8.1)
- Consider donating publicly traded securities or other assets (2.8.1)
- Combine your family's medical expenses on one return (2.8.2)
- Choose your own 12-month period for medical expense claims (2.8.2)
- Plan for the timing of your family's medical expense payments (2.8.2)
- Political contributions—take advantage of Canada's most generous tax break (2.8.3)
- If you're planning to move, arrange to meet the tests for deducting your moving expenses where practical (2.9.1)
- If you have friends and relatives visiting from outside Canada, have them claim the sales tax rebate for visitors (2.10.4)

In this chapter we highlight some commonly available and sometimes overlooked deductions and credits that can be claimed on your income tax return, depending on your family status and personal circumstances.

2.1 Background

2.1.1 The tax calculation

To understand how deductions and credits work, you need to understand the basic tax calculation. We'll describe it briefly here. (For Québec residents, the provincial tax calculation is completely separate and not as described below. See Chapter 15.)

You start by adding up your various kinds of income: employment, business, interest, grossed-up dividends, taxable capital gains, etc. This gives you **total income**. From this figure you subtract certain deductions, some of which we'll look at in this chapter, and reach **net income**. The net income figure is used for certain purposes later. Then some additional deductions are allowed, primarily loss carryforwards, giving you **taxable income**.

You then calculate your **federal tax** using the formula shown on Schedule 1 of your tax return. Then you subtract various **non-refundable tax credits** (see 2.1.2), and certain others such as the dividend tax credit (see 6.1.1). This gives you **basic federal tax**.

To the basic federal tax figure you add the **federal surtax** (3% of basic federal tax, plus an additional surtax of 5% for high-income earners). You also add the **provincial or territorial tax**, which is a percentage (anywhere from 45% to 69%, varying by province or territory) *of the basic federal tax*. Then, depending on the province, you may also have to add a provincial surtax, health care levy and/or flat tax. If you are self-employed, you may also be required to add your Canada Pension Plan ("CPP") contribution on your self-employment income at this point.

Next, you claim as a credit any other non-refundable credits that are federal only, such as the political contributions credit (see 2.8.3), and you end up with two figures: your federal tax for the year and your provincial tax for the year.

Finally, you record all source deductions of tax (withheld by your employer, for example) and instalments paid, both of which are credited to your account. Along with these are the **refundable credits**—the Child Tax Benefit (see 2.3.1), the Goods and Services Tax ("GST") Credit (see 2.10.3) and the GST rebate (see 2.10.4)—which are given the same treatment so that they can effectively be refunded to you even if you pay no tax for the year. (Some provinces also provide refundable tax credits.) The bottom line is your **balance due** or **refund claimed**, and that will be the cheque you send in on April 30 or receive when your return is assessed.

You can see why the non-refundable credits are given that name. They can reduce your tax to zero, but they are not paid to you if you have no tax to pay for the year. They *can* trigger a refund, however, in the sense of refunding tax that was taken off at source or paid by instalment.

2.1.2 Deductions versus credits—what's the difference?

Before we get into the specific deductions and credits available, you need to understand the different effects of a deduction and a credit. You can refer back to the calculation in 2.1.1 as we go through this.

A **deduction** reduces your taxable income, on which your federal tax is calculated. The combined effect of the federal and provincial taxes and surtaxes means that, as long as you are still paying some tax, a deduction is worth about 27% where your taxable income is under $29,590; about 41% where it is between $29,590 and $59,180; and about 50% where it is over $59,180.

In other words, a $100 write-off (of, say, deductible moving or child care expenses) is worth about $27 to $50 in tax savings, depending on your tax bracket.

A **credit**, on the other hand, is a direct reduction in tax; $100 of a credit such as the credit for political contributions (2.8.3 below) is worth exactly $100 to you.

There is a twist, however. Most of the credits are calculated as part of getting to basic federal tax, *before provincial tax and federal surtax are calculated.* As a result, these credits are worth about 50-75% more than they would otherwise be, because the provincial tax, provincial surtaxes and federal surtax are reduced as well.

> Example:
> Richard calculates his federal tax for 1997 as being $6,000. Federal surtax is 3% of federal tax. Richard lives in Ontario where the effective provincial tax for 1997 is 48% of the federal tax. Richard's total tax bill is $9,060 ($6,000 federal tax, $180 federal surtax, $2,880 provincial tax).
>
> Richard discovers that he is able to claim an additional credit, which he had not thought of. The credit is $100 against federal tax. Now his federal tax is $5,900, the 3% surtax is only $177 and his provincial tax is 48% of $5,900, or $2,832. His total tax bill is now **$8,909**.

As you can see, the $100 federal credit is actually worth $151 because of the reduced surtax and provincial tax—even though there is no explicit provincial credit to be claimed. The additional $51 is actually 3% + 48% (the federal surtax and provincial tax rate) on the $100. (The impact of provincial surtaxes, such as Ontario's Fair Share Health Care Levy on taxable income over about $52,300, can magnify this effect still more.)

Finally, note the distinction between refundable and non-refundable credits. Because they are treated as having been paid by you, just like source withholdings and instalments, refundable credits are always worth what they say they are. Non-refundable credits, like deductions, become worthless once you reach the point of paying no tax at all for the year.

2.1.3 Transferring credits between spouses

Some of the non-refundable credits outlined below, such as charitable donations (see 2.8.1), can be transferred between spouses if not otherwise usable (see Schedule 2 of the T1 General Return).

The higher-income spouse should claim credits to reduce high-income surtax.

Where you have a choice as to which spouse will claim certain credits note that credits are worth slightly more to very high-income individuals. That is because of the additional surtax that applies to individuals with high "basic federal tax". This additional surtax is an extra 5% of basic federal tax in excess of $12,500. Almost all provinces also have surtaxes on high levels of provincial tax, which can boost the effect of credits still further.

If you are paying any of these surtaxes and your spouse is not, it is better for you to claim most of the credits that can be allocated between the two of you.

2.2 Personal, spousal and dependent credits

Every individual gets a basic federal credit of $1,098, which offsets the federal tax on your first $6,456 of taxable income. (On your income tax return, it is a claim for a "basic personal amount" of $6,456, which you later multiply by 17%.)

2.2.1 Spousal and "equivalent-to-married" credits

If you are married, you can claim a further federal credit of $915 if your **spouse's** income is under $538, or a reduced amount if your spouse has income between $538 and $5,820.

If you're unmarried, don't miss out on the "equivalent-to-married" credit.

If you are single, widowed, divorced, or separated, and you support another family member (such as a child) in your home, you can claim that person under the "**equivalent-to-married**" credit. This will allow you the same claim as if that person were your spouse. (It cannot be used to claim a common-law spouse, however.) The credit will be worth about $1,460.

Common-law spouses who meet certain criteria (below) are treated identically to legally married couples for all purposes relating to income tax. This means that the spousal credit can be claimed for a dependent common-law spouse. It also means that a taxpayer who has a common-law spouse cannot claim the "equivalent-to-married" credit for a child.

Common-law spouses are treated as spouses if they are two people of the opposite sex who "cohabit in a conjugal relationship", where either they have had a child together, or they have cohabited for at least 12 continuous months. Separation is not considered to terminate this "cohabiting" unless the couple separates for at least 90 days because of a breakdown in their relationship.

2.3 Children

There is no tax credit available for **dependent children** under 18—this was eliminated in 1993 with the introduction of the Child Tax Benefit. There is a $400 credit for disabled dependants aged 18 and over (see 2.6.1).

2.3.1 Child Tax Benefit and Working Income Supplement

The "Child Tax Benefit" is a monthly non-taxable payment that replaced the former family allowance, Child Tax Credit and dependent child credit in 1993. Aimed at low and moderate income families, the Child Tax Benefit provides an annual basic benefit of $1,020 per child, an extra $75 for the third and each later child, and an extra $213 for each child under seven if no child care expenses are claimed. It begins to be phased out once family income exceeds $25,921. Depending on the number of children you have and whether you claim child care expenses, you can still receive a portion of the Child Tax Benefit even when your family income is quite high.

To help low and moderate income working parents cover some of the extra cost of working, the government also provides a "Working Income Supplement" (WIS) for families with family incomes up to $25,951. As of July 1997, WIS payments are calculated on a per-child basis, rather than a per-family basis. Maximum payments are $605 for one-child families, $1,010 for two-child families, and $1,010 plus $310 for the third and later children for larger families.

These changes to the WIS are part of the federal government's plans to replace the federal Child Tax Benefit with a National Child Benefit system in cooperation with the provinces in July 1998.

2.3.2 Child care expenses

For two-parent families, child care expenses can be deducted, usually by the spouse with the **lower income**, subject to various limitations. (The assumption is that the lower-income spouse would otherwise stay home with the children.) Single parents can deduct child care expenses from their own income, subject to the same limitations. Common-law couples who meet certain criteria are treated the same as spouses for purposes of calculating child care expenses (as well as for all other tax purposes—see 2.2.1). As of

1996, single parents who are full-time students and two-parent families where both parents are full-time students can also deduct their child care expenses.

Working parents, single parents attending school and two-parent/student families— claim your child care expenses.

You can claim child care expenses for your child, your spouse's child, or a child who was dependent on you or your spouse and whose net income in 1997 is less than $6,457.

Child care expenses include baby-sitting, day nursery services, day camps, boarding schools and camps.

For child care expenses to be claimed, they have to have been made to allow you or your spouse to work, carry on business, attend school "full-time" or carry on grant-funded research. "Full-time" attendance at school for these purposes means that you must be enrolled in a secondary or post-secondary program that is at least three consecutive weeks long and requires you to spend at least 10 hours per week on course work.

Assuming you are a single parent or the lower-income spouse, the deduction for child care expenses is limited to $5,000 times the number of your children who are under seven at the end of the year, plus $3,000 times the number of children seven and over but under 17. It is also limited to two-thirds of your "earned income" (basically salary and business income). For single parents and two-parent families where both parents are attending school, child care expenses are deductible against all types of income.

The deduction is based on when the services are provided rather than when the amounts are paid, so prepaying in December does not give you the deduction a year earlier.

Payments to a boarding school or camp are limited to $150 per week that the child attends the school or camp, for children under seven, and $90 per week for children over six but under 17.

Example:

Rick and Arlene are married and have two children under seven. Arlene earns $70,000 and Rick earns $21,000. They pay $12,000 in 1997 to a nanny to take care of their children while they are working.

Rick must be the one to claim the expenses, since he is the lower-income spouse. His deduction is the least of: (a) the amount paid— $12,000; (b) $5,000 per child—$10,000; and (c) two-thirds of his earned income—$14,000. He can therefore claim $10,000 as a deduction against his $21,000 of employment income. This will reduce his tax bill by about $2,700.

If Arlene was a single parent, she could claim the same amount as a deduction against her own income of $70,000 and reduce her tax bill by about $5,000.

Where a child, at any age, has a severe and prolonged mental or physical impairment for which the disability credit can be claimed (see 2.6.1), special rules allow a deduction as though the child were under seven. If the child is older than 16, but has a less severe mental or physical infirmity, you are entitled to the same deduction as that allowed for children aged 7 to 16.

There are also special circumstances where the lower-income spouse is not expected to care for the children. These are: where the spouse is disabled; where the spouse is in prison or hospital; confined to bed or a wheelchair, for at least two weeks; where the spouse attends full-time high school or post-secondary education; or where the spouses have separated. In such cases, the higher-income spouse can claim the deduction for up to $150 per child under seven ($90 per child seven and over) for each week that the condition continues.

Note that as a result of a 1993 Supreme Court decision (the *Symes* case), you cannot claim your child care expenses as a business expense. If you made this claim in past years, expect it to be disallowed by Revenue Canada if it is found on audit.

The tax treatment of child care expenses for Québec purposes is discussed at 15.2.2.

2.4 Students—tuition fees and educational status

Tuition fees qualify for a 17% federal credit if you pay them for yourself. Tuition fees paid for your child or other person cannot be claimed by you, subject to the transfer rules discussed below.

To be eligible for a credit, the fees must be paid to a Canadian university, college or other post-secondary educational institution, or to an institution certified by Employment and Immigration Canada. Fees paid to post-secondary institutions in other countries may qualify as well. Any fees you claim must total more than $100 per institution.

Along with admission fees, eligible tuition fees include library and lab charges, examination fees, application fees, mandatory computer service fees, charges for certificates and diplomas, and the cost of books included in the fees for a correspondence course. The 1997 budget extended eligibility for the credit to cover mandatory ancillary fees for health services, athletics and various other services (but not to student association fees, fees covering goods of value that you retain, or ancilllary fees at institutions sanctioned by the Ministry of Human Resources Development).

Note that fees paid to private schools for grade-school or high-school education will not entitle you to a tax credit. However, religious private schools may be able to provide a tax receipt for some of your tuition fees, treating that amount as a charitable donation (see 2.8.1) made toward the school's religious instruction.

As a separate credit from the tuition fees, you are entitled to a further **educational status** credit for each month you are in full-time attendance at a post-secondary educational institution. For 1997, the credit is $25.50 (federal) per month (up from $17 per month in 1996). In 1998 and later years, the credit rises to $35 per month. Disabled students qualify for this credit even if they attend the institution only part-time.

If you are not able to use your tuition and education credits (because you have no tax to pay), up to $850 ($680 in 1996) in federal credits for the two combined may normally be transferred to your spouse or to a parent or grandparent. Alternatively, for 1997 and later years, you can carry-forward any unused and untransferred tuition and education amounts and claim them against your taxable income in any later year. Note, however, that such amounts carried forward cannot be transferred—only the student can claim them in a later year.

Full-time students who are single parents or married with both parents attending school may be able to deduct child care expenses paid to attend school; if you are the working spouse of a full-time student, you may be able to deduct them on your own return (see 2.3.2). In certain cases, students may also be able to deduct their moving expenses (see 2.9.1).

If you are a student who lives in Québec, see 15.2.5.

2.5 Seniors

In the year 2001, the government is proposing to replace the current Old Age Security, pension income credit and age credit system (discussed below) with a new Seniors Benefit. If you were over 60 at the end of 1995, the government guarantees that your income (and your spouse's, regardless of his or her age) from government pension payments under the new system will be at least the same as it is now. Lower-income seniors will gain an additional $120 annually. The benefit will be reduced for seniors with income above $45,000 and will not be available for seniors earning more the $52,000 individually (or $78,000 for both spouses combined). Once it's in place, the Seniors Benefit will be tax-free and fully indexed to inflation.

2.5.1 Age credit

If you are 65 or older by the end of the year, you get an additional federal credit of up to $592. However, this credit is now linked to your income. It is phased out by 2.55¢ for each dollar that your net income (see 2.1.1) exceeds

$25,921. Thus, the credit completely disappears once your net income reaches $49,134. (Your spouse's net income does not affect this calculation.) The Québec age credit is discussed at 15.2.6.

Aim for at least $1,000 of pension income for both spouses.

You are entitled to a federal tax credit of 17% of your pension income, up to $1,000 of pension income for the year. A similar credit is available in Québec—see 15.2.6.

Pension income does not include Canada Pension Plan, Old Age Security or Guaranteed Income Supplement payments. It basically means private pension income received through a life annuity. If you are over 65 or are receiving payments as a result of your spouse's death, it also includes annuities out of an RRSP or DPSP, a payment out of a RRIF (see 3.2.4), or the income portion of a regular annuity.

To make the most of this credit, you should aim to have at least $1,000 of qualifying "pension income" annually, plus another $1,000 for your spouse if possible.

Old Age Security is paid monthly to most Canadian residents who are 65 or over. For high-income taxpayers, these payments are completely taxed back through a special tax, known informally as the "clawback". The tax applies to taxpayers whose net income (after most deductions such as RRSP contributions) is over $53,215. Spouses' incomes are not pooled; each taxpayer's income is considered separately.

The tax on Old Age Security benefits is deducted from your monthly benefits cheque. The amount withheld is based on your income in the prior two years. For example, for the first six months of 1997, your tax withheld was based on your 1995 income while your tax withheld for the last half of 1997 is based on your 1996 income. If too much tax is withheld, the excess will be applied to reduce your taxes owing or refunded to you after you file your return for the year. If the tax withheld falls short of your liability, you will have to repay the difference.

If you suffer from a severe and prolonged mental or physical impairment, you get an additional federal credit of $720. Your status must be certified by a medical doctor (or by an optometrist in cases of visual impairment or by an audiologist in cases of hearing impairment).

To qualify as having a severe and prolonged impairment, your ability to perform a "basic activity of daily living" must be "markedly restricted", and the impairment must have lasted or be expected to last for at least a year. The *Income Tax Act* has specific definitions to determine whether you qualify. The rules can be found on Revenue Canada's disability credit certificate, Form T2201. If you are disabled and reside in Québec, see also 15.2.11.

If Revenue Canada challenges your disability claim, consider objecting.

However, it is often difficult to determine whether one qualifies or not, and the Tax Court of Canada has issued a large number of decisions interpreting these rules. In some cases, the Court has found Revenue Canada's view to be incorrect. Therefore, if you believe you fit within the *Income Tax Act*'s definition of disabled, you should consider pursuing your claim if it is denied.

If you have a dependent child who qualifies for the disability credit but does not earn enough income to be able to use all of it, the child's unused credit can be transferred to your return. As well, if you support a dependent child age 18 or over who is disabled, you can claim an additional federal credit of $400 ($270 for 1995 and prior years). This credit is reduced by 17% of your infirm dependant's income over $4,103.

You may also be able to claim a portion of your medical expenses for the medical expense credit (see 2.8.2) and for the new refundable medical expense supplement (see 2.8.2).

2.6.2 Attendant for disabled person

If you are disabled, you can deduct some or all of the costs of an attendant needed to allow you to earn income. The deduction is limited to two-thirds of your "earned income" (basically salary and business income). As an alternative, expenses of an attendant can generally be claimed for purposes of the medical expense credit (see 2.8.2), even if you are not earning income.

Weigh the benefits of deducting the costs of an attendant or claiming the costs for purposes of the medical expense credit.

Before 1997, this deduction was capped at $5,000, generally making it more beneficial for moderate to high income disabled persons to claim these costs as medical expenses. Now that the $5,000 ceiling has been eliminated, you should calculate and compare the net tax results of claiming these costs through the attendant care deduction and the medical expense credit, which credit could be claimed on either spouse's return if the disabled person is married, to determine which option generates greater tax savings.

Marital breakdown

If you're separating, co-operate to minimize your joint tax bill.

While marriage breakdown is often an occasion for bitter disputes, you and your spouse (through your lawyers, if necessary) should co-operate to minimize your joint tax bill and share the resulting savings.

In May 1997, a new system for taxing child support payments took effect for federal and Québec tax purposes. Although these changes were designed to address the widespread perception that the former system was unfair to custodial parents, many divorced or separated couples with child support arrangements may be worse off under the new system than they would have been under the old system.

If you are a party to a child support agreement or court order finalized before May 1997, you can still take advantage of the tax savings available under the old system (see 2.7.2), but you and your spouse or ex-spouse may have to work together to preserve your ability to do so (see 2.7.3). If your support agreement or order was finalized on or after May 1, 1997, the payments will generally be treated under the new rules discussed in 2.7.1.

2.7.1 New tax treatment for child support payments

Under the pre-May 1, 1997 system, alimony and spousal and child support payments are deductible to the payer and taxable to the recipient if they meet the strict criteria set out in 2.7.2.

Under the new rules, child support paid under orders or agreements made or varied after April 30, 1997 will no longer be taxed as income to the recipient, or deducted from income by the paying parent. The government has also introduced new guidelines for the courts to follow when setting child support awards. Generally, the child support amount will be calculated as a percentage of the support-paying parent's income, and adjusted to account for the impact of federal and provincial taxes, certain special child care expenses and undue hardship.

Bear in mind that the new rules only deal with child support payments. Alimony and spousal support payments will remain deductible to the payer and taxable to the recipient under the rules discussed in the next section. The same rules apply when a common-law couple separates, if they meet the criteria for common-law spouses outlined in 2.2.1.

If you were in the midst of divorcing or separating in April 1997, you and your spouse or ex-spouse may still be able to have the old child support rules apply to your post-May 1, 1997 payments even if your support agreement or court order is made afterwards—but only if interim support payments were made before May 1, 1997 and the agreement or court order is signed before

1999. In this case, the order or agreement should be drafted so that it specifically provides for the pre-May 1997 payments. This will cause any interim support payments made in that year and the year before to be treated as having been paid under the post-May 1, 1997 agreement or order for tax purposes. It will also cause the agreement or order to be treated as having been made on the date of the first payment, instead of the date of signing, allowing pre-May 1997 treatment for all payments made under the order or agreement. If you are in this situation, be sure to obtain advice from a tax advisor on the appropriate drafting of your separation or divorce agreement.

2.7.2 Child support paid under pre-May 1, 1997 arrangements and alimony

Alimony and spousal maintenance payments are deductible to the payer and *taxable* to the recipient if they meet a number of well-defined and strict criteria. Child support paid under arrangements reached before May 1, 1997 are treated the same way. This system is generally of benefit to the separating or divorcing couple, since the person making the payments is often in a higher tax bracket than the recipient (see 2.7.3).

Note that your ability to claim a deduction does not depend on whether the recipient actually reports the income. Provided you meet all of the requirements, you can go ahead and claim the deduction, and it is up to Revenue Canada (or Revenu Québec) to take action if the recipient does not include the payments for tax purposes.

To be deductible, any payments must be an *allowance* which has been established in advance as a recurring payment. The amounts payable must be predetermined. (However, if they are required to be adjusted for inflation, they can still be considered predetermined.)

The further requirements are:

- the allowance must be paid under a written agreement or under a decree, order or judgment of a competent tribunal; and
- it must be payable on a periodic basis for the maintenance of the recipient (your spouse or ex-spouse) and/or the children of the marriage; and
- you must be living apart from your spouse or ex-spouse, at the time the payment is made and throughout the rest of the year. If the payments are alimony (rather than maintenance) and the marriage breakdown occurred before 1993, you must also be separated pursuant to a divorce, judicial separation or a written separation agreement.

Payments to former common-law spouses may be deducted on the same basis, where the recipient is an individual of the opposite sex who cohabited with you "in a conjugal relationship" or you are the natural parent of that person's child. However, if the common-law breakup occurred before 1993, the maintenance payments must be paid under a court order to be deductible.

2/ Tips for Your Tax Return

Note that the "periodic basis" requirement excludes one-time payments and transfers of property in settlement of rights of the marriage.

Payments made directly to third parties, rather than to your spouse or ex-spouse, are allowed in limited circumstances. Such payments can include medical bills, tuition fees and mortgage payments for your spouse or ex-spouse's home. Among other requirements, the court order or written separation agreement must specifically provide for the payments and must specifically provide that the relevant tax rules will apply, to make the payments deductible to you and taxable to your spouse or ex-spouse. For court orders and agreements made after 1992, these rules also apply to most common-law relationships.

In general, you also may deduct payments made before obtaining a court order or signing a written separation agreement, provided the order or agreement is signed by the end of the year following the year in which the payment is made, and that it specifically provides that the amounts paid earlier are to be considered as paid and received pursuant to the agreement.

If you pay alimony or child support to a non-resident of Canada, you used to have to withhold up to 25% of each payment and remit it to Revenue Canada. Since child support is no longer taxable under the new system, the government eliminated this withholding tax rule for all child support payments as of May 1, 1997, no matter when the child support arrangement was reached. Alimony payments are also now exempt because the government decided that the amounts involved did not justify Revenue Canada's expenses in collecting alimony withholdings.

If you **receive** alimony or maintenance payments in circumstances where they are deductible to the payer (i.e., under a pre-May 1, 1997 child support agreement or court order), they are taxable to you. If you receive child support from a resident of the **United States**, however, it will not be taxed due to the Canada-U.S. tax treaty (see 16.2.3).

2.7.3 New rules for child support—should you opt in?

The purpose of the elimination of the "deduction/inclusion" system for child support payments was to make the system fairer to custodial parents. However, all other things being equal, divorced and separated couples will probably pay more in combined taxes under the new rules, particularly in the usual case where the support-paying spouse is in a higher tax bracket than the recipient spouse.

For example, under the old system, if the payer is in the 41% tax bracket (taxable income from $29,590 to $59,180) and the recipient is in the 27% bracket (income under $29,590), then for each $1,000 paid in child support, the payer would save $410 and the recipient would pay $270, for net overall tax savings of $140 for each $1,000 payment.

Under the new system, the payer would bear tax of $410 on the entire $1,000 payment while the recipient would pay nothing. As a result, the separated family would pay $140 more in tax for each $1,000 payment than they would under the old system.

Aim to preserve pre-May 1997 child support arrangements where practical.

Because of this result, if you are a party in separation or divorce agreement entered into before May 1997, you should aim to preserve your ability to use the current inclusion/deduction system where practical. The new system generally will not apply to court orders made before May 1, 1997 unless a new court order or agreement made after that date changes the amount of child support payable under your existing order or agreement, or unless you and your spouse both sign and file a form with Revenue Canada (or Revenu Québec) stating that the new tax rules will apply to payments made after a specified date (which cannot be earlier than April 30, 1997).

2.8 Other commonly available credits

2.8.1 Charitable donations

Charitable donations entitle you to a two-tier credit. The first $200 of donations for the year (total to all charities) gives you a 17% federal tax credit, worth about 27% when provincial tax is taken into account. All donations above that level give you a 29% federal tax credit, worth about 50% when provincial tax is factored in (see 15.2.9 if you live in Québec).

For federal purposes, charitable donations above $200 for the year are therefore given the same treatment as if they were deductible, if you are in the top tax bracket (over $59,180 in taxable income). If you are in a lower bracket, the credit for large donations is worth far more than a deduction.

To claim charitable donations, you must submit official receipts which show the recipient organization's charitable registration number. Revenue Canada's administrative policy is to allow you to claim receipts made out in either your name or your spouse's.

Take advantage of the increased charitable donations limits.

In 1997 and after, the maximum amount of donations you can claim in a year is 75% of your net income (in 1996, the limit was 50%). To the extent you have receipts for more than this amount, or if you choose not to claim a donation for any other reason, you can save the receipts and claim the credit in any of the following five years.

The annual limit for donations in the year of death and the year before (including bequests and legacies) is 100% of net income for the year. A number of other special rules relating to charitable donations, and creative techniques for use of the credit for donations, are discussed in 13.7, in the chapter on Estate Planning.

Combine two or more years of charitable donations into one year.

If you donate only small amounts over a year, consider combining two or more years of donations into one year to put yourself over the $200 threshold. A $100 donation above the $200 level for the year costs you only about $50 instead of about $73 below that level.

If you're married, combine your charitable donations and claim them on the higher-income spouse's return.

If you and your spouse donate separately, you should combine your receipts and claim them all on one return (Revenue Canada's administrative practice is to permit this), to avoid having to get the low-rate credit on $200 twice. Due to the operation of the federal and provincial high-income surtaxes, the higher-income spouse should claim all the donations.

Once you are over the $200 level, consider making extra contributions in December rather than early in the new year. Your tax saving through the donations credit will come one year earlier.

Consider donating publicly traded securities or other assets.

Instead of donating cash, you should also consider the potential benefits of donating property such as publicly traded securities, artwork or real estate. The tax treatment of donations of property—or "gifts in kind"—is somewhat more complex but may result in greater tax savings for you and may enhance the value of your gift to the charity. Gifts in kind are discussed in 13.7.3.

2.8.2 Medical expenses

Medical expenses over a certain threshold entitle you to a tax credit. The threshold is 3% of your net income, or, if your net income exceeds $53,800, a flat $1,614. All qualifying medical expenses above this amount give rise to a 17% federal credit, worth about 27% when provincial tax is counted (if you live in Québec, see also 15.2.10).

Example:

Ben's net income is $30,000. He spends $1,500 on qualifying medical expenses in 1997.

Given that 3% of Ben's net income is $900, the remaining $600 qualifies for the medical expense credit. The federal credit is 17% of that, or $102. Ben's provincial tax and federal surtax will be reduced by about $60 as a result. So of his $1,500 in medical expenses, he will get back about $162 in tax.

Starting in 1997, a new "medical expense supplement" can be claimed by low-income workers with higher than average eligible medical expenses and earned income of at least $2,500. This refundable tax credit is available for 25% of the portion of your medical expenses allowable for the medical expense credit, to a maximum of $500. The credit is reduced by 5% of family net income over $16,069. Claiming the supplement will not affect your ability to claim the medical expense credit.

You can claim expenses for yourself, your spouse and any close relative dependent on you for support, including your child, grandchild, parent, grandparent, brother, sister, uncle, aunt, niece or nephew; or any of those relatives of your spouse (including a qualifying common-law spouse as outlined in 2.2.1). Except for your or your spouse's child or grandchild, the person must be resident in Canada.

To the extent any close relative dependent on you for support has net income over $6,456, any claim for the medical expense credit will be reduced. If the dependant has net income under $6,456, you can claim the medical expenses without restriction. To the extent the dependant has net income exceeding $6,456, the medical expenses you can claim are reduced by 68% of that excess. If a dependant has sufficiently high income, you will not be able to claim that person's expenses at all, since the reduction will exceed the total value of that dependant's medical expenses. (Note that it doesn't matter who *paid* the expenses; what matters is who the "patient" was.)

The list of qualifying medical expenses is very long, and you should refer to Revenue Canada's Interpretation Bulletin (see 2.11) if you need specific details. The list includes:

- payments to medical practitioners, dentists and nurses, hospital fees not covered by public health insurance, and diagnostic procedures
- prescription drugs
- premiums to a drug or dental plan
- travelling expenses and meals and lodging, in some cases
- institutional care (e.g., nursing home)
- part-time attendant for disabled person (up to $10,000, see also 2.6.2)
- guide dogs (both purchase cost and upkeep cost)

- eyeglasses, hearing aids and dentures
- home renovations required for someone with a mobility impairment
- a long list of specific devices, ranging from crutches to insulin needles, wheelchair lifts, speech synthesizers, visual fire alarm indicators and TDD devices for the deaf.

For 1997 and later years, this list has been expanded to include:

- 50% (to a maximum of $1,000) of the cost of air conditioners required by persons with chronic respiratory ailments
- 20% (to a maximum of $5,000) of the cost of adapting a van for transporting a person using a wheelchair
- sign language interpreter fees
- costs of moving to accessible housing
- driveway alterations made to provide access for persons with severe mobility impairments to a bus.

Combine your family's medical expenses on one return.

Because of the threshold of 3% of net income, you should combine all of the family's medical expenses on one return. It is normally better for the lower-income spouse to make the claim, provided that spouse has enough tax to pay to use up the credit, since the 3% threshold will be smaller. On the other hand, the credit might be slightly more valuable to a high-income spouse because it will reduce the application of high-income federal and provincial surtaxes (see 2.1.3).

Choose your own 12-month period for medical expense claims.

When claiming medical expenses, you can pick any 12-month period ending in the year. If, for example, you made no claim for 1996, and you have large medical expense bills in February 1996, January 1997 and November 1997, you might be better off to use January 1997 as the end of your 12-month period, claim the February 1996 and January 1997 expenses for 1997, and leave the November 1997 expenses to be claimed on your 1998 return.

Plan for the timing of your family's medical expense payments.

You can also plan for the timing of medical expenses, since they are based on when they are *paid*. If you are using a December end for the 12-month period, and you have pending expenses (perhaps for medical equipment purchases or large dental bills) that are due early in the new year, consider prepaying them so that you can claim them one year earlier.

2.8.3 Political contributions

Political contributions—Canada's most generous tax break.

If you are interested in the greatest "bang for your buck", consider a contribution to your favourite federal political party or election candidate. Contributions to federal political parties and to candidates in federal election campaigns entitle you to a credit, which is federal only. A donation of $100 will cost you only $25.

In addition, many of the provinces have their own credits for contributions to *provincial* parties and candidates. The Québec credit for political donations is discussed at 15.2.12.

Note that contributions to a candidate in a federal leadership campaign are not eligible for the credit. However, political parties sometimes set up funds that allow you to contribute to the party itself and direct that your contribution be used to support a particular leadership candidate.

To encourage small political donations by many people, the federal credit is most generous at the lowest levels. The credit is 75% for the first $100 of donation; 50% for the next $450; and 33.33% for the next $600. There is no additional credit for donations beyond $1,150.

Example:

Mark contributes $200 to a federal political party in 1997.

Mark's political contribution credit for 1997 will be 75% on the first $100 ($75) plus 50% on the next $100 ($50), for a total of $125. There is no reduction in provincial tax resulting from this credit.

2.8.4 Other credits

There are a number of other credits with a provincial component available when computing "basic federal tax" (thereby reducing provincial taxes and surtaxes, as discussed in 2.1.2). One of them is the dividend tax credit, explained in 6.1.2.

Other federal-only credits include the investment tax credit, which is an incentive for those carrying on business to invest in particular regions or sectors of the economy (see 8.2.13); the labour-sponsored funds tax credit (see 6.3.8 and, if you live in Québec, 15.3.5); and the foreign tax credit (also available in Québec), which offsets the impact of foreign tax paid on one's income from a foreign source, to reduce double taxation.

2.9 Other commonly available deductions

2.9.1 Moving expenses

Moving expenses are often overlooked as a deduction. If you start working at a new location of employment, or start a new business, and you move to a home that is 40 km closer to your new work location than was your old home (to the new work location), you can deduct substantial amounts for tax purposes. The 40 km distance is measured by the shortest normal route of travel, including roads, bridges and ferries, rather than "as the crow flies." Expenses incurred in moving from another country to Canada, or from Canada to another country, are not deductible for Canadian tax purposes (unless you are a student receiving scholarship or grant income; see below).

Except to the extent you are reimbursed by your employer, you can deduct the following:

- reasonable travelling costs, including meals and lodging, to move you and the members of your household
- the moving costs for your household effects, including storage charges
- the cost of meals and lodging near either the old or the new home for up to 15 days
- lease cancellation costs
- selling costs in respect of your old home, *including real estate commissions*
- where you are selling your old home, the legal fees and land transfer tax payable when you buy a new home. (GST and QST were allowable as well, but due to a retroactive change introduced in April 1995, any GST and QST you pay on buying your new home will not be allowed, even for past years going back to 1991.)

The real estate commissions alone can easily run into many thousands of dollars.

If you're planning to move, arrange to meet the tests for deducting your moving expenses where practical.

So when considering a move, ensure if possible that your move coincides with a new employment location or a new place of business, and that your move meets the 40 km test.

If you are a student, you can also claim moving expenses, if you move when you begin a job (including a summer job) or start a business. If you are moving to attend full-time post-secondary education (whether or not in Canada), you can deduct the expenses, but only to the extent you have scholarship or research grant income.

2.9.2 Legal fees

Whether or not you can deduct legal fees you have paid depends on why you paid them.

Legal fees are generally deductible if they are paid for the purpose of earning income from business or property. Legal fees to acquire or preserve a capital asset are normally not deductible, though there are a number of exceptions.

Legal fees associated with an objection or appeal of your income tax assessment (see 14.5) are deductible. This includes the costs of negotiations with Revenue Canada officials prior to filing a formal Notice of Objection. The fees are also deductible if you are appealing a Québec income tax assessment or an income tax assessment of a foreign government, or an Employment Insurance or Canada/Québec Pension Plan decision.

Legal fees to collect unpaid salary or wages owed to you by your employer or former employer are deductible.

Legal fees can be deducted where they are incurred to obtain a "retiring allowance" (including severance pay) or a pension benefit (see 7.10.6), but only up to a limit of your income from those sources (in the current year or past years).

Finally, legal fees to enforce an existing right to alimony or maintenance that is taxable in your hands (see 2.7 above) are deductible. They are not deductible, however, when incurred to *establish* a right to alimony or maintenance, except for maintenance for which you must sue your spouse or former spouse in a Family Court or under certain provincial legislation. (See also 15.2.8 if you live in Québec.)

2.9.3 Northern residents

If you live in northern Canada, a special deduction is available to help offset the higher costs of living and the hardship and isolation relative to the more populated parts of the country. The deduction is limited to 20% of your net income. A similar deduction is available for Québec tax purposes if you live in northern Québec.

If you live in the "prescribed northern zone", the federal deduction is $15 per day ($5,475 per year). If you live somewhat further south, in the "prescribed intermediate zone", you can only claim half as much. As well, if your employer pays the cost of travel for you and your family (e.g., an annual trip to southern Canada), a deduction is available to offset part or all of the taxable benefit that is thereby included in your income. See 7.10.9.

2.9.4 Other deductions

Some other common deductions are covered in other chapters. See, for example, 3.1.3 (contributions to RRSPs), 5.3.2 (allowable business investment losses), 5.4 (capital gains deduction), 6.2.3 (interest paid) and

7.10 (deductions available to employees). Some of the deductions relating to self-employment (carrying on business) are discussed in Chapter 8.

2.10 Canada/Québec Pension Plan, Employment Insurance and GST

2.10.1 CPP/QPP contributions and EI premiums

A federal credit of 17% of all Canada (or Québec) Pension Plan ("CPP/QPP") contributions and Employment Insurance ("EI") premiums is available, effectively giving you back about 27% of these amounts when provincial tax and surtax are factored in. If you are employed, these amounts are normally taken off your paycheque at source by your employer. If you are self-employed, you will normally have to calculate and remit CPP/QPP (but not Employment Insurance) contributions on your net self-employment income.

2.10.2 EI clawback

If you receive Employment Insurance benefits and your net income exceeds $58,500 in 1997, a portion of your benefits received during the year will be taxed back through a special tax, commonly called a "clawback", paid through your income tax return.

However, the total amount you pay back will never exceed 30% of the benefits. The remaining 70% remains taxable in the normal way.

2.10.3 GST Credit

The GST Credit is aimed at low-income families. It is designed to offset the GST paid by consumers on most goods and services. This credit is normally $198 per adult (but up to $303 in some cases) and $105 per child in the family, reduced by 5 cents for each dollar that the parents' income exceeds $25,921. The credit is prepaid in quarterly instalments to qualifying families, based on their previous year's income.

Many provinces also have sales tax credits for low-income taxpayers. For the Québec credit, which parallels the GST Credit, see 15.2.13.

Example:
Jeffrey and Margaret are married and have two dependent children. Their combined income is $25,000.

For 1997, their combined GST Credit will be $606 ($198 for each parent and $105 for each child). Since their combined income is below $25,921, the credit is not reduced. The $606 effectively offsets the GST paid on $8,657 of taxable goods and services purchased during the year. Thus, although the credit is paid through the income tax system, it operates to alleviate the effects of GST on low-income families.

2.10.4 GST rebate

In addition to the GST Credit described in 2.10.3, certain employees and members of partnerships can claim a GST rebate on their income tax returns. The rebate is available to employees who claim income tax deductions relating to their employment expenses, and partners who claim deductions on expenses they incur outside the partnership to earn partnership income. (See 7.11, 8.2.4 and 8.3.7 for more details; see also 15.2.13 if you live in Québec.)

Friends or relatives visiting from outside Canada should claim the visitors' sales tax rebate.

Non-residents are eligible for a full refund of the 7% GST and the 15% Harmonized Sales Tax ("HST"—see 8.2.5) paid on most goods they take back with them (but not alcohol and tobacco), as well as hotel accommodation while in Canada. The minimum rebate claim for non-resident visitors is $200 in purchases of goods and accommodation.

Your visitors should keep receipts and apply for a refund once they get home. They can also claim their refunds at duty-free stores at many land border points (all the airport duty-free shops have opted out of the refund program, not being able to handle the volume). Telephone 1-800-66VISIT from within Canada for information on this Visitors' Rebate Program.

The refund does not apply to purchases or services consumed in Canada, such as restaurant meals, gas or haircuts.

Many provinces also provide a refund of provincial sales tax on goods taken out of the province. For Québec and Manitoba, this is handled by Revenue Canada on the same form on which the GST/HST refund is claimed.

2.11 References

The following publications can be obtained (in person or by telephone request) from your nearest Revenue Canada District Taxation Office. Some of Revenue Canada's guides, brochures and forms are also available from Revenue Canada's Internet site at www.revcan.ca.

Interpretation Bulletin IT-99R4, "Legal and accounting fees"
Interpretation Bulletin IT-110R2, "Deductible gifts and official donation receipts"
Interpretation Bulletin IT-118R3, "Alimony and maintenance"
Interpretation Bulletin IT-178R3, "Moving expenses"
Interpretation Bulletin IT-495R2, "Child care expenses"
Interpretation Bulletin IT-513, "Personal tax credits"

Interpretation Bulletin IT-515R2, "Education tax credit"

Interpretation Bulletin IT-516R2, "Tuition tax credit"

Interpretation Bulletin IT-517R, "Pension tax credit"

Interpretation Bulletin IT-519R, "Medical expense and disability tax credits and attendant care expense deduction"

Interpretation Bulletin IT-523, "Order of provisions applicable in computing an individual's taxable income and tax payable"

Information Circular 75-2R4, "Contributions to a registered political party or to a candidate at a federal election"

Brochure, "Alimony or Maintenance"

Brochure, "Are You Moving?"

Brochure, "Students and Income Tax"

Brochure, "Tax Refund for Visitors to Canada"

Brochure, "Tax Information for People with Disabilities"

Guide, "Your Child Tax Benefit"

Form T1-M, "Claim for moving expenses"

Form T778, "Calculation of child care expense deduction for 19___"

Form T929, "Attendant care expenses"

Form T1157, "Election for child support payments"

Form T1158, "Registration of family support payments"

Form T2201, "Disability tax credit certificate"

Form T2202A, "Tuition and education credit certificate"

Form T2222, "Calculation of Northern Residents Deductions"

RRSPs and other tax deferral plans

▪ Contribute as much as you can to an RRSP (3.1.7)

▪ Contribute early in the year instead of the following February (3.1.7)

▪ Consider a self-directed RRSP for greater flexibility (3.1.6)

▪ Think about transferring shares that you already own to your self-directed RRSP (3.1.6)

▪ Think about boosting your self-directed RRSP's foreign content (3.1.6)

▪ Consider shares of a labour-sponsored venture capital corporation for your RRSP (3.3.5)

▪ Think about holding your own mortgage through your RRSP (3.1.6)

▪ Withdraw funds from your RRSP in low-income years (3.2.7)

▪ Contribute to your spouse's (or common-law spouse's) RRSP, if your projected income on retirement will be higher (3.3.1)

▪ Make spousal RRSP contributions in December instead of the following February (3.3.1)

▪ Transfer retiring allowances or severance pay to your RRSP (3.3.2)

▪ Top up your RRSP with a non-deductible $2,000 overcontribution (3.3.4)

▪ Consider Home Buyers' Plan withdrawals to buy or build your first home (but be sure to weigh the loss of RRSP growth) (3.3.6)

▪ Convert your RRSP to annuity or RRIF when you reach your retirement age limit (3.2.6)

▪ Consider contributing to your RRSP instead of a money purchase RPP (3.4.1)

▪ Find out about the vesting of your pension benefits, especially before making a career change (3.4.1)

▪ Think about establishing an "individual pension plan" (3.4.2)

▪ Consider setting up an RESP for your child's education (3.6)

Deferred income plans, particularly RRSPs and registered pension plans, are the most widely-used tax shelters in Canada. Put simply, almost everyone should have one.

The concept of deferred income plans is quite simple, although the particular rules can get rather complex. In this chapter, we'll take you through the basic rules, so you understand the system in general. We also discuss the options you have and steps you can take for tax planning.

The rules are essentially the same for Québec tax purposes.

3.1 Registered retirement savings plans—RRSPs

3.1.1 What is an RRSP?

You hear a lot about RRSPs every February, when the annual contribution deadline approaches. Although the acronym stands for Registered Retirement Savings Plan, an RRSP does not necessarily have anything to do with retirement. It can be used simply as a tax deferral tool.

The concept behind an RRSP is quite simple. If you agree to put some of your salary away and not have immediate access to it, the tax system will tax that income—along with all the interest and other income it earns—when it is *received* rather than when it is *earned*.

Example:

If you earn $60,000, you pay tax on $60,000.

Suppose you earn $60,000 but you put $2,000 of that into an RRSP. You will be taxed on only $58,000—the amount you have **received**.

If, some years later, the $2,000 you put away has grown (in a tax-free environment) to $3,000, you can take the $3,000 out of your RRSP, and it will be taxed (added to your income) at that point. Again, the original $2,000, now grown to $3,000, is being taxed in the year it is **received** rather than when it was **earned**.

The rules governing RRSPs are more complex than the above example indicates, of course. The amount you can contribute to an RRSP is limited in various ways.

3.1.2 How do you set up an RRSP?

An RRSP can be set up easily at almost any bank or trust company or through a stockbroker or life insurance agent. Basically, you just fill out a form and contribute money to the plan. Some institutions will give you your official tax receipt immediately; others will mail it to you some weeks later, in time for you to file it with your tax return.

3.1.3 How much can you contribute?

Contributions to an RRSP are deductible for any given year if they are contributed *in the year* or within *60 days after the end of the year.* So if you contribute by March 1, 1998, you can get a deduction for your 1997 tax return (and any resulting refund will come sometime in the spring of 1998 after you have filed your return).

There are three factors that limit the amount you can contribute to an RRSP: a dollar limit, which is $13,500 for 1997; a percentage (18%) of the previous year's "earned income"; and your "pension adjustment". We'll look at each of these in turn.

Dollar limit

The RRSP contribution limit has been frozen at $13,500 until 2003. The limit is scheduled to rise to $14,500 for 2004 and $15,500 for 2005, after which the limit will be indexed.

Percentage of previous year's earned income

The annual deduction (subject to the $13,500 dollar limit and pension adjustment) is limited to 18% of the **previous** year's earned income. That is, 18% of your 1996 earned income will be used to determine your 1997 contribution (made by March 1, 1998).

"Earned income" for most employees is the same as "salary"—the gross amount of salary, before deductions for income tax, EI, CPP, etc., which are withheld at source. "Earned income" includes business income, if you are self-employed or are an active partner in a business. It also includes:

- research grants, net of deductible related expenses
- royalties from works or inventions that you wrote or invented
- taxable alimony, maintenance and child support received (see 2.7)
- net rental income from real estate
- disability pension income received under the CPP/QPP.

Earned income is *reduced* by:

- deductible alimony, maintenance and child support you pay
- most deductible employment-related expenses, such as union dues and travelling expenses (but not pension plan contributions)
- rental losses.

Earned income does not include most investment income, such as interest or dividends, or capital gains. Nor does it include pension benefits, retiring allowances, severance pay, death benefits or amounts received from an RRSP, RRIF or deferred profit-sharing plan.

If your 1996 earned income was more than $75,000, your 1997 contribution will be limited to $13,500 (minus the pension adjustment as discussed below). Otherwise, you will be limited by the 18% factor.

Pension adjustment

Once you have calculated your maximum contribution limit as 18% of your previous year's earned income, subject to the dollar limits discussed above, you must subtract your **pension adjustment**, if any. This figure represents the deemed value of your pension earned for the previous year. In other words, the more that has been put aside (by you and your employer combined) towards your retirement pension, the less the *Income Tax Act* allows you to contribute to an RRSP.

If you are *not* a member of an employer's pension plan or deferred profit-sharing plan, your pension adjustment is zero, and you can contribute the full

18% of your previous year's earned income (subject to the annual $13,500 dollar limit).

Otherwise, your pension adjustment for 1997 should appear on your 1996 T4 slip, as well as on your Notice of Assessment received in the spring of 1997 following the filing of your 1996 return.

For "money-purchase" pension plans (see 3.4.1), the pension adjustment is the total contributions made towards your pension by you and your employer combined. The same applies to deferred profit sharing plans (see 3.5), except that the contributions are made only by your employer. For "defined benefit" pension plans (the type of pension plan most employees belong to), the pension adjustment is based on a calculation that takes into account the benefit you may receive on retirement based on the past year's employment.

In some situations, the calculation of your RRSP limit may also be reduced by a **past service pension adjustment** ("PSPA"). In general terms, a PSPA can arise when your pension benefits under a defined benefit pension plan are improved on a retroactive basis.

Example:

Melanie is a chemical engineer who belongs to her employer's pension plan. Her 1996 earned income was $60,000. Her pension adjustment for 1997, as reported to her on her 1996 T4 slip and her 1996 assessment received from Revenue Canada in mid-1997, is $3,200.

Before accounting for her pension adjustment, Melanie's contribution limit for 1997 is 18% of her 1996 earned income, to a maximum of $13,500. For 1996, 18% of her earned income is $10,800. From this amount she must deduct her pension adjustment of $3,200. Melanie may therefore contribute up to $7,600 to an RRSP by March 1, 1998 for a deduction on her 1997 tax return.

If you terminate your employment before retirement in 1997 and later years, you may be entitled to a **pension adjustment reversal** ("PAR"). The PAR is designed to give you back some of the RRSP contribution room lost due to PAs (pension adjustments) while you were a member of a company pension plan.

If you were a member of a defined contribution plan or deferred profit sharing plan, your PAR will be the total of all PAs reported by your employer since 1990 that have not yet "vested" (see 3.4.1). If you were a member of a defined benefit plan and you have not reported any PSPAs, your PAR will be equal to your total PAs since 1990 less the post-1989 portion of any lump sums paid to you or transferred to an RRSP or money-purchase pension plan (if you have reported any PSPAs, your PAR calculation will be more complex but, whatever your plan, your employer's pension plan administrator will figure it out for you). You will not be entitled to a PAR if you will be receiving any periodic pension payments from the plan.

PARs for 1997 terminations will increase your 1998 RRSP room, while PARs for post-1997 terminations will increase RRSP room for the year of termination. Since the PAR is new for 1997 and later years, employers do not have to report PARs for 1997 and 1998 terminations until 1999. If you are ending company pension plan membership in 1997 and 1998, you may want to encourage your employer to report your PAR earlier so you can make use of the related extra RRSP room as soon as possible.

Carry forward of unused deduction room and undeducted contributions

If in any year you contribute less than the maximum to an RRSP, you can "carry forward" the extra deduction room and make that much more contribution in any following year. As well, if you contribute an amount for a year but choose not to deduct the amount for that year, you can claim the deduction in any subsequent year (provided you still have contribution room).

> Example:
> Melanie, from the example above, has $7,600 of contribution room for 1997. She chooses to contribute only $5,000 to an RRSP for the year.
>
> Melanie has unused RRSP contribution room of $2,600 to carry forward. As a result, she may increase her contribution by that amount in any following year. If Melanie's contribution limit for 1998 is again $7,600, she can contribute up to $10,200 for deduction in 1998.

You should carefully review your assessment from Revenue Canada to make sure the contribution limit reported is correct, before relying on it. A wrong statement from Revenue Canada will not entitle you to deduct a contribution you would otherwise be entitled to.

In some cases you might contribute more than you can actually deduct. We discuss overcontributions in 3.3.4.

3.1.4 What's your contribution worth?

What is your contribution worth in tax savings? It depends on your marginal tax rate. The rates vary among the provinces due to different provincial tax rates (see Appendix II), but they are *approximately*:

> 27% on income up to $29,590
> 41% on income from $29,591 to $59,180
> 50% on income over $59,180

In the example above, if Melanie's taxable income, after other deductions, would be between $34,590 and $59,180, her contribution of $5,000 to an RRSP will save her about 41% of that amount, or $2,050, in tax for 1997. For someone whose taxable income stays over $59,180 even after making the RRSP contribution, the same $5,000 contribution would be worth about $2,500. Clearly, RRSPs are more tax-effective to those with higher incomes.

You should keep the value of your deduction in mind and try to take maximum advantage of the carry-forward mechanism in claiming your RRSP deductions. In a low-income year, for example, it may be advantageous to make your maximum RRSP *contribution*, but to defer claiming the *deduction* until a later year when your income is taxed at a higher marginal rate. However, beware of any potential exposure to minimum tax (see Chapter 12) if you are claiming a very large RRSP deduction in any single year.

3.1.5 What happens to the funds in the RRSP?

While your funds are in the RRSP, they are not subject to tax at all. No matter what amounts of interest, dividends, capital gains—or losses—result, there will be no tax effect until you withdraw the funds. (As we shall see in 3.2, you must close out the RRSP by the end of the year in which you reach your retirement age limit, but even then the tax effects can be partially deferred.)

The effects of having income compound without tax are quite dramatic. Compare the following two situations: A, where you invest $5,000 of your salary in an RRSP for 10 or 20 years at 10%, and B, where you earn the same 10% but it is subject to tax. The example assumes a 50% marginal tax rate.

	1997	2007	2017
A. Invest $5,000 in an RRSP After withdrawal	$5,000	$12,969 $6,484	$33,637 $16,818
B. Do not put the $5,000 in an RRSP, so you are immediately taxed on it as salary and on the income it earns	$2,500	$4,072	$6,633

In case A, you pay 50% in tax when you withdraw the funds, but they have grown substantially in the meantime. After 20 years, your $5,000 is worth $16,818 *after* tax. In case B, since the annual 10% interest is taxed, you have only 5% to reinvest for compounding purposes. The fact that you can use the $6,633 (after 20 years) directly in case B, without having to pay 50% tax on it as in case A, doesn't come close to making up for the tax-free compounding of interest.

Of course, if you are paying non-deductible interest such as mortgage interest, that interest also effectively compounds on a pre-tax basis, and you might be better off to pay down your mortgage rather than contribute to an RRSP. In such a case, you can generally use all your unused RRSP contribution room by making and deducting a "catch-up" RRSP contribution in a later year, when you have the funds to contribute.

As we mentioned earlier, your RRSP can be invested in a number of different forms. The simplest, and usually lowest-paying, is a deposit account that pays interest monthly or twice a year. Many people invest instead in longer-term Guaranteed Investment Certificates ("GICs") or term deposits. Equity mutual funds are growing increasingly popular as a method of indirectly investing RRSP funds in a number of companies, but they do entail a higher level of risk. See 1.2.5 for tips on choosing investments and advice on developing an appropriate investment strategy.

3.1.6   Self-directed RRSPs

Consider a self-directed RRSP for greater flexibility.

If you're ambitious and willing to take a little more risk with your funds by investing in stocks or bonds of your own choosing, you can set up a **self-directed** RRSP. This is normally done through a stockbroker or financial institution, subject to an annual fee in the $100-150 range (plus normal commissions on any stock trades). You then decide what your RRSP invests in. There are restrictions—the system tries to ensure that your money, while not necessarily "safe", is at least invested in reasonable places. "Qualified investments" for an RRSP include:

- cash
- government, Crown corporation or municipal bonds
- GICs, term deposits and treasury bills ("T-Bills")
- certain government-insured mortgages
- shares or bonds of corporations listed on Canadian stock exchanges
- RRSP-eligible mutual funds
- shares listed on certain foreign stock exchanges, bonds of certain foreign governments and mutual funds investing in foreign markets (however, as discussed below, no more than 20% of an RRSP may be invested in foreign assets)
- certain small business shares.

The rules governing the details (e.g., which mortgages and small business shares are qualified investments) are extremely complex, and you should consult a professional advisor if you wish to do more with your self-directed RRSP than simply buy, say, T-Bills and Hydro bonds (which are generally regarded as good safe investments, incidentally). However, if you have the time to give it the attention it needs, a self-directed RRSP can prove to be much more rewarding in the long run. The control you will gain over investment decisions will diversify your risk and give you the flexibility to pursue a different range of investment opportunities—including some that are generally only possible through self-directed RRSPs, like stripped bonds, mortgage-backed securities and other less common RRSP investments.

The broader range of investment options you may acquire with a self-directed RRSP comes with a higher level of risk. It is generally prudent to spread your investments over a wide range of options and to ensure that at least a portion of your investments have fixed rates of return, such as GICs.

Think about transferring shares that you already own to your self-directed RRSP.

Consider contributing shares (or interest-bearing investments) that you already own to your self-directed RRSP in lieu of cash contributions. Shares in small businesses can be contributed in limited circumstances (for example, you must not be a controlling shareholder of the corporation). However, most shares and bonds of Canadian public corporations are fair game. If you have shares that you intend to hold for a long time, you can contribute them to your RRSP and get a tax deduction without any cash outlay.

Note that capital gains and dividends are effectively fully-taxed when withdrawn from an RRSP, since you're taxed on the total amount withdrawn. So if you contribute shares (or buy shares inside your RRSP), any capital gains and dividends will eventually be taxed at a higher rate than if you earned them directly (see 5.2 and 6.1.2). If you leave the funds in the RRSP for long enough, the deferral of tax and tax-free compounding of interest should more than make up for the tax rate differential, however.

A transfer of investments to your RRSP can trigger a capital gain (see 5.2), since the transfer will be deemed to take place at fair market value. However, you are prohibited from claiming a capital loss (see 5.3) on the transfer of investments to your RRSP.

A self-directed RRSP allows you to invest in shares listed on certain foreign stock exchanges, certain foreign government bonds and other foreign properties, within limits. Generally, only 20% of the cost amount of all property held by your RRSP can be invested in foreign property. The calculation is performed at the end of each month. Foreign property values over the 20% threshold are subject to a special tax of 1% per month payable by the RRSP. The 20% limit is generally based on the property's cost at the time of purchase, not its current market value. Your RRSP's administrator should monitor your RRSP's foreign content holdings and warn you if it is in danger of going off-side.

Consider boosting your RRSP's foreign content.

With the right investment mix, you can boost your self-directed RRSP's foreign content to a maximum of 40% of the cost amount of property held by it. To assist small businesses in obtaining equity financing, a special rule permits you to increase your RRSP's holdings of qualifying foreign property without penalty by $3 for every $1 that you invest in a certain Canadian small business corporation. That means a 6.67% holding of a qualifying small business property will enable you to increase your foreign property holdings by 20% (3 × 6.67%), up to the 40% maximum.

However, if you own more than 10% of the shares of a small business, your RRSP's ability to invest in that business may be restricted or denied. Since these restrictions and the rules governing the types of small businesses that qualify are quite complex, you should consult your tax advisor if you are considering increasing your self-directed RRSP's foreign content through small business investments.

Another indirect way of further increasing your self-directed RRSP's foreign property content is to invest in a qualifying mutual fund trust. As long as the trust meets certain conditions, the mutual fund trust in which you invest can also invest up to 20% of the cost amount of its holdings in foreign property.

Think about holding your own mortgage through your RRSP.

It is even possible for you to arrange for your RRSP to hold your own mortgage—in other words, you put funds into your RRSP, receive a tax deduction, and lend the funds to yourself. This is not easy to do, however; the mortgage must be federally insured, and various other restrictions apply.

Investing in your own mortgage may make you feel good, but does not always make sense financially. Since the investment must be at the market rate, you may be no better off depending on the size of the mortgage, once all fees (legal, appraisal, etc.) are taken into account. As a general rule of thumb, to be a worthwhile investment, the mortgage's principal should be in the $50,000 to $100,000 range with a term of at least five years. Alternatively if you don't have that much cash in your RRSP, some financial institutions offer a program through which the mortgage is "shared" between your RRSP and your institution.

3.1.7 How to make the most of your RRSP

If you have cash in the bank earning interest, even if you are young and not yet concerned about retirement, you should contribute as much as possible to an RRSP. The example we saw in 3.1.5 above shows how valuable it is to have your funds earning tax-free income.

RRSPs—contribute early and often.

If possible, you should contribute early, rather than waiting till the deadline. Your 1997 contribution, for example, may be made any time until March 1, 1998 if you intend to deduct it on your 1997 tax return. If you contribute at the beginning of 1997, all of the income earned for that extra year will accumulate tax-free. The effect of early contributions over several years will be dramatic. Do ensure, however, that you have enough contribution room before you commit your contribution for the year, and remember that each year's contribution will be limited to 18% of your *previous year's* earned income.

You can store up any unused RRSP contribution room if you can't afford to make a contribution now, and make your contribution and claim the deduction in later years.

If you have the cash and the contribution room, but do not want to claim a deduction in the current year because you are already in a low tax bracket, make the contribution but delay the deduction. As discussed in 3.1.3, you can claim the deduction in any later year. If you are confident of being in a higher tax bracket within the next year or so, this strategy can maximize the tax-free growth of funds while also maximizing your tax savings.

For cash-flow purposes, you may wish to set up a monthly transfer of a few hundred dollars from your regular bank account to your RRSP account. That will ensure steady contributions to the RRSP over the course of the year.

When considering investments within your RRSP, bear in mind the one major drawback of long-term investments such as five-year GICs. If you decide to withdraw the funds sooner for tax purposes (see 3.3.4), or to use the Home Buyers' Plan (see 3.3.6), you may have a problem.

3.2 How do you get money out of an RRSP?

There are basically four routes for getting your money out of an RRSP—you must make use of one of these options described in this section by the end of the year in which you reach your age limit.

3.2.1 New age limit for maturing RRSPs and other plans

If you will be celebrating your 69th, 70th or 71st birthday in 1997, you'll have to decide what to do with your RRSP before the end of 1997. That's because the 1996 budget lowered the age limit for maturing RRSPs, registered pension plans and deferred profit sharing plans from 71 to 69 (with a year's grace allowed for those who turned 69 or 70 in 1996).

If you are 68 or younger at the end of 1997, you will have to decide what to do with your RRSP by the end of the year in which you turn 69.

3.2.2 Withdraw the funds

The first, and easiest, way to cash out your RRSP is simply to **withdraw the funds**. The amount withdrawn from the RRSP is included in your income for the year in which you do so. It is taxed as ordinary income, just as if it were salary, even if some of the value of the RRSP represents capital gains (which outside an RRSP are normally only partially taxed and, in some cases, could be entirely exempt). A percentage to cover tax will be withheld at source by the financial institution and remitted to Revenue Canada (and Revenu Québec if appropriate) on your behalf (see 3.2.7). You will then report the income and amount of tax withheld on your annual income tax return and either receive a refund or, if not enough tax was withheld, pay the difference.

3.2.3 Purchase an annuity

The second method is to purchase an **annuity**. None of the RRSP proceeds will be taxed immediately, but the annuity payments will be taxed as you receive them. (As discussed in 2.5.2, up to $1,000 per year of the income may effectively be exempted through the pension income tax credit.)

There are three general kinds of annuities: "term-certain", payable to you or your estate for a fixed number of years; "single life", payable to you as long as you are alive; and "joint and last survivor life", payable as long as either you or your spouse is alive. Numerous additional options are available, such as a guaranteed term as part of a life annuity, indexing for inflation, reduction of payment on the death of your spouse, reduction of payment when Old Age Security payments begin, and so on. You should discuss the available options, and their effect on the monthly annuity payment you receive, with your life insurance agent. (A life annuity may only be acquired from a life insurance company. Term-certain annuities are available from trust companies as well.)

If you purchased a deferred annuity before March 6, 1996, it will be exempt from the reduced RRSP age limits discussed in 3.2.1.

3.2.4 Convert RRSP to RRIF

The third thing you can do with your RRSP is to convert it into a **Registered Retirement Income Fund**, or RRIF (pronounced "riff"). A RRIF is somewhat like an RRSP, in that you can have it invested in various kinds of securities. However, you must withdraw at least a "minimum amount" from the RRIF each year, and report what you withdraw for tax purposes. (Again, up to $1,000 per year of such income may effectively be fully or partially exempted through the pension income tax credit, as explained in 2.5.2.)

For RRIFs set up before 1993, the amount that must be withdrawn from the RRIF each year up to age 78 is 1/N of the value of the RRIF at the beginning of the year, where N is the number of years left until you (or your spouse) turn 90. After age 78, and for all ages for RRIFs set up in 1993 or later, the amount is a fraction that increases gradually each year, levelling out at 20% once you turn 94.

Note that you should always pay investment management fees related to the management of your RRIF's assets with funds from within the plan. Revenue Canada considers payment of these types of fees to be a contribution to the plan, and, since RRIF contributions are not allowed, payment of investment management fees with funds outside the RRIF could result in the RRIF's deregistration, meaning that you will be subject to immediate tax on all of the RRIF funds in the year of deregisteration.

However, it does make sense to pay service fees for your RRIF's *administration* with funds outside the RRIF. Although you will not get a deduction for the amount of the administration fees, you will be able to preserve the amount of funds growing in the RRIF's tax-sheltered environment.

3.2.5 Convert locked-in RRSP to life income fund

A life income fund ("LIF") provides an alternative to a life annuity when certain individuals, who were formerly members of a registered pension plan, terminate employment or plan membership. The LIF is also an option for individuals who have transferred pension funds to a **locked-in RRSP** (see 3.3.2).

A LIF is a RRIF for tax purposes (see 3.2.4) with additional restrictions. Like any other RRIF, a minimum amount must be withdrawn each year. As well, under a LIF there is a *maximum* amount that can be withdrawn each year until age 80. (Thus, the funds remain "locked in", just like a pension or locked-in RRSP.) The remaining balance of funds in the LIF must be used to purchase a life annuity by December 31 of the year in which the individual turns 80.

A LIF can offer an attractive income alternative to a life annuity option. LIFs are now available in all provinces except Prince Edward Island and they can be purchased with funds governed by either federal or provincial pension regulations. You should consult your professional advisor to determine whether this option is available to you.

3.2.6 Maturing your RRSP—what's the best option?

By the end of the year in which you reach your age limit (see 3.2.1), you will have to decide what to do with your RRSP. A straight withdrawal will rarely be the best option, since you will be taxed on the total income—and none of it will be eligible for the pension tax credit (see 2.5.2).

Convert your RRSP to RRIF or annuity when you reach your retirement age limit.

Instead, if you wish to have some control over the investments, you should purchase a RRIF (see 3.2.4). If you prefer simply to have a steady monthly income that you don't have to worry about, contact your life insurance agent and purchase an annuity (see 3.2.3).

If you are setting up an annuity, consider the effect of the tax brackets on your income. Your main goal, of course, is to ensure that you have enough income each month to meet your needs. If you can satisfy those needs with a longer-term annuity that keeps your income below the high-tax brackets, you may be better off.

3.2.7   Early withdrawals—your RRSP as a tax averaging tool

As discussed in 3.1.5, the funds in your RRSP are not taxed until the year in which you withdraw the funds. As a result, RRSPs can be used as a tax averaging tool rather than just a mechanism for retirement saving. If you are still fairly young and not too worried about retirement income, you can withdraw funds from your RRSP whenever there is a tax advantage to doing so.

Withdraw funds from your RRSP in low-income years.

Suppose you plan to take some time off to care for your young children, for example, or to go on an extended vacation or take up some other activity. During such years, where your employment income will be low, you can withdraw funds from your RRSP and perhaps pay tax at the 27% rate instead of 41% or 50%. The advantage of low-rate taxation will have to be balanced against the advantage of tax-free growth available by leaving the funds in the RRSP.

In an anticipated low-income year following a high-income year, you can even consider contributing in February, claiming a deduction (say at 41%) for the previous year, and withdrawing the funds, to be taxed at the low (27%) rate.

You will need to plan around the withholding tax on RRSP withdrawals, however. For federal purposes, a withdrawal of up to $5,000 is subject to 10% withholding; over $5,000 and up to $15,000, 20%; and over $15,000, 30%. In Québec, a withdrawal of up to $5,000 is subject to 21% withholding (25% as of 1998); over $5,000 and up to $15,000, 30% (33% as of 1998); and over $15,000, 35% (38% as of 1998). You may be able to arrange withdrawals so that they incur the least possible withholding tax, leaving you with the use of the funds until you file your tax return the following April.

Bear in mind, however, that you may have a tax liability to settle up on April 30 to the extent that your tax rate on the income exceeds the withholding tax rate.

3.3 Special RRSP rules

A number of rules deal with special situations with respect to RRSPs. We will refer to them only briefly; you should consult your professional advisor if you are in these situations.

3.3.1 Spousal plans

Contribute to your spouse's (or common-law spouse's) RRSP, if your projected income on retirement will be higher.

The RRSP rules allow you to contribute to an RRSP for your spouse, and claim the deduction yourself. Your total contributions (to your own and your spouse's plans) are still subject to your normal limits (18% of your previous year's earned income or $13,500 for 1997, minus any pension adjustment). The advantage is that your spouse will ultimately be the one who reports the income for tax purposes, when the funds are withdrawn on retirement or otherwise. If your spouse has less income than you either on retirement or at some earlier time (including, for example, due to expected maternity leave), this can result in significantly less tax on the income.

Make spousal RRSP contributions in December instead of the following February.

To prevent spousal RRSPs from being used for "income splitting" (see Chapter 4), the amount you contribute will be taxed back to you (rather than your spouse) to the extent any amount is withdrawn by your spouse in the year *in which* you contribute *or in the next two calendar years*. See 3.3.12.

Example:

Jon and Nancy are married. Jon contributes $5,000 to Nancy's RRSP in February 1998, and claims the deduction on his 1997 tax return.

If Nancy withdraws the funds at any time up to the end of 2000, $5,000 of the amount withdrawn will be treated as Jon's income, not Nancy's. (If, however, Jon's contribution had been made in December 1997, this would only be the case until the end of 1999.)

This rule does not apply if the spouses are separated or divorced. We explore this planning idea in more detail at 4.3.9, in the chapter on Income Splitting.

If you are over the age limit for maturing your RRSP (generally age 69, see 3.2.1) and have "earned income" in the previous year, this will create new RRSP room for you in the current year. As long as your spouse is 69 or younger, you can still claim a deduction for a spousal RRSP contribution.

In general, there will be little effect on the real ownership of the funds under provincial law if you and your spouse separate or divorce. The rule in most provinces is that such funds will be pooled and shared between the spouses. There are rules in place to allow a tax-free division of RRSP funds in such situations.

3.3.2 Transfers to and from RRSPs

RRSPs can generally be transferred, with no tax consequences, to other RRSPs or to RRIFs, by simply filling out a form.

Transfer retiring allowances or severance pay to your RRSP.

Under pension legislation you may be prevented from immediately withdrawing pension benefits from your employer's plan on your departure from the company. This legislation is commonly referred to as "locking-in" legislation. Pension benefits subject to these rules may be transferred to a locked-in RRSP. Locked-in RRSPs are essentially subject to the same restrictions on withdrawal of funds as was the original pension plan. For example, you cannot usually access the locked-in plan funds until you are within ten years of your normal retirement date. On the other hand, you do have more flexibility in deciding how to invest the funds. A locked-in RRSP may be convertible to a LIF (see 3.2.5).

Where the pension legislation permits a transfer from a registered pension plan to a locked-in RRSP or LIF, there are generally no tax consequences to such transfers, though the tax rules may restrict the amounts that can be transferred from a "defined-benefit" pension plan.

Special rules allow a "retiring allowance" (which, as defined for tax purposes, includes severance pay and amounts received for wrongful dismissal) to be transferred tax-free to an RRSP, rather than taxed as income when received. The amount that can be transferred is normally limited to $2,000 for each calendar year (or part year) of employment before 1996, plus $1,500 for years of employment before 1989 for which employer pension contributions have not vested. (If the amount you transfer this way is large, you could trigger minimum tax. See Chapter 11.)

3.3.3 Death

On death, a taxpayer is normally taxed on the entire amount of any RRSPs or RRIFs, except where the funds are left to the taxpayer's spouse, in which case they are included in the spouse's income (see 13.1.1). To the extent the funds come from an RRSP, they can be transferred to the spouse's own RRSP or RRIF for a deduction that offsets the income inclusion.The spouse can also use these funds to acquire an annuity. If there is no surviving spouse, and the RRSP or RRIF funds are left to a financially-dependent child or grandchild, the RRSP or RRIF funds can either be taxed in the hands of the child or grandchild or used to buy a term annuity to age 18. The executor of the deceased's estate should obtain professional advice on these matters.

See Chapter 13 for a general discussion of the tax effects of death.

3.3.4 Overcontributions

The RRSP contribution limits were discussed in 3.1.3. What happens if you contribute more than the maximum?

First, bear in mind that your financial institution will not prevent you from overcontributing. Your financial institution is not obliged to tell you how much you can or cannot contribute.

Second, any contributions over the maximum are **non-deductible**. However, once the funds are in your RRSP, they are taxable when withdrawn (whether on retirement or earlier), just like the funds that were deductible when you contributed them. Therefore, there is double taxation—once when you earn the income (and receive no deduction despite putting the funds into the RRSP), and once when you withdraw the funds from the RRSP.

Third, in certain rare circumstances, overcontributing might be valuable despite the double taxation, because of the huge beneficial effect of tax-free compounding (as illustrated in the table in 3.1.5).

Also, you can often deduct an overcontribution in a later year as new contribution room is created. There is therefore a rule preventing excessive overcontributions. Up to **$2,000** can be contributed without penalty. Above the $2,000 level, the excess is subject to a penalty tax of 1% per month.

Top up your RRSP with a non-deductible $2,000 overcontribution.

The $2,000 figure is designed to catch those cases where you might have miscalculated your pension adjustment (see 3.1.3) and contributed a little too much. However, as long as you are certain about your pension adjustment, you can use the $2,000 deliberately if you wish. So if you are already contributing your maximum for 1997, consider making an additional contribution of up to $2,000 to further benefit from the compounding of tax-free growth.

Until February 27, 1995, the overcontribution limit was $8,000. If you overcontributed before that date, you must use up the excess over $2,000 by deducting it against your RRSP contribution room in 1996 and on as new room becomes available.

As discussed at 3.3.1, new RRSP room continues to be created after you reach age 69 (see 3.2.1) if you have earned income. Thus, you may be able to claim a deduction for your undeducted $2,000 overcontribution after reaching age 70 if you have sufficient earned income in the previous year. Another idea is to consider making an RRSP contribution in December of the year in which you turn 69 equal to your new RRSP contribution room in the year you turn 70 (plus a $2,000 overcontribution if available). Although you will have to pay a 1% penalty tax for the month of December, your overcontribution will be eliminated on January 1 of the next year.

3.3.5 Labour-sponsored venture capital corporation shares

In most provinces, a combined federal/provincial credit of 30-35% (depending on the province) is available for an investment of up to $3,500 per year in shares of a "labour-sponsored venture capital corporation", or LSVCC (see 6.3.8 and 15.3.5). For LSVCC shares purchased before March 7, 1996, the combined credit is generally 40% with a maximum investment of $5,000 per year. In Newfoundland, Alberta and the Territories, only the 15% federal credit is available (or 20% for shares purchased before March 7, 1996). The parallel Québec tax credit is discussed at 15.3.5.

You can buy shares in a labour-sponsored venture capital corporation and contribute them to your RRSP. You can also generally have the shares bought directly by your self-directed RRSP (see 3.1.6), provided the RRSP uses "new" or previous contribution funds (but not earnings). Either way, you claim the credit on your personal income tax return.

Consider shares of a labour-sponsored venture capital corporation for your RRSP.

When combined with the deduction for the RRSP contribution, a $3,500 investment in an LSVCC may cost you as little as $595 after tax. Particularly if you are not otherwise making the maximum possible RRSP contribution, an investment in an LSVCC for your RRSP may be worth considering. Before taking the plunge and investing in an LSVCC, make sure you evaluate the relative merits from an investment perspective, as they are generally a higher risk and probably illiquid investment. (See also 6.3.8.)

3.3.6 The Home Buyers' Plan

Under the Home Buyers' Plan, if you qualify, you are allowed to withdraw up to $20,000 as a loan from your RRSP to buy or build a home, without counting the withdrawal as income. You must then repay the loan, without interest, over the next 16 years.

Who may use the Home Buyers' Plan?

The Plan may only be used by what the government calls a "first-time buyer". You are not a "first-time buyer" if you have owned and lived in a home as a principal place of residence at any time during the five calendar years up to and including the current year. (For the current year, you can use the Plan up to 30 days after you acquire a home.) If your spouse has owned and lived in a home during that period, and you have inhabited that home during the marriage, you also do not qualify. (Remember that "spouse" includes a common-law spouse as outlined in 2.2.1.) Furthermore, you generally cannot use the Plan if you have used it before.

How does the Plan work?

You can borrow (withdraw) up to $20,000 from your RRSP under the Plan. If you and your spouse each have RRSPs, you can thus borrow up to $40,000 between the two of you if you are taking joint ownership in the property. A qualifying home must be acquired before October 1 of the year following the year of the withdrawal. You must also begin or intend, not later than one year after its acquisition, to use the home as a principal place of residence. No tax will apply to the withdrawal.

When you withdraw the funds, you fill out Form T1036 (and TP-935.1-V for Québec purposes), certifying that you have entered into a written agreement to purchase a home, and stating its address. Once you have done this, the financial institution will not withhold tax when it pays the funds to you.

Note that the Home Buyers' Plan does not give you any right to withdraw funds from your RRSP if you didn't already have that right. If your RRSP funds are invested in term deposits or other long-term obligations, you will still need to negotiate with the financial institution to have the funds released as cash. Similarly, if your RRSP funds are in your employer's group RRSP or a "locked-in RRSP", you may not be able to get them out.

Once you borrow the funds, you must normally complete the purchase by September 30 of the *following* year. (A one-year extension may be available if the deal falls through and you buy a replacement property.) If you withdraw less than the $20,000 maximum, you can in many cases withdraw a further amount up to the following January 31 and treat the total as one withdrawal.

The requirement to repay the funds begins in the second year following the withdrawal. You can opt to make any year's repayment up to 60 days after the end of the year.

If you do not make repayments as required, you must include the shortfall in income for tax purposes. In effect, it's treated as a permanent withdrawal from your RRSP and you're taxed on it.

Example:

Olivia has $30,000 in her RRSP. She signs an agreement in September 1997 to purchase a new home. In November 1997 she completes Form T1036 and withdraws $15,000 from her RRSP. The purchase closes in January 1998.

No tax will be withheld from the $15,000 that Olivia withdraws, so she can use the full amount towards the home purchase. Since she withdrew the funds in 1997, Olivia must repay $1,000 (1/15 of the total) to her RRSP during 1999 or by February 29, 2000. If she repays only $600, she will have to include $400 in income for 1999 and pay tax on that amount.

If Olivia repays no more than $1,000 in 1999 (or by February 29, 2000), she will be required to repay 1/14 of the balance, another $1,000, in 2000 (or by March 1, 2001). Suppose she repays $8,000 in 1998, leaving a balance owing of $7,000? For 1999, she will still be required to repay 1/14 of the balance, or $500. The fact she has prepaid more than required will reduce but not eliminate her obligation to continue paying the balance in later years.

Contributions in the year you use the plan

If you contribute to an RRSP and withdraw the same funds within 90 days under the Home Buyers' Plan, you cannot deduct your contribution. For purposes of this rule, any balance that was already in your RRSP can be considered as withdrawn first. Thus, it is only to the extent the amount of your new contribution is needed for the withdrawal (within the 90-day period) that a deduction will be disallowed.

Home Buyers' Plan—some special situations

The Home Buyers' Plan may be used for building a new home on an existing lot that you own. Instead of an agreement to purchase the home, you must have an agreement in place to construct it.

If you withdraw the funds but your home purchase does not close, you can generally cancel your participation in the Plan and return the funds to your RRSP with no adverse tax consequences. Alternatively, if you buy another qualifying home as a replacement, you can remain in the Plan.

If you have contributed to a spousal RRSP, your spouse must normally wait two to three years before withdrawing the funds or they will be taxed back to you (see 3.3.1). However, with the Home Buyers' Plan, your spouse can borrow the funds to purchase a qualifying home, and to the extent they are not repaid over the 16 years, it is your spouse that must include the difference in income, not you. (Note, however, that if your spouse withdraws the funds and does not purchase a qualifying home, so that the full amount withdrawn is taxed in the current year, the attribution rule *will* apply and you, not your spouse, will be taxed on the withdrawal.)

If you become a non-resident of Canada, you must repay the entire outstanding balance to the RRSP within 60 days. Otherwise, the balance will be included in your income for the year that you became non-resident.

If you should die while you have an outstanding balance to repay, that balance will be included in your income for the year of death and tax will be payable by your estate (see 13.1.1). However, if you leave a surviving spouse, your executor and your spouse may make a special election to have your spouse take over the obligation to repay the funds over the remainder of the 15-year period, and the balance will not be included in your income for the year of death.

Should you use the Home Buyers' Plan?

Weigh the loss of RRSP growth before using the Home Buyers' Plan.

At first glance, the Plan seems attractive, since it gives you ready access to a potentially large chunk of cash. However, there are three costs to consider.

First, you lose the **tax-free compounding** in your RRSP (see the example in 3.1.5). Balanced against this is the fact that you have probably reduced the mortgage interest expense you would otherwise have to pay out of after-tax dollars. Nevertheless, the value of the RRSP may be significantly less, at your retirement, than it otherwise would have been. If you are depending on your RRSP for your retirement income, you will want to forecast the reduction in income that will result from withdrawing a large chunk of the funds now and repaying it to the RRSP over the next 16 years.

Second, you have to be able to sustain the **cash flow** to repay the RRSP; if you cannot, you will end up being taxed on the funds you have withdrawn. When figuring out the cash you need to handle your mortgage and property tax payments, don't forget the 1/15 minimum repayment to the RRSP in each year beginning with the second year after the withdrawal (due by 60 days after the end of the year). Of course, since you are repaying borrowed funds and not contributing new money to the RRSP, no deduction is available for the amounts you repay.

Third, you might not be able to make a contribution to your RRSP for the current year. This will depend on the balance in your RRSP. If your withdrawal does not exceed the value you had in the RRSP 90 days before the withdrawal, you have no problem. Otherwise, you may have to postpone the current year's contribution, and save it up for a later year. The result would be one less year for those funds to have earned tax-free interest, and higher tax to pay in the current year since you will not have a contribution to deduct.

Nevertheless, if you need the funds to help you purchase your first home, the Home Buyers' Plan may be a significant help.

Planning for the Home Buyers' Plan

If you're thinking about tapping your RRSP to purchase your first home but your RRSP is not yet at $20,000 and you intend to use the Home Buyers' Plan to its fullest, make your contribution early enough so that it can sit in the RRSP for 90 days before you withdraw the funds. Then the amount you contributed can be withdrawn as well without affecting your deduction for the contribution.

If you are planning to buy a new home and you are close to the four-year cutoff that will re-qualify you as a "first-time buyer", consider waiting and making your purchase at a time when you can use the Home Buyers' Plan. For example, if you sold your last home in 1993, you can use the Plan as of January 1, 1998.

If you are about to be married and your future spouse owns a home that you will be living in, consider borrowing funds under the Home Buyers' Plan before your wedding. Once you are married, you will not be able to do so. However, you are not restricted by a previous home owned by your spouse, as long as you do not live in it while married. Therefore, if you plan on buying a new home after your wedding, you should not (romantic considerations aside) move into your spouse's current home until you have made your withdrawal under the Plan.

The same applies if you have been living common-law for less than 12 months (and have not had a child together). Once you reach 12 months of living together, you are considered "married" for income tax purposes (see 2.2.1). If your mate owns your present home, but you are planning on "moving up" to a larger home, you should consider withdrawing funds under the Home Buyers' Plan before you have lived together for 12 months. However, you will have to take ownership (or at least part ownership) of the new home in your own name.

3.4 Registered pension plans—RPPs

3.4.1 Ordinary RPPs

A registered pension plan is set up by an employer for its employees. Virtually all large companies, and many smaller ones, have such plans. These are quite different from the Canada Pension Plan (or, in Québec, the Québec Pension Plan), to which all employed and self-employed taxpayers must contribute.

The employer contributes (and deducts for tax purposes) an annual amount on behalf of each employee. Unlike most other employment benefits, these amounts are not taxed as benefits from employment in the year they are contributed. Instead, employees are taxed on the income from the pension when they *receive* it, which is normally after retirement.

In some cases, employees may be required or permitted to make additional contributions to the plan, which they can deduct for tax purposes in the year contributed.

There are two general kinds of pension plans: money-purchase and defined benefit. **Money-purchase** plans are analogous to RRSPs, in the sense that whatever the funds earn determines the amount of the pension payments. The pension plans of most employees are **defined benefit** plans. With such plans, you know from the beginning how much your pension will be, usually based on a percentage of your actual salary over a specified number of years. It is up to the employer to contribute enough, and to the pension fund management to invest wisely, to make sure that the plan remains sufficiently well funded to make those payments.

Once an employee retires, or becomes otherwise eligible for the pension (e.g., on leaving for other employment after a certain number of years of being in the pension plan), the pension income is taxed as regular income as it is received (except for amounts transferred to a RRIF, as discussed below). Up to $1,000 per year may effectively be exempted through the pension income tax credit (see 2.5.2).

If you have a defined benefit RPP, you are allowed to transfer lump-sum amounts from the RPP to a RRIF (see 3.2.4). In the past, you were only allowed to do so before you turned 72 but, for 1996 and later years, the rules have been changed to allow you to make this transfer even if you are 72 or older. The amount you can transfer is limited to the amount of annual pension given up under the RPP multiplied by a factor based on your age at the date of the transfer. The factor is 9.0 if you are under 50, gradually rising to 12.4 at ages 64 and 65, and then decreasing to 3.0 once you are 96 or over.

Consider contributing to your RRSP instead of a money purchase RPP.

If you've been making voluntary contributions to your registered pension plan under a money purchase provision, consider contributing to an RRSP instead. The amount you can contribute will normally be the same, but the RRSP will give you much greater flexibility in the future. If you want to make sure you never have access to the funds before retirement, then by all means continue to contribute to your pension plan.

Find out about the vesting of your pension benefits before making a career change.

If you are a member of a company pension plan, find out how long it takes for your contributions to be "vested". Once they are vested, the pension you have earned becomes yours, and almost all employers will allow you to take the full pension benefits with you if you change jobs. On the other hand, if they are not vested, you get your own contributions back when you leave—but no pension down the road. The vesting of your pension benefits can be a major factor in career change decisions.

3.4.2 Individual pension plans—IPPs

An individual pension plan ("IPP") is exactly what the name implies—a registered pension plan designed and structured for one individual member. It is possible for owner-managers to meet the qualifications to have this type of pension plan registered with Revenue Canada.

The IPP concept is a two-pronged retirement saving strategy. First, your employer (or your own company, if you are an owner-manager) sets up a personalized, defined benefit, registered pension plan for you. Second, you also make the maximum allowable contribution to your RRSP (or your spouse's RRSP), although your maximum contribution amount will probably be zero until at least 2004 (see 3.1.3). The IPP concept is an alternative to the basic retirement saving strategy, which would be simply to make the maximum possible RRSP contributions (the "RRSP route").

Generally speaking, the IPP concept will be suitable for you if you are

- a key executive and/or owner-manager of a corporation
- over 53 years old; and
- earning a base salary of more than about $100,000.

An IPP may also be worth considering if you are already in your employer's group RPP but the benefits from that RPP are not as generous as you would like them to be.

At termination or retirement, any surplus in the IPP can be returned to the member after paying personal tax. The surplus is the excess of IPP assets over the actual cost of the defined benefit pension to be provided under the terms of the plan. Alternatively, the tax sheltering may be allowed to continue if your IPP is able to opt, upon your retirement, to "self-annuitize" (i.e., have the IPP pay you, the beneficiary of the plan, a life annuity rather than purchase one from a life insurance company). This can have the effect of stretching out the additional tax sheltering represented by any accumulated IPP surplus well into the years beyond retirement and quite possibly until the last of you and your spouse dies. However, some provinces do not allow self-annuitization in a plan with no active members, which will be the case for your IPP after you retire.

Weigh the advantages of establishing an "individual pension plan".

The main advantage of the IPP is that, if you are over 53, you and your employer will be allowed to make higher annual contributions than you would otherwise be entitled to under the RRSP route. In addition to maximizing tax savings, the higher allowable contributions under the IPP concept can be looked on as a form of forced savings. Your employer will be required to top up the funds in the IPP if investment performance is poor and there will be insufficient funds (as determined by an actuary) to pay you the defined benefit pension promised under the plan (which could be a point of concern to your employer). A further advantage is that an IPP is generally creditor-proof, while most RRSPs are not.

Depending on your particular circumstances, an IPP could also provide some scope for making past service pension contributions. This can further enhance the tax sheltering value of an IPP.

There are also significant potential disadvantages of an IPP which you should carefully consider. For example, you will lose the flexibility to split income on retirement, since contributions cannot be made to the IPP for your spouse, as can be done with RRSPs. In contrast to RRSPs, which can be cashed in any time, contributions made to the IPP will be locked in under pension benefits legislation until retirement, at which time they must be used to provide retirement benefits (usually in the form of a life annuity or life income fund). An RRSP, on the other hand, provides a variety of options, on termination or retirement (see 3.2). In addition, start-up and ongoing costs of administration of an IPP will be higher than those of your RRSP. This is due to the complex regulatory environment governing pension plans. For example, an actuarial valuation will be required at start-up and every three years thereafter; and certain forms must be filed annually.

The rules regarding IPPs are quite complex. You should consult your professional tax advisor for more information.

3.5 Deferred profit-sharing plans—DPSPs

Deferred profit-sharing plans are less common than registered pension plans. They operate the same way in that contributions are made by the employer and are only taxed in the employee's hands when received, normally on retirement.

Employer contributions to DPSPs are based on profits and are not usually expressed as a fixed dollar amount per employee each year. Such plans may be used, for example, by smaller companies which are not sure of profits and do not wish to commit themselves to large pension contributions, especially if they end up losing money for the year.

Employer contributions to DPSPs are generally limited to $6,750 for 1997 per employee. They also cannot exceed 18% of the employee's salary from the employer for the year. Your employer's contributions to a DPSP add to your pension adjustment, and they therefore reduce the amount you can contribute to an RRSP (see 3.1.3).

Employee contributions to a DPSP are not permitted.

DPSPs cannot be set up for employees who are also major shareholders (over 10% of any class of shares) in the employer corporation, or for members of their families. They therefore cannot be used for owner-managers of small businesses.

3.6 Registered education savings plans—RESPs

The RESP is a rather different animal from the other plans we have seen. Contributions to a RESP are *not* deductible. However, the income in the plan grows tax-free, so RESPs enjoy the effect of tax-free compounding of interest, which we illustrated in 3.1.5 above.

There are two basic ways of investing in a RESP. You may enroll in an existing group plan; there are two or three major ones which advertise heavily in baby magazines and pediatricians' offices. Or, if you prefer, you can set up an individual plan, in which case you will have control over the investment of the funds as well as choosing the beneficiaries of the plan.

One normally enrolls one's child or grandchild (or a friend or relative's child) while he or she is young. If the child goes to college or university, the RESP provides an income to help cover the child's expenses. The income will be taxable to the child, who normally will not have much other income and so will pay little or no tax.

Consider setting up an RESP for your child's post-secondary education.

Starting in 1997, the maximum contribution to RESPs by all taxpayers is limited to $4,000 per year (up from $2,000 in 1996) and $42,000 lifetime in respect of any one beneficiary. In addition, the maximum period over which income generated in an RESP may be sheltered from tax is 26 years. RESPs set up after February 20, 1990 may make payments only to individuals who are *full-time* students. As of 1997, RESP payments can also be made to beneficiaries enrolled in qualifying distance education courses, such as correspondence courses.

Family plans are subject to the same contribution limits per beneficiary, but if one of your children decides against post-secondary school, the funds you have contributed for this child and, as of 1997, the income earned on those contributions, can be re-directed to benefit your other children who do pursue post-secondary education.

In the past, many parents decided against the use of an RESP because, if their child chose not go on to post-secondary education, the family would only get back the amounts contributed to the RESP, while the income earned from it over the years would be forfeited.

The government has partially removed this disincentive for 1998 and later years in cases where none of the RESP's intended beneficiaries are post-secondary students by age 21 and the plan has been running for at least 10 years. You will be allowed to transfer up to $40,000 of RESP income during your lifetime to your RRSP (or your spouse's) tax-free to the extent you or your spouse has available RRSP contribution room (see 3.1.3). If you do not have enough RRSP room to fully offset the RESP income, you will be subject to an extra charge of 20% of the excess RESP income (plus an additional 10% if you live in Quebec), on top of the regular taxes on the amount (the extra charge is designed to make up for the taxes deferred while the funds were in the plan).

3.7 References

The following publications can be obtained (in person or by telephone request) from your nearest Revenue Canada District Taxation Office. Some of the brochures and forms are also available from Revenue Canada's Internet site at www.revcan.ca.

Interpretation Bulletin IT-124R6, "Contributions to registered retirement savings plans"

Interpretation Bulletin IT-167R6, "Registered pension funds or plans— Employee's contributions"

Interpretation Bulletin IT-307R3, "Spousal registered retirement savings plans"

Interpretation Bulletin IT-320R2, "Registered retirement savings plan— Qualified investments"

Interpretation Bulletin IT-337R2, "Retiring allowances"

Interpretation Bulletin IT-363R2, "Deferred profit sharing plans— Deductibility of employer contributions and taxation of amounts received by a beneficiary"

Information Circular 72-22R9, "Registered retirement savings plans"

Information Circular 77-1R4, "Deferred profit sharing plans"

Information Circular 78-18R5, "Registered retirement income funds"

Information Circular 79-8R3, "Forms to be used to directly transfer funds to plans"

Information Circular 93-3, "Registered education savings plans"

Guide, "RRSPs and Other Registered Plans for Retirement"

Brochure, "Home Buyers' Plan for 19___ Participants"

Form TIE-OVP, "Individual return for RESP overpayments"

Form T1023, "Calculation of earned income for 19___ "

Form T1036, "Applying to withdraw an amount under the Home Buyers' Plan in 19___ "

Form T1037, "Designating contributions you made to your RRSPs as your repayment under the Home Buyers' Plan for 19___"

Form T2097, "Identification of amounts transferred to an RRSP for 19___"

Form T2205, "Calculation of amounts from a spousal RRSP or RRIF to be included in income for 19___"

Reducing your family's tax bill through income splitting

- Beware of the "general anti-avoidance rule" (4.2.5)
- The higher-income spouse should pay household expenses (4.3.1)
- Pay your spouse's tax bills with your own funds (4.3.1)
- Pay the interest on your spouse's investment loans (4.3.1)
- Pay a salary or consulting fee to your spouse and/or children (4.3.2)
- Think about loaning business assets to your spouse or child (4.3.3)
- Consider making spousal investment loans when interest rates are rising (4.3.4)
- Have your spouse or child earn income on income from transferred funds (4.3.5)
- Shelter future gains by transferring property at fair market value (4.3.6)
- Shelter future gains by transferring capital assets to your children (4.3.7)
- Transfer shares that will pay capital dividends (4.3.8)
- Contribute to your spouse's RRSP (4.3.9)
- Make spousal RRSP contributions by December 31 (4.3.9)
- In the year your children turn 17, give them funds they can invest (4.3.10)
- Let your children invest their own earnings (4.3.11)
- Split income by assigning CPP/QPP benefits to the lower-income spouse (4.3.12)
- Claim baby-sitting wages paid to your adult children as child care expenses (4.3.13)

"Income splitting" is a term used to describe strategies to save taxes by shifting income from the hands of a family member in a higher tax bracket to the hands of a second family member in a lower tax bracket so that the same income is taxed at a lower rate of tax—or not at all if the second family member's income is low enough. In this chapter, we discuss the tax rules that are in place to prevent many forms of income splitting and point out some of the income splitting opportunities that remain available.

.

4.1 Why income splitting?

The Canadian tax system uses progressive tax rates, whereby the marginal rate of tax (tax on additional income) increases as taxable income increases.

The marginal rate of tax varies from province to province, but is *approximately*:

> 27% on income up to $29,590
> 41% on income from $29,590 to $59,180
> 50% on income over $59,180.

As can be seen, the tax payable on two $30,000 incomes will be significantly less than that on one $60,000 income—about $4,500 less, in fact. Taxpayers, therefore, have an incentive to "split" income between, for example, a high-income earner and a non-working spouse or children.

The federal *Income Tax Act* contains a number of measures to prevent the most obvious kinds of income splitting (similar rules apply for Québec purposes). However, some opportunities are available. We'll review the rules, so you understand the context in which to plan, together with a discussion of the planning opportunities that remain.

Note that most of this chapter will be irrelevant to you if you do not have funds invested and earning income that is subject to tax. One of the best tax planning techniques is to channel extra cash into paying off any non-deductible interest such as your mortgage or credit card balances.

4.2 Rules that prevent income splitting

4.2.1 Indirect payments

The *Income Tax Act* provides that a payment or transfer made "pursuant to the direction of, or with the concurrence of" a taxpayer to some other person is to be included in the taxpayer's income to the extent it would have been if paid to the taxpayer. So, for example, if you arrange for your employer to pay part of your salary to your spouse, the income will still be taxed in your hands and you will not have accomplished anything.

4.2.2 Attribution between spouses

Suppose you earn $90,000 per year and your spouse earns $10,000. Your marginal tax rate (tax on any additional income) is 50% and your spouse's is 27%. Assume you have $10,000 in bonds that generate $1,000 per year in interest and decide to give, or lend, the bonds to your spouse. As a result you hope to pay only $270 tax on the income instead of $500.

This is the kind of transaction that the **attribution rules** cover. These rules attribute income from property (in our example, the $1,000 of investment income each year) back to the person who transferred or loaned the property.

The attribution rules with respect to spouses provide that where *property* (including money) is *transferred or loaned, directly or indirectly* by you to your spouse (or a person who has since become your spouse), then all *income* or loss *from the property*, and any *capital gain or loss* on the disposition of the property will be *attributed back* to you. So, in our example, the $1,000 income on the $10,000 investment that you gave to your spouse must be reported on your tax return, not your spouse's—and so will be subject to tax of about $500 rather than about $270. This will be true year after year—as long as you and your spouse remain together, any income from the bonds will be taxed in your hands. If you transfer shares, for example, and your spouse sells the shares at some later time, any capital gain or capital loss relative to *your* original cost must be reported as *your* capital gain or loss, subject to the usual rules for capital gains (see Chapter 5).

Note that common-law spouses who meet the criteria outlined in 2.2.1 are considered spouses for tax purposes, and are therefore subject to these attribution rules as well.

There is an exception to these attribution rules; an exception that applies as well to the rules we will see later. If you transfer for fair market value consideration (e.g., sell the bonds to your spouse for $10,000 cash) and report the resulting gain, the rule will not apply. (If you realize a loss on the transfer, a special rule deems the loss to be zero. However the denied loss can be added to your spouse's cost for tax purposes.) If the consideration includes indebtedness (e.g., you sell the bonds for a $10,000 promissory note), or if you simply lend funds or property to your spouse, then to avoid the attribution rule you must charge (and, of course, report!) interest on the loan. The interest rate must be at least equal to Revenue Canada's prescribed interest rate at that time (see 14.3) or a commercial rate of interest. For this exception to apply, the interest must actually be *paid* in each year, or by the following January 30. If the January 30 deadline ever passes without the interest being paid, that year's income and *all* future income from the loaned property will be attributed back to the lender.

Example:
On January 1, 1997 you lend $10,000 cash to your spouse, who puts the money in the bank and earns $800 interest over the course of the year.

If you do not charge interest, then the $800 will be attributed back to you and taxed in your hands. Suppose you do wish to charge interest. The minimum rate would have to be either:

- the rate that would apply between two arm's length parties (assume 6% for this example); or
- Revenue Canada's rate at the time the loan was granted (assume 4%).

If your spouse is required to pay interest on the anniversary date of the loan and actually pays you at least $400 in interest by January 30, 1998, then the $800 interest will not be attributed back to you.

Revenue Canada's (and Revenu Québec's) prescribed rate, which is set quarterly, is for this purpose 4% lower than the rate that applies to late payments of tax (see 14.3).

4.2.3 Attribution between parents and children

Suppose you lend $10,000 in bonds to your daughter, who is in high school and can earn $1,000 in interest without paying any tax at all.

The attribution rules apply to children under 18. Where property is transferred or loaned, there will be attribution of income (or loss), but *not* of capital gains or losses. The attribution applies only for years in which the child is still under 18 *at the end of* the year.

Not all children under 18 are caught by the rule. It depends on the child's relationship with the taxpayer who transfers or lends the property. Attribution applies where the taxpayer and the child "do not deal at arm's length", a phrase that is defined to include all persons who are "related" as defined in the *Income Tax Act*. Generally, this will cover one's child, grandchild, great-grandchild (including one's spouse's child, one's child's spouse, etc., where "spouse" includes a common-law spouse as outlined in 2.2.1) or brother or sister (including brother-in-[common]-law and sister-in-[common]-law). This rule also specifically applies to nieces and nephews. For other relationships, it is a "question of fact" whether two taxpayers deal at arm's length.

Although the attribution rule with respect to minors does not apply to capital gains and losses, the transfer of the property to the minor itself will generally be deemed to take place at fair market value. So any capital gain or loss accruing up to the time of the transfer will be triggered immediately in the transferor's hands, and it is only the gain or loss accruing *after* the transfer that when realized will be taxed in the child's hands.

The exceptions that we saw in 4.2.2, where the transferred property is acquired for fair market value or where interest is paid on any indebtedness or loan, also apply to this attribution rule.

4.2.4 Attribution on loans to adult family members

One further rule applies to loans (but not transfers) of property to other persons with whom the taxpayer does not deal at arm's length—such as, for example, one's children who are over 18, or one's in-laws or grandparents. If one of the main reasons for the loan was to achieve income-splitting and thereby reduce taxes, the income will be attributed back to the lender. So if you lend $10,000 to your adult son who is in university, and the purpose is to allow him to earn the $1,000 interest and pay little or no tax on it (rather than, say, to allow him to use the $10,000 to pay for his tuition), the $1,000 of interest will be attributed back to you. The exception where interest is charged and paid, as outlined in 4.2.2, applies in this case.

4.2.5 Special anti-avoidance rules

If you are creative and devious enough, you may have thought of some possible ways around the rules we have just described. Don't bother. The federal and Québec tax laws contain a number of special rules designed to thwart the loopholes that creative tax planners exploited in years past. We will summarize them only briefly; basically, anything you can think of has probably been thought of before.

(1) *Substituted property.* If property is substituted for transferred or loaned property, the attribution rules will apply to income or capital gains from the substituted property, and so on *ad infinitum* (to the extent that attribution would have applied to income from the original property). So if you give $10,000 in bonds to your spouse, who then sells them and buys $10,000 in stocks, any dividends and capital gains on the stocks will be attributed back to you.

(2) *Transfers to a trust or corporation.* In general, transfers to a trust will result in the same application of the attribution rules as if the transfer were made directly to the beneficiaries of the trust. Transfers to a corporation which result in a benefit to a "designated person" (spouse or related minor children, using the same definition we saw in 4.2.3) are also caught in most cases. So, for example, if you and your spouse each own half the shares in a corporation, and you give $10,000 to the corporation so that your spouse will benefit, you will be taxed as though you had received interest from the corporation. This attribution rule does not apply where the corporation is a "small business corporation" (see 5.3.2).

(3) *Back-to-back loans and transfers.* If you lend or transfer property to a third party, who then lends or transfers it to a "designated person" (your spouse or related minor children), it will be treated as though you had lent or transferred the property directly.

(4) *Guarantees.* If you arrange for a third party (e.g., a bank) to lend funds to a "designated person" on the strength of your guarantee, it will be treated as though you had lent the funds directly.

(5) *Repayment of existing loan.* If you lend funds to a "designated person", and they use the funds to pay off another loan that they used to buy property, your loan will effectively be treated as if it had been used to buy that property. (This is the flip side of the "substituted property" case covered in (1) above.) So, for example, if your spouse borrows $10,000 to invest in bonds, and you then lend your spouse $10,000 which is used to pay off that loan, the interest from the bonds will be attributed back to you.

(6) *Reverse attribution.* The attribution rules can be ignored if you try to use them to turn the tables on Revenue Canada and have them apply in the opposite direction from that intended.

Beware of the "general anti-avoidance rule".

(7) *General anti-avoidance rule.* The Act provides a general anti-avoidance rule ("GAAR"), applicable to all transactions. If you come up with a way of avoiding the attribution rules that is not caught by the existing rules but is a misuse or abuse of the *Income Tax Act*, it may be caught by GAAR.

4.3 Income splitting opportunities

In this section we discuss the planning opportunities available to achieve income splitting. For many of these to work, you need to keep careful documentation. Separate bank accounts for spouses will allow you to trace each one's funds properly. (Under provincial family law, this will not normally affect either spouse's rights to the family's funds on marriage breakdown.)

4.3.1 Increasing the lower-income spouse's investment base

The higher-income spouse should pay household expenses.

The simplest technique is to make sure that daily living expenses (groceries, mortgage or rent payments, credit card bills, etc.) are paid by the higher-income spouse. This will allow the lower-income spouse to maintain a larger investment base for earning future income that is taxed at a low rate.

Pay your spouse's tax bills with your own funds.

Another way to effectively transfer funds is for you to directly pay your spouse's income tax liability—both in April and any instalments that are due during the year. Simply make sure that the cheque paying your spouse's taxes is drawn on your own account. Since the amount you pay goes directly to the government and is not invested by your spouse, there is no property from which income can be attributed. The result is that any funds your spouse would otherwise use to pay income taxes can be invested without the income being attributed back to you.

Pay the interest on your spouse's investment loans.

If your spouse has taken out an investment loan from a third party, consider providing him or her with the funds to pay the interest. There will be no attribution provided you do not pay any principal on account of the spousal loan. (Since the amount you pay is not actually invested by your spouse, there is no property from which income can be attributed.) The interest payment will be deductible on your spouse's tax return. This technique will preserve your spouse's assets and thereby increase his or her investment income.

4.3.2 Employing your spouse and children

Pay a salary or consulting fee to your spouse and/or children.

If you carry on a business, either personally or through a corporation, rather than having purely employment income, consider paying a salary to your spouse and/or children. The salary must be "reasonable" in light of the services they perform for the business. Such services might include bookkeeping, filing, other administrative work, business development planning and acting as a director of the corporation. Revenue Canada and Revenu Québec auditors are usually fairly flexible in interpreting what constitutes a "reasonable" salary, provided services are genuinely being provided.

The impact of payroll taxes, Canada Pension Plan contributions and Employment Insurance premiums should be weighed against any potential tax savings expected from implementing this strategy.

Consider also whether your spouse can provide services on a contract (consulting) basis rather than as an employee. This would allow your spouse the advantages of self-employment income (see Chapter 8), including writing off expenses. This is an aggressive tactic and should only be implemented with appropriate professional advice.

Another possibility is to bring your spouse into partnership with you. Taxation of partnerships is discussed in 8.3.

4.3.3 Transfers of business assets

Think about loaning business assets to your spouse or child.

The attribution rules, as we have noted, apply to income from *property*— such as interest, dividends, rent and royalties. They do not, however, apply to income earned from a *business*. So if you can transfer or lend business assets in such a way that your spouse or child carries on business on a regular and continuous basis to earn income from business rather than from property, there will be no attribution. Such a step should only be undertaken with proper professional advice, to ensure that the legal steps required to effect the transfer are properly completed and that the possibility of the general anti-avoidance rule applying is minimized.

Note that this generally cannot be done for a passive interest in a partnership (including an interest in a limited partnership). Income from the partnership's business is technically business income, but it is deemed to be property income for purposes of the attribution rules unless the taxpayer is actively engaged in the partnership's business or is carrying on a similar business.

4.3.4 Spousal loans

As we saw in 4.2.2, the attribution rules do not apply where property or funds are loaned and interest is charged at a minimum rate, provided the interest is actually paid. Where assets are expected to produce a return that is well in excess of the minimum rate (the lower of a reasonable commercial rate and the Revenue Canada prescribed rate), it may make sense to lend the funds or assets and charge a rate of interest sufficient to avoid the application of the attribution rules. The excess yield from the assets over the amount of interest charged will then effectively be transferred to the lower-income taxpayer and not attributed back to the lender.

Consider making spousal investment loans when interest rates are rising.

If interest rates are rising, the current Revenue Canada prescribed rate may be relatively low, since there is a time lag before it is set each quarter. Where such an opportunity arises, consider making a loan to your spouse on which interest is charged, "locking in" at the low prescribed rate, and having your spouse use the funds to invest at current market rates.

4.3.5 Reinvesting attributed income

We have seen that attribution applies to the income from property that is transferred or loaned. But what about the income from that income (secondary income)? Suppose you give $10,000 to your spouse, who earns $1,000 in interest in the first year, and the $1,000 is attributed back to you. In the second year, your spouse invests the $1,000 as well as the $10,000, and the $1,000 generates a further $100 in interest.

Have your spouse or child earn income on income from lent or transferred funds.

This "secondary income" is not attributed back to you, as it is not income from the property that was transferred. It is thus taxed in your spouse's hands. Over time, a significant stream of such secondary income can be built up. However, accurate records must be maintained. You may wish to have your spouse keep two bank accounts, one for the income that is attributed back to you and one into which all income from the first account is deposited. Only the income from the first account would be reported on your return.

4.3.6   Transfers for fair market value

Shelter future gains by transferring property at fair market value.

As we have seen, the attribution rules also do not apply where property is transferred in exchange for consideration equal to the property's fair market value. (Where the consideration includes indebtedness, such as a promissory note, interest must be charged as outlined above.) A transfer at fair market value may be beneficial where the assets are expected to produce a high yield or to increase in value in the future.

4.3.7   Transferring capital property to children

Shelter future gains by transferring capital assets to your children.

As we saw in 4.2.3, the attribution rules with respect to minor children do not apply to capital gains. If you have assets that are expected to increase substantially in value (such as shares of a corporation), consider transferring them to your children or to a trust for your children. Any dividends will be attributed back to you as long as your children are under 18 at the end of the year in which the dividend is paid, but capital gains on sale of the assets will not be.

For example, suppose you own shares in your private business corporation. You invested $10,000 originally, and they are now worth $20,000. But you expect the corporation to do well over the coming years. If you give the shares to your children, you will be deemed to have disposed of them at $20,000, but the capital gain may be shielded by the $500,000 capital gains exemption (see 5.4.1). If, a few years later, your children sell the shares for $100,000, the $80,000 capital gain will be taxed in their hands, not yours, and possibly taxed at a lower marginal rate, even if the $500,000 capital gains exemption is no longer available at that point.

Other assets that might be appropriate for transfer to children are those which will normally generate capital gains but not income. Examples include jewellery, art and shares in speculative public companies.

Transfers to children should be done with proper professional advice. In some provinces there is a question as to whether minors can legally own property such as shares. You may need to set up a trust for this purpose.

4.3.8 Payment of capital dividends

Normally, dividends that are paid on shares you transfer to your spouse or minor children will be attributed back to you. However, the tax system provides for "capital dividends", which are always tax-free. Such dividends include a distribution of the untaxed 1/4 of a corporation's capital gains. (For an example, see 9.2.4.)

Transfer shares that will pay capital dividends.

If you transfer shares of a corporation, and the shares subsequently pay capital dividends, there will be no attribution of the income because it is not taxed in anyone's hands in the first place. As well, any income earned from reinvesting the dividends will not be attributed. This technique can work well for shares of private holding companies, but must be undertaken with proper professional advice to minimize the application of various anti-avoidance rules which could turn the dividends into taxable dividends.

4.3.9 Spousal RRSP

Contribute to your spouse's RRSP.

A contribution to your spouse's RRSP, as we saw in 3.3.1, is specifically allowed for federal and Québec tax purposes. When the funds are turned into an annuity or RRIF on retirement, there will be no attribution of the income back to you.

A further technique can be used at any time before retirement. Contributions to your spouse's RRSP, if withdrawn by your spouse, are taxed back in your hands to the extent you have made any spousal contributions in the year of withdrawal or in the two previous years. This means that you can split income, provided you can wait 24-36 months and not make spousal contributions in the meantime. It also means foregoing the benefits of leaving the funds to grow tax-free in the RRSP (see 3.1.5).

Example:
On December 31, 1997 you contribute $13,500 to an RRSP for your spouse.

This entitles you to a deduction of $13,500 for 1997 (assuming you have adequate contribution room—see 3.1.3—and have made no contributions to your own RRSP for 1997). Any withdrawals of up to $13,500 from your spouse's RRSPs in 1998 or 1999 will be attributed back to you; but on January 1, 2000, your spouse can withdraw the full $13,500, which will be taxed to your spouse as the recipient provided you make no further spousal RRSP contributions in 1998, 1999 or 2000.

Of course, when you contribute to a spousal RRSP you lose your own RRSP contribution room, so the tax advantages of this technique are somewhat limited in scope, but it does achieve income splitting over the long term. You must also consider, however, whether your spouse having a higher income at retirement will affect eligibility for the Age Credit (see 2.5.1) and will trigger the Old Age Security clawback (see 2.5.3).

Make spousal RRSP contributions by December 31.

Note also that in this example, if you contributed for 1997 on January 1, 1998 rather than December 31, 1997, your spouse would have to wait until January 1, 2001 to withdraw the funds without attribution back to you. Contributions to spousal plans should thus not be put off to January or February, as is often done with one's own contributions.

4.3.10 When your children turn 17

In the year your children turn 17, give them funds they can invest.

Consider giving your children funds that they can invest. If your child turns 17 in the year you make the gift, the funds can be invested in a one-year (or longer) term deposit or certificate, which will not require interest to be reported until the year in which the child turns 18, and thus no attribution will follow. (If the investment is for more than one year, interest must still be reported annually—see 6.2.1.) Do not simply loan the funds without considering the special attribution rule discussed in 4.2.4.

You might also consider a gift of enough funds so that the income earned on the funds will cover the child's university tuition and residence over four (or more) years. Of course, you must be prepared to lose the funds, since they will legally belong to your child and not to you. Consider the use of a trust (with proper legal advice) if this is a concern.

4.3.11   Your children's employment income

Let your children invest their own earnings.

Consider lending your child, interest-free, an amount equal to what he or she earns over the summer and would otherwise spend. This will allow the child to earn investment income on his or her own earnings, and the investment income will not be attributed back to you.

Suppose you have a daughter who attends university and who earns $10,000 over the summer, and your normal arrangement with her is that she uses her income to pay for her tuition and basic expenses. If you lend her $10,000 interest-free, she can use the funds you lend her to pay her tuition and living expenses, and invest her summer earnings. Since the $10,000 invested represents her own funds, the income earned on that amount will not be attributed back to you and will be taxed at her marginal rate (or not taxed at all if her income is low enough). You could then repeat this process through several years of university, and have your daughter pay back the entire amount of the loan when she graduates, using the funds she has invested from her own earnings. Alternatively, you could lend her less money each year, as she will have her investment income available as an additional source of funds.

4.3.12   Assignment of CPP/QPP benefit payments

You may direct that up to 50% of your Canada Pension Plan ("CPP") benefits be paid to your spouse, provided both of you are over 60. If either of you does this, a portion of the other spouse's CPP is assigned automatically back to the first spouse.

If both spouses are eligible for maximum CPP benefits, assignment will not change anything, since each will assign half of the maximum to the other. But if one has high CPP benefits and the other has low benefits or none, the assignment can effectively transfer up to half of the CPP income.

Split income by assigning CPP/QPP benefits to the lower-income spouse.

The attribution rules specifically do not apply to an assignment of CPP benefits. If you and your spouse are both over 60, and you have higher CPP benefits and are in a higher tax bracket, you should consider such an assignment, which is done by completing a form available from Human Resources Development Canada. This assignment might not be advantageous, however, if it affects your spousal tax credit claim (see 2.2.1).

Benefits from the Québec Pension Plan ("QPP") can be assigned to your spouse by completing a form available from Régie des rentes du Québec.

4.3.13   Paying children over 18 for child care

Claim baby-sitting wages paid to your adult children as child care expenses.

The deduction for child care expenses was discussed in 2.3.2. No deduction is allowed for payments you make to a person related to you who is under 18. Once your older children turn 18, if you are the lower-income spouse you can pay them for child care or baby-sitting services that permit you to earn employment or business income. Your adult child will need to give you a receipt and report the income for tax purposes.

4.4   References

The following publications can be obtained (in person or by telephone request) from your nearest Revenue Canada District Taxation Office. Forms and brochures may also be available from Revenue Canada's Internet site at www.revcan.ca.

Interpretation Bulletin IT-295R4, "Taxable dividends received after 1987 by a spouse"

Interpretation Bulletin IT-307R3, "Spousal registered retirement savings plans"

Interpretation Bulletin IT-335R, "Indirect payments"

Interpretation Bulletin IT-369R, "Attribution of trust income to settler"

Interpretation Bulletin IT-510, "Transfer and loans of property made after May 22, 1985 to a related minor"

Interpretation Bulletin IT-511R, "Interspousal and certain other transfers and loans of property"

Form T2205, "Calculation of amounts from a spousal RRSP or RRIF to be included in 19___ income"

Capital gains and losses

■ Classify your gains as capital gains and your losses as business losses, where possible (5.1)

■ Make the Canadian securities election to ensure capital treatment for gains on your stock market trades (5.1)

■ Consider delaying the sale of all or part of an asset until after the year end to defer capital gains tax (5.2)

■ If you have unused net capital losses, carry them back or forward to offset taxable capital gains (5.3.1)

■ Carryover unused "allowable business investment losses" to reduce taxable business income (5.3.2)

■ "Purify" your corporation to create qualified small business corporation shares eligible for the $500,000 exemption (5.4.1)

■ Plan around your CNIL balance when using the capital gains exemption (5.4.3)

■ Amend or cancel your capital gains election before 1998 where warranted (5.4.4)

■ If you've sold an asset but not received all the proceeds, claim a capital gains reserve (5.5.1)

■ Consider changing principal residence ownership to shelter gains on recreation properties (5.5.2)

■ Make the election to treat rented-out property as principal residence (5.5.2)

■ If you're emigrating from Canada, be sure to utilize your remaining $500,000 capital gains exemption (5.5.4)

Capital gains and losses are given special treatment in the federal income tax system. Capital gains are effectively taxed at a lower rate than regular income; and individuals are entitled to an exemption for capital gains on certain kinds of property. The rules are substantially the same for Québec purposes. In this chapter we'll describe the rules in general and take a look at some of the planning opportunities that are available.

5.1 What is capital?

Before we get into the rules that apply to capital gains and losses, it helps to understand what we mean by "capital". Capital property is property that, if sold, will lead to a capital gain (or capital loss). The alternative is property that, when sold, leads to full income inclusion of any gain as income from business. For example, if you speculate on real estate, and you buy and sell a number of properties, your gains on the sales will probably be business income rather than capital gains.

There are no clear rules defining capital property. The *Income Tax Act*'s only comment is to define a "business" as including "an adventure or concern in the nature of trade". The courts have developed guidelines over the years, from which a general picture emerges. If you buy property with the intention of reselling it, and particularly if you sell it quickly and engage in many such transactions, your profit is likely to be considered income from business. If you buy property with the intention of earning income (e.g., rent or dividends) from it, and particularly if this is an isolated transaction and you hold the property for a long time, any gain on a sale is likely to be a capital gain.

Classify your gains as capital gains and your losses as business losses, where possible.

As we'll see in 5.2, most capital gains are only three-quarters taxed (and gains on certain small business shares and farm property are eligible for the $500,000 capital gains exemption—see 5.4), so it is therefore much better to have capital gains than regular income. On the other hand, capital losses are of limited use since they can only be used to offset capital gains (see 5.3), while business losses can be deducted against other income.

To the extent possible within the law, therefore, you should try to classify your gains as capital gains and your losses as business losses. For example, if you buy and sell a commodity on the stock market, how you classify the transaction may depend on whether you have a gain or a loss. Where you are near the borderline between income and capital, you have some leeway to classify the transaction as either. Of course, you should be consistent; you could not take two essentially identical trades and call one a capital gain and the other a business loss.

For example, if you are buying and selling real estate and doing well at it, try to gather data for your files that will support your claim to be engaging in capital transactions. For example, you will want to show that you are purchasing properties purely for their investment value as rental properties, and that any sales were not originally planned but were required by a change in circumstances.

Revenue Canada may well reassess you on your classifications, if you are audited. At that point you would have to decide whether to fight the assessment via a Notice of Objection (see 14.5.1), or to accept it and pay the tax that you would have paid in the first place, plus interest. If you are unsure as to whether property you own is capital property or not, you should consult your professional advisors.

Make the Canadian securities election to ensure capital treatment for gains on your stock market trades.

If you wish to ensure that your trades on the stock market will always result in capital gains rather than business income, you may file an "Election on Disposition of Canadian Securities" (federal Form T123 and Québec form TP-250.1-V) with any year's tax return. This will prevent Revenue Canada or Revenu Québec from claiming that you are buying securities for the purpose of selling them and therefore earning business income rather than capital gains.

Once you do so, *all* "Canadian securities" you ever own will be considered to be capital property for the rest of your life. This includes, generally, shares in Canadian corporations, investments in mutual funds, and bonds, debentures or other debt issued by individuals or corporations resident in Canada (except a corporation related to you). Certain taxpayers, such as traders and dealers, are not allowed to make this election.

The downside of making the election is that you will never be able to claim losses on Canadian securities as business losses in the future. Since this is generally hard to do in respect of shares anyway, this may not be a problem for you. You should consider your entire financial position and possibly obtain professional advice to determine the likely effects of the election.

5.2 Capital gains

Capital gains occur only when property is sold (or deemed to have been disposed of under special rules, which we'll see in 5.5.3 and 5.5.5). So if you own, say, a rental property that has increased in value tenfold, you do not pay any tax on the increase until you actually sell the property. The capital gain is taxed only in the year of the sale.

The basic calculation of a capital gain is easy to understand: proceeds of disposition (normally the sale price), minus any selling expenses (e.g., real estate commissions), minus the "**adjusted cost base**", equals the capital gain. In most cases the adjusted cost base is simply your cost of the property, but this figure is "adjusted" in various ways. (For the adjusted cost base of an interest in a partnership, see 8.3.5.) Where you have used the election to trigger part of your capital gains exemption (see 5.4), your adjusted cost base will be higher than the actual cost.

Capital gains are, in effect, taxed at a lower rate than regular income. This is done by including in income only the **taxable capital gain**, which is three-quarters of the capital gain.

Example:

Jennifer paid $5,000 (including commission) for shares of the TD Bank in 1992. In 1997, she sells the shares for $6,100, of which her broker keeps $100 as commission.

For 1997, Jennifer has a capital gain of $1,000. The taxable capital gain is three-quarters, or $750, and this amount is included in her income for tax purposes.

We have mentioned in earlier chapters the marginal rates of tax on ordinary income. With three-quarters taxation of capital gains, the effective rates of tax are *approximately*:

Income level	Salary income	Capital gain (3/4)
$0-$29,590	27%	20%
$29,591-$59,180	41%	31%
$59,181 and up	50%	37%

The exact rates vary by province.

If you have very large capital gains, minimum tax may apply—see Chapter 12.

Consider delaying the sale of all or part of an asset until after year-end to defer capital gains tax.

If you sell an asset after the end of the year, any tax on the capital gain will apply one year later, giving you the use of the funds for an extra year except to the extent you are required to make quarterly tax instalments (see 14.2.2). A sale on December 31, 1997 will require tax to be paid by April 30, 1998; a sale on January 1, 1998 will require tax to be paid by April 30, 1999.

Note that most stock and bond market transactions normally settle three business days after the trade is entered. (This is standard practice in the brokerage industry and is recognized by Revenue Canada.) Because weekends and public holidays may affect the determination of "business days", if you intend to do any last-minute 1997 trades, consider completing all trades before Christmas and be sure to check the settlement date with your broker.

In some circumstances, you may wish to sell half of an asset at the end of December and the other half at the beginning of January. Doing this will split your capital gain across the two years. This can be beneficial for two reasons. First, you may be able to reduce the marginal rate which applies in both years, by keeping your total taxable income below about $59,000 for each year. Second, you may be able to avoid minimum tax, due to the

$40,000 minimum tax exemption available for each year ($25,000 for Québec tax purposes).

5.3 Capital losses

5.3.1 Ordinary capital losses

A capital loss occurs when the capital gain calculation produces a negative amount; that is, the adjusted cost base is greater than the proceeds of disposition minus the selling expenses. Just as capital gains are less heavily taxed than regular income, capital losses are less useful to you than regular (business) losses.

An **allowable capital loss** is *three-quarters* of a capital loss. This amount can be offset against taxable capital gains. In normal circumstances, if you have no taxable capital gains, the loss *cannot* be used against other income.

Example:
Brent earns an annual salary of $40,000. In October 1997, Brent sells some shares of a mining company, which cost him $2,000 several years before, for $6,000 after commission. In November 1997, he sells some bars of gold he bought in 1982 for $18,000, and receives only $10,000 since the price of gold has come down.

Brent has a $4,000 capital gain on the shares, which is a $3,000 taxable capital gain. He also has an $8,000 capital loss on the gold, which is a $6,000 allowable capital loss. This completely wipes out the taxable capital gain, but the extra $3,000 of allowable capital loss cannot be used to reduce his salary income of $40,000. It can only be used against taxable capital gains of other years, as outlined below.

If you have unused net capital losses, carry them back or forward to offset taxable capital gains.

Allowable capital losses that can't be used in any given year, as in this example, can be **carried back** and applied against taxable capital gains of any of the previous three years, subject to whether the capital gains exemption was used in that prior year. They can also be **carried forward** indefinitely; this balance is known as "net capital losses" and can be used against taxable capital gains in any future year.

If you have any net capital losses that cannot be used in the current year, look into whether you can carry them back to any of your three prior years' returns. Revenue Canada and Revenu Québec are required to reopen and reassess your return when you make such a claim. Make sure as well that you keep track of any such losses that you can't carry back, and carry them forward to use in future years.

Before May 23, 1985, up to $2,000 per year of allowable capital losses was allowed to be used against other income (such as employment income). If you disposed of any capital property at a loss before that date, you may still use this $2,000 deduction per year. Your unused pre-May 23, 1985 net capital losses less any capital gains exemption claimed since then is called your "pre-1986 capital loss balance".

5.3.2 Allowable business investment losses

There is an exception to the general rule that allowable capital losses cannot be used against ordinary income. It applies to **allowable business investment losses**. These arise when there is a loss on shares of, or debt owing by, a **small business corporation**.

The term "small business corporation" has a very specific meaning in the *Income Tax Act*. It need not, in fact, be small. The corporation must meet a number of tests, which are that it be resident in Canada, a private corporation, not controlled in any manner by non-residents or public corporations, not listed on a Canadian or any of about 25 foreign stock exchanges, and, most importantly, that substantially all (taken by Revenue Canada to mean 90% or more of the value) of its assets be used in an active business carried on primarily in Canada. Shares and debts in other small business corporations can qualify as such assets.

A capital loss on the shares or debt of a small business corporation (including, in some cases, simply determining that the debt has gone bad and will not be repaid) is called a "**business investment loss**". Three-quarters of this amount, the "allowable business investment loss" ("ABIL"), can be deducted against any other income such as employment income or investment income. However the amount of the ABIL that can be deducted against other income must be reduced by any capital gains exemption claimed in prior years. In addition, if an ABIL is deducted against other income, you must realize an equal amount of taxable capital gains in later years before you can use the capital gains exemption again. The availability of an ABIL is an extra incentive to investment in private Canadian businesses.

Example:

Janet carries on business as the proprietor of a clothing store, from which she nets $50,000 per year in business income. In 1987, Janet invests $10,000 in shares in XYZ Jewellery Inc., a corporation run by her brother which meets the definition of "small business corporation". In December 1997, the corporation goes bankrupt and Janet's shares become worthless.

Janet has a $10,000 business investment loss in 1997, resulting in a $7,500 allowable business investment loss. She can use this against her $50,000 business income, and so will be taxed in 1997 as if she had earned only $42,500.

Carryover unused ABILs to reduce taxable business income.

Allowable business investment losses that can't be fully used (because you have already wiped out all of your income) are given the same treatment as business losses (see 8.4). That is, they can be carried back and used to offset income in any of the three previous years (even though you have already filed returns and paid tax for those years), or they can be carried forward and used to offset income in any of the next seven years. Any unused balance remaining after the seventh year is reclassified as an allowable capital loss.

5.4 The capital gains exemption

Every individual (but not a trust or corporation) is entitled to a lifetime **$500,000 "capital gains exemption"** on certain small business shares and farm property.

The general **$100,000 capital gains exemption**, which applied to all kinds of property, was eliminated as of February 22, 1994. An election was available to use up your exemption for gains accrued to that date, but your last chance to make the election was April 30, 1997. As we shall see below in 5.4.4, if you did make the election, you have until the end of 1997 to change or revoke it.

Technically, under the *Income Tax Act* and on Revenue Canada's forms, the exemption is called the capital gains *deduction*. Where it applies, the taxable capital gain is still included in income for tax purposes (see 5.2), but an offsetting deduction from net income is allowed when computing "taxable income", the last step on the tax return before calculating tax and tax credits (see 2.1.1).

Note that your $500,000 exemption is limited to the *total* gains on both small business shares and family farms (plus any other exemption claimed up to February 22, 1994, as discussed in 5.4.4 below) over your lifetime. If, for example, you have already claimed an exemption in respect of, say, $420,000 of gain on small business shares, the maximum exemption available to you for farm property would be $80,000.

5.4.1 Qualified small business corporation shares

Up to $500,000 of capital gain on "qualified small business corporation shares" can be exempt.

The meaning of "small business corporation" was discussed in 5.3.2. The definition of "qualified small business corporation share" is very complex. In very general terms:

■ the business must use substantially all (considered by Revenue Canada to mean 90% or more of the value) of its assets in carrying on an active business in Canada, except for shares and debt in other small business corporations

- nobody but you or a person "related" to you can have owned the shares for the two years before you sell them

- throughout the two-year period, more than 50% of the corporation's assets must have been used principally in an active business carried on in Canada, or invested in other small business corporations.

Consult your tax advisor for the specific details as they apply to any shares you own.

Example:

Arnold has not used any of his capital gains exemption in the past. He owns all the shares of a corporation. The shares, which are "qualified small business corporation shares", originally cost him $30,000. In 1997, Arnold sells the shares for $230,000.

Arnold's capital gain is $200,000. Three-quarters of the gain, or $150,000, goes into Arnold's income for 1997, but an offsetting capital gains deduction of $150,000 is allowed in computing his "taxable income"—so he pays no extra tax, except possibly for minimum tax (see Chapter 12). Of his $500,000, Arnold still has $300,000 of capital gains ($225,000 of taxable capital gains) that can be exempt in the future.

As you can see from the example, it doesn't matter whether you think of the exemption as covering **$500,000** (in the example, $200,000 plus $300,000) of **capital gains**, or **$375,000** ($150,000 plus $225,000) of **taxable capital gains**. It comes to the same thing.

"Purify" your corporation to create qualified small business corporation shares.

If you own shares in a small business, and are considering selling them, or transferring them to your children, you should investigate whether the corporation's shares qualify for the $500,000 capital gains exemption. There may be steps you can take to "purify" the corporation so that it meets the criteria discussed above.

It is also possible to transfer the assets of a business which you carry on personally (as a proprietor) into a corporation on a tax-free basis in order to take advantage of the $500,000 exemption. This procedure, known as a "section 85 rollover", requires professional advice, as do other mechanisms for "crystallizing" the exemption (see 9.1).

There is also a special election that lets you take advantage of the exemption for qualified small business corporation shares if the corporation goes public, without having to actually sell the shares. (Once the corporation becomes a public corporation, the shares will no longer qualify for the exemption.)

5.4.2 Qualified farm property

The $500,000 exemption generally applies to **family farms** and **farm quotas** that meet certain conditions. In general terms, if you acquired the property before June 18, 1987 and it was used in the business of farming by you or a member of your family either in the year you sell it or in any five previous years, it will be qualified farm property. If you acquired it after June 17, 1987, you normally have to have owned it for at least two years, been engaged in farming on a regular and continuous basis, and have earned more gross income from farming than from other sources. Similar rules also apply to allow the exemption to be claimed for gains realized on the sale of shares of a **family farm corporation** or an interest in a **family farm partnership**.

If you own farm property that you are considering selling, you should obtain professional advice to determine whether you are eligible for the $500,000 exemption.

5.4.3 Restrictions on use of the exemption

The *Income Tax Act* provides rules to prevent people from taking what is considered unfair advantage of the capital gains exemption. The exemption is supposed to exempt capital gains from being taxed. If, however, you are able to use the system of capital gains taxation to claim capital-related losses against other income, the rules prevent you from getting the exemption as well. We'll look at the details in this section.

Capital losses deducted against other income

There are two kinds of allowable capital losses that can be written off against ordinary income. These are allowable business investment losses (see 5.3.2) and a much rarer bird, pre-1986 capital losses, which can still be used up at $2,000 per year (see 5.3.1).

If you have either of these kinds of losses, you will lose your capital gains exemption to the extent that the losses are or can be written off against your ordinary income. The idea is that such losses should effectively be netted against your taxable capital gains first. In other words, you cannot both have a gain that is sheltered by the capital gains exemption, and also use certain capital losses against your other income.

Cumulative net investment loss ("CNIL")

As discussed in 6.2.3, interest paid on a loan is deductible if you use the loan to invest in shares. Even though your real reason for buying the shares may be to obtain capital gains, the fact that the shares *could* pay dividends (which are income from property) is generally considered enough to make the interest on the loan deductible as interest on funds borrowed to earn income from property.

Tax policy-makers considered it unfair for people to be able to take out large loans, write off the interest, and use the funds to buy shares which would increase in value, giving them a capital gain which was tax-free due to the capital gains exemption. This kind of "double-dipping" was stopped in 1988.

Your capital gains deduction (normally taken, as we have seen, when calculating your "taxable income") is therefore *reduced* by the amount of your **cumulative net investment loss**, or CNIL (pronounced "senile"). The basic idea is that if you borrow money, buy an investment and the investment goes up in value, you shouldn't be able to get both the capital gains exemption and your interest write-off.

The actual calculation is rather more complicated. Your CNIL is the total of your **investment expenses** minus all your **investment income**, cumulative since January 1, 1988. "Investment expenses" includes interest you have deducted, investment counsel fees, partnership losses (except where you are an active partner), losses from rental property, and most tax shelter write-offs. Investment income includes interest, dividends ("grossed-up" by one-quarter as explained in 6.1.2), rental income and income from a partnership where you are not an active partner.

Example:
Arnold has not used any of his capital gains exemption in the past, but has claimed a total of $10,000 in net investment expenses since 1988, so his CNIL balance is $10,000. He owns all the shares of a corporation. The shares, which are "qualified small business corporation shares", originally cost him $30,000. In 1997, Arnold sells the shares for $230,000.

Arnold's capital gain is $200,000. Three-quarters of the gain, or $150,000, goes into Arnold's income for 1997. Because of his $10,000 CNIL balance, the offsetting capital gains deduction is only $140,000, not $150,000.

In effect, Arnold must "eat through" his CNIL balance and pay tax on the $10,000 before he can start to use his capital gains exemption.

Note that the CNIL limitation applies even though the investment expenses and the capital gain are unrelated. However, taxable capital gains that are actually taxed, because you cannot or do not offset them with your capital gains exemption, effectively reduce the impact of the CNIL balance.

Plan around your CNIL balance when using the capital gains exemption.

Note also that the calculation of the exemption (and CNIL) is done at the *end* of the year. It is therefore possible to realize a capital gain that you think is exempt, but for which you cannot claim the exemption because you create a CNIL balance later on in the same year. So if you have a CNIL balance, consider reducing or eliminating it before the end of the year. This can be done by increasing your investment income. For example, if you are the owner-manager of an incorporated business (see Chapter 9), you may be able to reduce your salary and increase your dividends from the corporation to use up your CNIL balance. There may also be situations where you can advance interest receipts to before the end of the year, or defer deductible interest payments until after December 31, to reduce your CNIL.

5.4.4 **The $100,000 exemption and the election as of February 22, 1994**

Until February 22, 1994, there was a general $100,000 exemption for capital gains on any property (except for investment real estate acquired after February 1992). The $100,000 was included in the total $500,000 allowed over an individual's lifetime for all property (including farms and small business shares).

The February 22, 1994 federal budget eliminated the regular exemption for gains after that date. However, the budget also introduced an **election** for gains accrued to February 22, 1994. To the extent you would otherwise have been able to claim the exemption (see 5.4.3), you could have *elected* to treat any property as if you had sold it on budget day at a particular price (up to the property's fair market value) and immediately bought it back at the same price. (The exemption was also eliminated for Québec tax purposes and a virtually identical election was introduced.)

The election was generally due by May 1, 1995. Revenue Canada accepted late elections until April 30, 1997, as long as a late-filing penalty was paid.

Amend or cancel your capital gains election before 1998 where warranted.

If you made the election, you still have the opportunity to amend or revoke it until **December 31, 1997**. You can only file an amended election in respect of the same property upon which you originally elected. This rule stops you from transferring the bumped-up portion of the adjusted cost base of one asset to another asset.

If you file an amended election to report a larger taxable capital gain for a particular property, you'll have to pay a penalty of 0.33% of any additional taxable capital gain that results from increasing your election, for each month or part month that the amended election is filed past the original May 1, 1995 deadline. No penalty will result if you cancel your election or amend it to reduce the elected capital gain.

Changing or cancelling your election will make retroactive changes to your 1994 return, not your 1997 return, and may have some side effects. For example, amending your election to elect to report a higher capital gain on the property will increase your 1994 "net income", which can result in a reduced age credit (see 2.5.1), medical expense credit (see 2.8.2), Child Tax Benefit (see 2.3.1) and GST Credit (see 2.10.3). Among other things, you could also find yourself liable for minimum tax (see Chapter 12).

Flow-through entities—mutual funds and others

Certain investments can have capital gains calculated at the investment level and then flowed through to you so that you report the capital gain on your personal income tax return. These are called "**flow-through entities**". They include mutual funds (see 6.1.6), segregated funds (similar to mutual funds, but offered through life insurers), partnerships (see 8.3.3), investment corporations, mortgage investment corporations, employee profit sharing plans and certain other special trusts.

You can have capital gains on flow-through entities in two ways. First, gains incurred in the entity are flowed through to you. Second, you can sell your interest in the entity.

If you made the election to trigger your capital gains exemption in respect of holdings in flow-through entities, the effect is very different than for other property. Rather than increasing your cost base in the investment, your election created an "**exempt capital gains balance**" that you can use until the year 2004 to reduce any capital gain resulting from either the sale of the property or capital gains flowed through to you. Thus, you can shield "flow-through" gains in future years, even though you may not have sold the investment. This balance will only apply until the year 2004, after which the effect of the election will be lost (subject to any future changes in the rules).

Note that you will have to track the "exempt capital gains balance" for each mutual fund or other investment on which you make the election. You cannot use the balance from one fund to shield capital gains distributions from another fund.

If you sell all of the units of a property, any remaining exempt capital gains balance is added to the adjusted cost base of the last units of the flow-through entity to be sold, which will enable you to realize a capital loss at that time.

Example:

David owned 100 units of a mutual fund on February 22, 1994 which he had purchased in 1993 for $1,000 per share, or $100,000, and which had a fair market value of $120,000 on February 22, 1994. David filed the capital gains election with his 1994 return with respect to that fund, electing proceeds of $120,000. The election created a $20,000 "exempt capital gains balance". In 1997, David sold all of the units for $105,000.

At the time of the sale, David's $20,000 exempt capital gains balance would increase the adjusted cost base of the units to $120,000, triggering a $15,000 capital loss which David could apply to other taxable capital gains.

When the exempt capital gains balance was originally introduced in 1994, you could not use the balance to create a capital loss. If all of the units of a property were sold, any remaining exempt capital gains balance simply disappeared. In July 1996, the government eliminated this restriction retroactive to 1994. Under the old rule, David in the above example would only have been able to use his $20,000 exempt capital gains balance to shield his $5,000 capital gain on the shares from tax and his remaining balance would have become zero.

Since this amendment is retroactive to 1994, if you sold all of the units of a flow-through entity but were unable to fully use up your exempt capital gains balance, you should amend your return for the year in which you sold the units to realize your capital loss. This change will be particularly important for executors of the estates of taxpayers who died owning units or shares of flow-through entities and who may have realized significant capital gains on death on other assets.

5.5 Special cases

5.5.1 Reserves

If you've sold an asset but not received all the proceeds, claim a capital gains reserve.

If you sell a property for a capital gain but do not receive all of the proceeds right away, you may be able to claim a **reserve**, to defer recognition of the gain for tax purposes.

Suppose, for example, you sell a house you have been renting out. The house cost you $100,000 and you sell it for $300,000. But you take back a mortgage for $150,000. You can normally claim a reserve on the capital gain, reflecting the fraction of the purchase price that you haven't yet received. In this case, since you haven't received half of the purchase price, you would only have to recognize half of the gain in the year of sale.

Under the reserve rules, you must recognize at least 1/5 of the gain each year (cumulatively), so that the entire capital gain must be accounted for by the fourth year after the year of sale.

Claiming a reserve might not be beneficial where you may be in a higher tax bracket in later years.

5.5.2 Principal residence

As you probably know, a gain on selling your home is normally completely exempt from taxation. The exemption is based on the definition of "principal residence". This term includes, among other things, a house, a condominium and a share in a co-operative housing corporation. It also includes the land around the house, but normally only up to 1/2 hectare (about 1.2 acres).

You, or your spouse or child, must have "ordinarily inhabited" the residence for it to qualify, so you can't use the exemption on property you rent out without ever having lived in it, or for vacant land. However, it need not have been your "principal" residence in a literal sense. It can be a cottage, for example.

Since 1982, each family unit is limited to one "principal residence" at a time. For this purpose, the family unit means you, your spouse (including a common-law spouse as outlined in 2.2.1), and any unmarried children under 18. So if you designate your house as your principal residence for a period of several years, your spouse cannot also designate your cottage as a principal residence over the same period. (The designation is only made when you file your tax return for the year in which you sell the property, so you can decide at that point which property to claim the exemption on.)

Consider changing principal residence ownership to shelter gains on recreation properties.

Where you and your spouse or another member of your family unit have owned two residences (such as a regular home and a summer cottage) since before 1982, it may be possible to structure your holdings so that the pre-1982 portion of the capital gain on the second residence will be exempt. That is because each taxpayer was entitled to a principal residence exemption before 1982—the "family unit" concept wasn't yet in place. In such a case, the gain accruing to December 31, 1981 may continue to be exempt. Consult a professional adviser on this matter.

If you have adult children, consider giving them the ownership of a second residence. If you own your house and your 19-year-old son owns the cottage, he can designate it as his principal residence when he sells it. However, at the time you transfer it to him you will have to recognize any increase in value since you purchased it (subject to a reduction if you made an election to use your capital gains exemption on it). You should also be sure you are satisfied with the *legal* effect of what you are doing—giving away your cottage—before you embark on such a transaction for tax purposes.

Make the election to treat rented-out property as your principal residence.

An exemption is also available in some cases where you rent the property out, either before or after you use it as your own residence. If you move out of your home and rent it out, you can continue to designate it as your residence for up to four years (provided you do not claim any other property as your principal residence and you file a special election with your tax return for the year in which you begin to rent the property). If you move due to relocation of your or your spouse's employment, the four-year period can normally be extended indefinitely, provided you move back to the home upon leaving that employment.

If you acquire property and rent it out, and then move in at some later date, you can file a special election with your tax return for the year in which you move in, to defer the capital gain that would normally apply when you change the property from income-earning to personal-use. If you do this, you may be able to get an exemption for four years during which you rented the property.

5.5.3 **Death**

When you die, you are generally deemed for tax purposes to have sold your capital property for its current fair market value, thus triggering a capital gain on all of the increase in value that has accrued since you purchased it. This prevents gains from accruing indefinitely without ever being taxed. In fact, although there are no estate taxes or succession duties in Canada, the taxation of accrued capital gains on death is thought by some to be a close equivalent.

Example:
Morris bought shares in Bell Canada in 1977. When he dies in November 1997, the shares will be worth $20,000 more than he paid for them (after all commissions).

Morris will be deemed to have sold the shares before his death for a capital gain of $20,000, three-quarters of which ($15,000) will be included in his income for the year of death.

Where property is left to your spouse, the gain will be put off until your spouse's death, at which point the entire capital gain will be taxed in your spouse's hands. A trust set up for your spouse can also be used to defer the gain, if certain conditions are met. However, your executor in both situations may elect to have this rule not apply to one or more of your properties, so as to use up your unused net capital losses and give your spouse a higher cost base for the assets.

Any net capital losses carried forward from previous years, which as we saw in 5.3.1 can normally only be used only against capital gains, can be used against all other income for the year of death and for the immediately preceding year, except to the extent the capital gains exemption has been claimed.

For further details on the treatment of capital gains on death, see 13.1.2.

5.5.4 Emigrating from Canada

If you leave Canada and become non-resident, you are deemed to have sold most of your assets at fair market value, and will have to recognize any resulting income or capital gains. Before October 2, 1996, this rule did not apply to some assets (unless you elected otherwise), such as Canadian real estate and shares in private Canadian corporations (technically known as "taxable Canadian property"), since any capital gains on such property will be taxed by Canada even when you are non-resident. However, for such assets, a tax treaty between Canada and the country to which you emigrated often prevents Canada from taxing the gain when you do sell the property (see 16.4.9).

On October 2, 1996, the government announced a series of proposals that make emigrating from Canada potentially much more expensive. Among other things, the broad exception for "taxable Canadian property" has been eliminated. The range of assets treated as having been sold for fair market value on emigration now includes *all* property, except for Canadian real estate, certain pensions and a few other specific exceptions.

New emigrants will have to pay tax on the resulting income or capital gains immediately. You can opt to defer payment of the tax until the property is sold, but only if you post acceptable security with Revenue Canada for the later payment. Acceptable security could be a letter of credit, a mortgage or a bank guarantee. At the time of writing, Revenue Canada has not yet finalized its conditions for accepting less negotiable forms of security, such as shares of private corporations.

Under new information reporting rules, if you emigrate from Canada in 1996 or later and you own property with a total value of $25,000 or more, you must also file an information return with Revenue Canada listing all of your signficant assets.

These proposals had not been made law at the time of writing, so details on aspects of the proposals are not yet available or may be changed before enactment. If you are becoming non-resident, professional advice is a must. Aside from the effects of Canadian tax law, the foreign tax law and any tax treaty between Canada and the country you are moving to must all be considered.

If you're emigrating from Canada, be sure to utilize your remaining $500,000 capital gains exemption.

Once you are non-resident, you cannot use the $500,000 capital gains exemption. So if you still have room in your exemption, and you own qualifying farm property (which includes Canadian real estate), you may wish to make steps to "crystallize" your gain before you emigrate. That way, you will trigger a gain that is absorbed by the $500,000 exemption which would not otherwise be available after you have emigrated, and only the increase from the current fair market value will be taxed in Canada when you, as a non-resident, eventually dispose of the property.

Alternatively, if you realize gains on the deemed disposition of qualified farm property or shares in a qualified small business corporation, you will want to make sure you apply any of your remaining $500,000 exemption against these gains.

Since qualifying farm property and small business shares are "taxable Canadian property", the deemed disposition on emigration will occur automatically if the emigration tax proposals discussed above are enacted. You will not need to make a special election and you can claim the exemption on your return for your year of emigration.

5.5.5 Other rules

Pre-1972 property—If you have property that you have owned since before 1972, when capital gains were not taxed at all, only the gain accruing since the end of 1971 will be taxed. For publicly-traded shares, valuation is easy; for real estate and shares in private businesses, valuation as of December 31, 1971 may be difficult to accomplish. When you report such a gain, you will need to estimate the value of the property on that date, and use that as the cost of the property (assuming it is higher than your actual cost).

Non-arm's length transfers—When you give or sell property to a member of your family, you are normally deemed to have received fair market value for it, triggering recognition of any accrued capital gain (or loss) for tax purposes. However, if you transfer property to your spouse, it is normally deemed to have been sold at your cost unless you elect to realize a gain. This rule also applies to common-law spouses who meet the criteria outlined in 2.2.1.

Personal-use property—No capital loss is available on personal-use property, except for "listed personal property" (jewellery, works of art, stamps, coins and rare books) losses which can be used only against listed personal property gains. As well, capital gains on personal-use property only apply to the extent the sale price exceeds $1,000.

If you change a property from personal use to income-earning use, you are normally deemed to have sold it at its fair market value, requiring you to recognize for tax purposes any accrued capital gain.

Options—Special rules apply to determine capital gains where you purchase or grant options (e.g., on the stock market).

Superficial loss—If you sell property (e.g., shares) to trigger a capital loss, and you or your spouse or a corporation controlled by either of you acquire identical property within 30 days before or after your sale, the capital loss will be called a "superficial loss" and ignored for tax purposes. The denied loss will be added to the cost of the identical property.

Insurance or expropriation proceeds—If property of yours is lost or destroyed, or expropriated, any insurance settlement or expropriation payment is considered to be proceeds of disposition, for purposes of the calculation described in 5.2.

5.6 References

The following publications can be obtained (in person or by telephone request) from your nearest Revenue Canada District Taxation Office. Forms and brochures may also be available from Revenue Canada's Internet site at www.revcan.ca.

Interpretation Bulletin IT-78, "Capital property owned on December 31, 1971—Identical properties"

Interpretation Bulletin IT-84, "Capital property owned on December 31, 1971—Median rule (Tax-free zone)"

Interpretation Bulletin IT-107, "Costs of disposition of capital property affected by the median rule"

Interpretation Bulletin IT-120R4, "Principal residence"

Interpretation Bulletin IT-133, "Stock exchange transactions—Date of disposition of shares"

Interpretation Bulletin IT-170R, "Sale of property—When included in income computation"

Interpretation Bulletin IT-218R, "Profits, capital gains and losses from the sale of real estate, including farm land and inherited land and conversion of real estate from capital property to inventory and vice versa"

Interpretation Bulletin IT-232R2, "Non-capital losses, net capital losses, restricted farm losses, farm losses and limited partnership losses— Their composition and deductibility in computing taxable income"

Interpretation Bulletin IT-236R3, "Reserves—Disposition of capital property"

Interpretation Bulletin IT-387R2, "Meaning of identical properties"

Interpretation Bulletin IT-456R, "Capital property—Some adjustments to cost base"

Interpretation Bulletin IT-459, "Adventure or concern in the nature of trade"

Interpretation Bulletin IT-479R, "Transactions in securities"

Interpretation Bulletin IT-484R2, "Business investment losses"

"Capital Gains Election Package"

"Capital Gains Tax Guide"

Form T123, "Election on disposition of Canadian securities"

Form T664, "Election to report a capital gain on property owned at the end of February 22, 1994"

Form T657, "Calculation of capital gains deduction for 19___ on all capital property"

Form T936, "Calculation of cumulative net investment loss to December 31, 19___ "

Form T2091 (IND), "Designation of principal residence"

Form T2091 (IND)-WS, "Principal residence worksheet for 19___ "

Investments and tax shelters

- Consider acquiring preferred shares to enhance after-tax yield (6.1.2)
- Use your exempt capital gains balance for mutual fund investments (6.1.7)
- If you're the higher-income spouse, consider electing to report your spouse's dividend income on your own return (6.1.8)
- Defer tax by acquiring investments that mature shortly after year-end (6.2.1)
- Structure your investments to make interest deductible (6.2.3)
- Consider investing in tax shelters—but don't let tax write-offs drive your decision (6.3)
- Before investing in a tax shelter, obtain its Identification Number (6.3.1)
- Look into investing in LSVCC shares—a new $3,500 investment may only cost you $595 after tax (6.3.8)
- Think about setting up a trust for your children (6.4)
- Consider the merits of acquiring an exempt life insurance contract (6.5)

In this chapter we look at how investment income is taxed, how interest expense can be written off, and the various types of tax shelters, along with a number of tax planning ideas that you should keep in mind. For advice on developing an appropriate investment strategy, see 1.2.5.

6.1 Dividends

6.1.1 What is a dividend?

A dividend is a distribution of profits to the shareholders (owners) of a corporation. A corporation may have many classes of shares. **Preferred shares** are shares on which dividends must generally be paid first, before dividends can be paid on a corporation's **common shares**.

Preferred shares typically pay a fixed annual or quarterly dividend. In some ways, they are similar to bonds or other debt, since the return is a fixed percentage. However, a corporation is not *required* to pay dividends on its preferred shares as long as it does not pay dividends on its common shares. If the corporation suffers losses, its board of directors may well decide not to pay dividends on preferred shares.

From a tax point of view, for individuals, preferred shares are identical to common shares (which typically pay dividends that bear some relationship to the corporation's profits).

6.1.2 How is a dividend taxed?

Dividends received by individuals from Canadian corporations are taxed in a rather peculiar manner, designed to reflect the fact that the corporation paying the dividend has already paid tax on its profits. The amount included in the individual's income is "grossed-up" to reflect the total amount of *pre-tax* income that the corporation is presumed to have earned. The individual then receives a credit to offset the tax the corporation is presumed to have paid (at about 20%). In no case, however, is the *actual* income earned or tax paid by the corporation taken into account.

Canadian dividends received are **grossed-up** by one-quarter. That is, you add 25% to the amount received, and show the total as income from dividends on your tax return. The offsetting federal dividend tax credit is then two-thirds of the amount of the gross-up—two-thirds of that 25%, or, if you like, 13.33% of the total you showed as dividend income. For most provinces, this dividend tax credit is then augmented by about half as much again, since the provincial tax is calculated on a reduced federal tax. In Québec a separate dividend tax credit is available for 8.87% of the grossed-up dividend. (In the example below, we use 50% as the provincial tax rate for illustrative purposes.)

Example:

Melissa earns $35,000 per year. She also owns shares in Canadian Inc., which pay her a dividend of **$1,000** in 1997.

Melissa's income for 1997 will be $35,000, plus the $1,000 dividend, plus a gross-up of one-quarter of the dividend, or $250. Her tax will be calculated on this income of **$36,250**. From the tax, she will deduct her regular credits (see Chapter 2) and a dividend tax credit of **$166.67** (two-thirds of the $250 gross-up). When her provincial tax and federal surtax are calculated, at 56% and 3% of the federal tax respectively, her tax will be reduced by a further **$98.34**, since the federal tax has been reduced by the credit. Melissa's $1,000 dividend is therefore taxed at about 41% of $1,250, but then reduced by a total of about **$265** in dividend tax credit and reduced provincial tax and surtax. The net result is that the dividend is taxed at about 25% instead of 41%.

(See 9.2.1 for more detail on the dividend tax credit from the perspective of the corporation.) The effect of the dividend tax credit is to tax dividends at *approximately* the following rates:

Income level	Salary income	Dividend income
$0-$29,590	27%	7%
$29,591-$59,180	41%	25%
$59,181 and up	50%	33%

The exact numbers vary by province. Remember that these numbers apply only to dividends from Canadian corporations. Dividends on foreign corporations are taxed as ordinary income.

Consider acquiring preferred shares to enhance your after-tax yield.

Since preferred shares pay dividends rather than interest (which is taxed like regular income, as we'll see in 6.2), preferred shares may offer a better after-tax rate of return than many interest-earning investments while still coming close to a guaranteed yield. While the yield is never completely guaranteed, many major public companies will continue to meet preferred share dividend expectations even when they suffer losses.

The yields on preferred shares usually reflect the fact that dividends are less heavily taxed than interest (as well as the fact that dividend payments are not deductible to the corporation). If current interest rates are around 8%, preferred share yields may well be around 6%. You will have to monitor preferred share prices on the market to find the best yields.

6.1.3 Stock dividends

A corporation will sometimes pay a **stock dividend** by issuing new shares to pay the dividend rather than giving you cash. In such a case, the gross-up and dividend tax credit still apply, and you must pay tax on the stock dividend even though you have received no cash. The amount of the dividend on which the gross-up is calculated is the increase in the paid-up capital resulting from the issue of new shares.

6.1.4 Capital dividends

You may also receive **capital dividends** from private corporations. They are completely tax-free (see 4.3.8). A capital dividend is generally a distribution of the untaxed one-quarter of capital gains. As we saw in 5.2, that fraction of the capital gain is not taxed at all. The capital dividend mechanism is used to distribute the untaxed portion without any tax consequences to the shareholder. (For an example, see 9.2.4.)

6.1.5 Dividends received by a corporation

Intercorporate dividends are normally tax-free. The assumption is that once a corporation has paid tax on its income, its profits can be distributed through a chain of holding corporations with no further tax consequences until an individual receives a dividend at the end of the chain. However, a special refundable tax—"Part IV tax"—can apply to intercorporate dividends in some circumstances, including most dividends received on investments in public corporations. The Part IV tax is 33 1/3%.

6.1.6   Mutual funds

Mutual funds are pools of assets that are invested by professional managers, either in general investments or in a particular sector (such as real estate or natural resources). A mutual fund corporation will pay dividends, but may designate all or a portion of the dividends as "capital gains dividends", to reflect capital gains earned by the mutual fund. From the taxpayer's point of view, such dividends are treated as capital gains rather than dividends, and subject to the usual capital gains treatment discussed in Chapter 5.

6.1.7   Mutual funds and your exempt capital gains balance

If you own any mutual funds that qualify as **"flow-through entities"**, you may have made the election to trigger the $100,000 capital gains exemption in respect of them (see 5.4.4). If so, making the election has created an **"exempt capital gains balance"** for each mutual fund, which you can use to offset capital gains from that fund—both gains from selling it and gains flowed through to you from it.

Use your exempt capital gains balance for mutual fund investments.

Where a mutual fund (or any other flow-through entity) has **allocated** capital gains to you for the year, make sure to use the exempt capital gains balance to claim a deduction on your return to offset the taxable capital gain that you have reported. It is up to you to remember that this balance is available to offset such gains until 2004. After that time any remaining exempt capital gains balance is added to the adjusted cost base of the mutual fund. If you sell all of the units of the fund before 2005, any remaining exempt capital gains balance will be added to the adjusted cost base of the units, creating a capital loss (see 5.4.4).

6.1.8   Election to transfer dividends from spouse

Since the dividend tax credit is a credit against tax owing, it is worthless if there is no tax to pay. If your spouse's income is very low, and you claim a credit for your spouse as a dependant (see 2.2.1), a relatively small amount of dividend income, when grossed-up by 25%, can take your spouse over the $538 income threshold and thereby reduce your spousal tax credit. At the same time, since your spouse does not pay any tax, the dividend tax credit is of no use.

If you're the higher-income spouse, consider electing to report your spouse's dividend income on your own return.

In such a case, you may elect to report all of your spouse's dividend income on your own tax return. While this may result in the income being taxed at a higher rate, it will avoid the erosion of the spousal tax credit. You will have to calculate tax both ways to see which is better. This election is done by including the dividends directly on Schedule 5 (Investment income) on your tax return, not Schedule 2 (Amounts transferred from spouse). If you live in Québec, you can make the same election for Québec tax purposes.

6.2 Interest income

Interest income is taxed at the same rates as employment or business income.

6.2.1 Accruing interest

Suppose you acquire a seven-year term deposit for $1,000 which will return $1,700 after seven years. When do you report the $700 in interest?

The answer depends on when you acquired the investment. If you bought it in 1990 or later, you must declare, **each year**, the interest accrued to the anniversary date of when you acquired it. Your financial institution should issue you a T5 slip showing the interest accruing on all such long-term investments.

If you acquired the investment before 1990, you must report the accruing interest at least **every three years**, though you have the option of reporting it annually if you wish.

The accrual rules apply to almost all kinds of investments, including stripped bonds (see 6.2.2 below), Canada Savings Bonds, and mortgages or loans to relatives on which interest is allowed to accrue.

Example:
In 1992, Christine lent $10,000 to her cousin, who is attending university and needed the funds for tuition and residence. Her cousin agreed in writing to pay 10% annual interest (not compounded) on the loan, but that he will not pay back the loan or the interest until after he has graduated and secures a job.

Christine is required to report and pay tax on $1,000 of accrued interest income each year beginning in 1993. If in 1997 her cousin pays her $15,000 to cover the loan and all interest, she will only report $1,000 as income in 1997, since she will have already reported $4,000 over the previous four years.

Defer tax by acquiring investments that mature shortly after year-end.

As a general deferral technique, acquire investments that mature shortly after year-end rather than before. For example, if you are investing in T-Bills on July 15, and you can choose between maturity dates of December 29 and January 2, then you should choose January 2 if all else is equal. That way you will defer reporting and paying tax on the income by one year. Of course, tax considerations should not override normal investment considerations, such as the available rates of return and the question of when you will need access to the funds.

6.2.2 Stripped bonds and clipped coupons

Stripped bonds are long-term government or government-backed (e.g., provincial hydro) bonds which pay interest when their coupons are cashed in. A typical bond might have a 20-year term, have a face value of $100,000 and come with coupons paying $5,000 in interest, cashable every six months. At the end of the 20 years one simply redeems the bond for $100,000.

Brokerage firms often acquire such bonds and split up the bond and its coupons, selling them separately. The $100,000 bond maturing in 20 years, in our example, might be sold for $15,000, while the forty $5,000 coupons would be sold at prices reflecting the length of time until their maturity.

For tax purposes, the difference between the discounted price of the bond (or coupon) and the amount you receive when it is redeemed is considered to be interest. Because of the annual (or three-year, if bought before 1990) accrual rule, such bonds generally are unattractive to many taxpayers—you have to pay tax annually on interest that you will not receive for some time. However, they can be excellent investments for self-directed RRSPs and other tax-deferred plans (see Chapter 3).

One should be cautious when acquiring stripped bonds or clipped coupons— or, for that matter, any long-term bond. If you need to sell them before they mature, you will find that their value fluctuates considerably due to trends in interest rates. If interest rates in general have gone up, the resale value of your bond or coupon will likely have gone down.

6.2.3 Deductibility of interest expense

As a general principle, interest is deductible for tax purposes as long as the loan was used **for the purpose of earning income** from a business or property. So, if you borrow money to buy shares on the stock market, or to invest in a business, the interest you pay is generally deductible. Such expenses are also called **carrying charges**.

On the other hand, if you buy an investment with a fixed interest rate, you cannot deduct interest on your loan beyond the rate that your investment pays. For example, if you borrow at 15% and lend the funds to a relative at 10%, you can only deduct 10% interest on your loan. Where the investment is in preferred shares, it is the grossed-up amount of the dividend (see 6.1.2) which determines the amount of interest that can be deducted. If the dividend rate is 8%, being effectively 10% when grossed-up by 25%, then once again only the first 10% of interest on the loan can be deducted.

Interest is not deductible where the loan was taken out for some purpose other than to earn income subject to tax. Examples include:

- home mortgage, except to the extent you use a home office for business purposes (see 8.2.11);
- car loan, where the car is used solely for personal use;
- credit cards, except to the extent the charges are for business expenses;
- loan to contribute to an RRSP;
- interest on late income tax or instalment payments.

If you dispose of the property that you borrowed money to acquire, you can continue to deduct the interest in certain cases even though the underlying source of income has been lost. The rules in this respect are complex, and professional advice may be required if you are in this situation.

Interest on a car loan, where the car is used for your employment or business purposes, is limited to the employment or business portion of $250 or $300 per month, depending on when the car was purchased—see 7.10.1 and 8.2.8.

Structure investments to make interest deductible.

Since interest on consumer loans and home mortgages is normally not deductible, while interest on loans taken out to purchase income-generating investments is deductible, you should therefore try to ensure that all loans you take out are for a deductible purpose.

For example, if you have a home mortgage as well as investments that can be easily sold, consider whether you can sell the investments, pay off the mortgage, and borrow new funds (secured by the same mortgage, if necessary) for the purpose of purchasing new investments. You will of course be required to recognize any capital gains on the sale of the investments (beyond the level you may have elected for capital gains exemption purposes effective February 22, 1994—see 5.4.4). There is a possible danger of this plan being in contravention of the general anti-avoidance rule—consult a tax professional to minimize the chances of the rule applying.

Revenue Canada often pays special attention to deductions for interest expenses. It is wise to keep on file, along with your tax return, accurate records showing the amount of the loan, the purpose of the loan and the interest paid during the year, along with the relevant financial statements and possibly a confirming letter from your financial institution. It may be appropriate to file this information with your tax return if you have done so in previous years.

For minimum tax purposes, interest expense must be added back to your income if it relates to tax shelters or other "tainted" deductions. See 12.2.

6.3 Tax shelters

Tax shelters are no longer as important to tax planning as they were some years ago. For a variety of reasons, there are now relatively few publicly-offered vehicles for sheltering your ordinary income from tax.

Contrary to popular perception, tax shelters are generally not "loopholes" in the system. Preferences are given to certain types of investment as a deliberate move by the government to stimulate economic activity in a particular area. Whether it is investment in Cape Breton Island, scientific research or exploration for oil and gas or computer software, the specific write-offs and credits in the *Income Tax Act* are put there to encourage you, the taxpayer, to invest funds in a particular sphere.

Don't let tax write-offs drive your decision to invest in tax shelters.

One should only invest in a tax shelter if, after taking the tax benefits into account, there is a reasonable expectation of profit from the shelter. The tax benefits alone should rarely control your investment decision. Further, Revenue Canada is becoming increasingly aggressive in challenging tax shelter-related deductions on the basis that there is no reasonable expectation of profit from the shelter.

There are relatively few tax shelters around, even compared to a year ago. Strict new rules that were released in 1995 and expected to become law in the fall of 1997 make many tax shelters unattractive (see 6.3.2). Another set of proposals announced on November 18, 1996 takes aim at certain types of tax shelter investments which have rights to receive future income, such as limited partnership structures involving mutual fund limited partnerships and film production services, curtailing the tax benefits of such investments for 1997 and later years.

When investing in tax shelters, one must be aware of the possible application of the **minimum tax** (see Chapter 12). Québec residents should also read Chapter 15. Finally, you must always be aware of the possible application of the general anti-avoidance rule discussed in 4.2.5.

We do not discuss RRSPs and other tax deferral plans in this section. They were dealt with in detail in Chapter 3.

6.3.1 Tax shelter identification number

Before investing in a tax shelter, obtain its Identification Number.

Anyone selling an interest in a tax shelter is required to obtain an identification number from Revenue Canada (and Revenu Québec, in some cases) and provide that number on all documents and financial statements relating to the shelter. *If you do not have the identification number, or if any penalties relating to the identification number are payable by the promoter and have not been paid, you will not be able to claim the benefits of the shelter.*

For the purposes of this rule, a tax shelter is defined, generally, as an investment that is advertised or represented as entitling you to write-offs or deductions over four years that will exceed your investment (net of any tax credits or other benefits you obtain). Flow-through shares (see 6.3.5) and the deferred income plans we saw in Chapter 3 (RRSPs, etc.) are excluded from the definition.

Because of this rule, caution is required when considering investments in tax shelters. Note, however, that the identification number does **not** indicate approval by Revenue Canada or Revenu Québec of the proposed benefits. It merely ensures that the shelter has been registered for administrative purposes, making audit and reassessment easier for Revenue Canada and Revenu Québec if they eventually decide to disallow some or all of the tax benefits.

Any deduction relating to an investment that requires a tax shelter identification number must be added back into income for minimum tax purposes. See 12.2.

6.3.2 Limited partnerships

A number of shelters involve the purchase of an interest in a limited partnership. A limited partnership is a **partnership**, in that you share the profits of the business with the other partners, and report a percentage of the partnership's income (or loss) directly as your income—whether or not you have received any of the profits. This is in contrast to corporate profits, which are reported only when distributed as dividends, as we saw in 6.1.2 above. However, a limited partnership is similar to a corporation in that you have **limited liability**—you cannot be sued for the partnership's debts. In general, you can only lose your original investment. (Note also that, while you may periodically receive draws from the partnership, you may be obliged to repay these amounts, up to your original investment, if the partnership suffers losses.)

Because you can report partnership losses directly on your own tax return, limited partnerships are an attractive investment where the partnership business is expected to have losses in its initial years (either real losses due to start-up costs, or tax-created losses due to high write-offs available on certain kinds of investments).

However, you may not write off more than the original cost of your investment. The *Income Tax Act*'s "at-risk" rules provide that you cannot deduct more than the amount you have at risk in a limited partnership. As well, draft legislation released in 1995 severely restricts the use of limited partnerships to create losses where there is "non-recourse" debt (i.e., you are required to contribute amounts to the partnership, but cannot be forced to do so from your own funds, only from the profits from your partnership interest).

Example:

Kevin invests $6,000 for 1/100 of a limited partnership undertaking bona fide business activities. In its first year, due to high expenses and special write-offs available, the partnership records a $1 million loss for tax purposes.

Although 1/100 of the loss is $10,000, Kevin may only deduct $6,000, being his "at-risk amount", on his tax return. The remaining $4,000 will be usable against Kevin's income from the partnership at any time in the future.

Losses from limited partnerships and the carrying charges related to the partnership units must be added back into income for minimum tax purposes. See 12.2.

6.3.3 Investments in income rights

Before 1997, investments in certain types of limited partnership structures offered significant tax deferral advantages. Unlike the limited partnership tax shelters discussed in 6.2.3, a passive investment in this type of limited partnership is used to finance another party's business expenses in exchange for the right to receive future income, or an "income right."

However, new proposals announced on November 18, 1996 will severely limit the tax deductions available for such investments made in 1997 and later years. The two most common forms of investment in income rights affected by these rules are limited partnership structures involving film production service and mutual fund selling commissions, but the new rules target most types of passive investments in income rights.

Specifically, the proposals apply to investments in rights to any income that is related to another taxpayer's activity, property or business, and that is computed with reference to the production or use of property and similar criteria (e.g., revenue, cash flow and commodity price).

For example, many mutual funds (see 6.1.6) are "no-load" funds, meaning that the investor pays no fee to buy into the fund, and pays no fee to have the units redeemed by the fund, provided the investor holds the units for some period of time (typically five to eight years). When a stockbroker (investment dealer) sells a unit of a mutual fund, the broker receives a commission of about 3% of the investment. Where the fund is a "no-load" fund, the investor is not supplying the cash to pay the broker's commission. This cash has to come from somewhere.

Mutual fund limited partnerships are limited partnerships (discussed above in 6.3.2) set up to fund these commissions. When you invest in a mutual fund limited partnership, your investment is used to pay commissions to brokers who sell units in a specific mutual fund. You then receive income from the mutual fund over several years in the form of "distribution fees".

Before July 31, 1997, the tax shelter benefits for passive investors in income rights were generally in the form of a tax deferral arising from the mismatching of the year in which the related expenses may be deducted and the later year(s) in which the related income is recognized. For passive investments in mutual fund selling commissions, you are permitted to claim your share of the limited partnership's selling commissions incurred after July 1995 and before 1997 as a deductible expense over three years on a straight-line basis. Your income from the fund is taxable in the years you earn it.

Pre-1997 investments in film production service limited partnerships offered an even greater tax deferral benefit—the film production expenditures are generally deductible against the revenue earned from the production. In addition, to the extent any undeducted expenses come to be considered unrecoverable, they may be deducted in the year this determination is made.

After 1996, your deduction for your share of certain expenditures will be spread over a period of time that more accurately matches the life of the related income right. Such "**matchable expenditures**" include the amount you spent to acquire the right and any amounts expended to fulfill related obligations or to preserve or protect the right. (Certain otherwise deductible amounts are excluded from this definition, including capital cost allowance, interest, annual fees and overhead costs.)

Under the new rules, deductions for matchable expenditures must be amortized according to a three-part formula. The minimum amortization period is five years and the maximum is 40 years, computed on a straight-line basis. However, the formula further reduces or eliminates the deduction if the cumulative income from the right is not at least equal to the cumulative amount of the otherwise deductible expenditures.

Example:

In 1997, Alison invests $1,000 in an income right that covers a five-year period. Her income from the investment is $350 in 1997, $100 in 1998 and $80 in 1999, for a three-year cumulative total of $530.

Alison can deduct $200 in 1997 and in 1998 ($1,000 divided by 5). But in 1998, Alison's deduction will be capped at $130 because her three-year total cannot be more than the $530 cumulative income from the right for that period. The $70 ($200 – $130) disallowed as a deduction in 1999 would be deductible in 2000, along with the $200 normally allowable for that year, as long as Alison receives at least $270 from the rights in 2000, which is the amount required for Alison to report a cumulative $800 in that year.

If the rights do not earn enough cumulative income to equal the matchable expenditures before the rights expire or are sold to unrelated third parties, you would be able to deduct the unamortized expenditures in that year, less any sale proceeds, essentially as a terminal loss (as long as the investment passes the general tests for deductibility, including the "reasonable expectation of profit" test discussed in 8.4).

If you invested in one of these types of shelters before 1997, your investment will probably be exempt from the new rules. However, you should check with a professional tax advisor to confirm your ability to claim any related deductions in 1997 and 1998. (We understand that the Department of Finance is considering delaying the application of these rules to production services limited partnerships beyond July 31, 1997, but no official announcement has been made at the time of writing.)

6.3.4 Resource activities

Two areas that receive special incentives from the federal tax system are mining, and oil and gas exploration (for details of the Québec incentives, see 15.3.7). Tax shelters in these areas usually involve either limited partnerships (see 6.3.2) or **flow-through shares**. However, their appeal over the last few years has diminished greatly.

Flow-through shares are treasury shares of the capital stock of a resource corporation that are issued to a person under a written agreement that specifies that the person will receive the common shares and resource tax deduction in exchange for the cash paid by the investor. Under the *Income Tax Act*, the corporation can "renounce" some of its resource expenses, and will not be able to claim them for tax purposes. In exchange, it passes the rights to these claims to the owners of the flow-through shares. The adjusted cost base (see 5.2) of a flow-through share is nil. If the corporation is in its early years and not making a profit anyway, the flowing-through of the deductions allows the shareholders to use write-offs which otherwise could not currently be used by the corporation.

Whether you invest in a limited partnership or flow-through shares, the particular deductions you get will depend on the classification of the partnership or corporation's income and expenses. You will receive a statement and/or an information slip indicating your share of some or all of: business income or loss (partnership only); investment income and dividends (partnership only); Canadian exploration expenses (fully deductible); Canadian development expenses (excluding mining property acquisitions for flow-through shares; 30% deductible on a declining balance basis); Canadian oil and gas property expenses (partnership only; 10% deductible on a declining balance basis); and resource allowance (25% of certain production and processing income).

Before investing in resource funds, be sure to examine the track record of the promoters, the geological and engineering expertise available, the type of exploration to be undertaken and the expected tax effects of the various types of expenditures.

At the time of investment in the shelter you can usually obtain a forecast of the expected expenses and their classification, along with the implications for your tax return.

6.3.5 Business ventures

Some tax shelters involve investing in ongoing business ventures such as computer software development, either through limited partnerships or through a direct purchase of property. These are cases where the property is eligible for a high rate of capital cost allowance (depreciation), thus giving you a substantial write-off relative to your cash investment.

The tax system restricts capital cost allowance claims available in respect of certain "leasing properties", such as nursing homes, recreational vehicles, hotels and yachts, in cases where you are not personally active in the day-to-day operation of the business. In general, the restrictions limit your claim to your income from that business, so you cannot use the capital cost allowance to shelter other income. Consult a professional advisor for details on the restrictions regarding any particular kind of asset.

6.3.6 Commodity straddles

If you are very aggressive and willing to risk the possible application by Revenue Canada of the *Income Tax Act*'s general anti-avoidance rule, you can consider commodity straddles and similar transactions.

In a commodity straddle, you would take both "buy" and "sell" futures positions on a particular commodity, where the positions are not exactly offsetting. By year-end, the commodity can be expected to have fluctuated in value, and you will have a loss on one of the contracts but a gain on the other. You then get out of the contract which has lost value before year-end, and either get out of the other contract in the new year or buy a new contract as a hedge at the time you get out of your loss position. The result will be a loss in the current year, offset by a gain in the next year—or, in other words, deferral of tax.

For the above technique to work, you have to consider yourself a speculator, so that the transactions result in business loss and income rather than capital losses and capital gains (as we saw in 5.3.1, capital losses are not very useful). Revenue Canada's position is that once you have treated such transactions as being on income account, you cannot revert to calling them capital transactions in the future. Note also that the general anti-avoidance rule discussed in 4.2.5 might be applied to your transactions.

6.3.7 Real estate investments

Investments in real estate can offer a reasonable rate of return, when the tax benefits are combined with rental income and capital appreciation. Mortgage interest expense, property taxes and maintenance costs can all be written off. Capital cost allowance (depreciation) for buildings is normally 4% per year on a declining balance basis, but cannot normally be used to create or increase a loss used against other income. (No capital cost allowance is available for land.)

6.3.8 Labour-sponsored venture capital corporations

Look into investing in LSVCC shares.

A "labour-sponsored venture capital corporation", or LSVCC, is a fund sponsored by organized labour that provides venture capital to start-up businesses. Although the government has curtailed the tax benefits of investments in LSVCC shares, they may still be an investment worth considering.

After March 5, 1996, an investment in an LSVCC of up to $3,500 entitles you to a special federal tax credit of 15% of your investment. Also, depending on the province you live in, you may get a further 15% or 20% credit against your provincial income tax which you claim on your provincial T1C form when filing your tax return (see 15.3.5 if you live in Québec). Where the provincial credit is less than 15%, the federal credit will be limited to the lesser amount; if the LSVCC is federally registered, however, the federal credit will not be reduced below 10%. No provincial LSVCC credit is available in Alberta, New Brunswick or Newfoundland.

For LSVCC shares acquired on or before March 5, 1996, the federal credit was 20% on a maximum investment of $5,000, and the provincial component, where available, was also 20%.

Like an RRSP contribution, an LSVCC investment can be made up to 60 days after the end of a year and still qualify for the credit for that year.

Generally, you may redeem your investment whenever you wish, but certain restrictions and charges may apply depending on which fund you invest in. You must repay the special credits if you do not keep your pre-March 6, 1996 LSVCC investment for at least five years, or two years if you reach age 65, retire or cease to be resident in Canada. LSVCC shares acquired after March 5, 1996 must be held for eight years, whether or not you were previously eligible for the two-year minimum holding period.

A new LSVCC investment of $3,500 may cost as little as $595 after tax.

As we saw in 3.3.5, an investment in an LSVCC can be transferred to your RRSP or bought by your RRSP with "new" funds you have contributed for that purpose.

If you live in a province that matches the federal credit and you invest in LSVCC shares after March 5, 1996, you receive 30% of your investment back in credits on your tax return (assuming a 15% provincial credit). If you invest the maximum $3,500 by March 1, 1998 for your 1997 taxation year, your actual cost is $2,450. If you then transfer the investment to your RRSP (or have the RRSP make the investment with "new" funds), you can deduct the full $3,500; if you are in a 53% tax bracket, this will save you a further $1,855.

The result is that the cash cost of a $3,500 investment can be as low as $595, if you have contribution room in your RRSP that you are not otherwise using. However, as previously noted in 3.3.5, you should carefully evaluate the relative investment merits of these funds before cutting the cheque.

6.4 Trusts

A trust is an arrangement whereby a trustee holds property for the benefit of one or more beneficiaries. A trust can be set up at any time, or on death by one's will.

Trusts are taxed as separate taxpayers. A trust created on death will be taxed at the same rates as an individual. All other trusts are taxed at a flat rate, which is the top rate of tax (about 50%, depending on the province).

Think about setting up a trust for your children.

Trusts can be a useful way of directing income to children for their education to provide for financial support, or to transfer funds to other relatives. To the extent a trust distributes its income to its beneficiaries, the beneficiaries rather than the trust pay tax on that amount.

Any arrangements involving trusts should be set up with proper legal and tax advice, particularly taking into account the attribution rules discussed in Chapter 4.

Trusts are discussed in more detail at 13.3.

6.5 Exempt life insurance contracts

The life insurance industry has developed attractive products that can help you meet two planning objectives at once: having insurance coverage, and providing retirement income from tax-sheltered growth.

Consider the merits of acquiring an exempt life insurance contract.

There are many issues to look at when considering whether to acquire such a contract, such as the underlying mortality costs and administrative expenses, a guaranteed minimum rate of return, comparison to a similar return in a non-tax sheltered environment, your required life insurance coverage, your income objectives and so on. Professional advice is a must when assessing the merits of this type of "investment".

Life insurance is discussed in more detail at 13.6.

6.6 References

The following publications can be obtained (in person or by telephone request) from your nearest Revenue Canada District Taxation Office. Forms and guides may also be available from Revenue Canada's Internet site at www.revcan.ca.

Interpretation Bulletin IT-66R6, "Capital dividends"

Interpretation Bulletin IT-67R3, "Taxable dividends from corporations resident in Canada"

Interpretation Bulletin IT-148R2, "Recreational properties and club dues"

Interpretation Bulletin IT-195R4, "Rental property—Capital cost allowance restrictions"

Interpretation Bulletin IT-232R2, "Non-capital losses, net capital losses, restricted farm losses, farm losses and limited partnership losses— Their composition and deductibility in computing taxable income"

Interpretation Bulletin IT-274R, "Rental properties—Capital cost of $50,000 or more"

Interpretation Bulletin IT-295R4, "Taxable dividends received after 1987 by a spouse"

Interpretation Bulletin IT-367R3, "Capital Cost Allowance—Multiple-unit residential buildings"

Interpretation Bulletin IT-381R3, "Trusts—Capital gains and losses and the flow-through of taxable capital gains to beneficiaries"

Interpretation Bulletin IT-394R, "Preferred beneficiary election"

Interpretation Bulletin IT-396R, "Interest income"

Interpretation Bulletin IT-445, "The deduction of interest on funds borrowed either to be loaned at less than a reasonable rate of interest or to honour a guarantee given for inadequate consideration in non-arm's length circumstances"

Interpretation Bulletin IT-503, "Exploration and development shares"

Interpretation Bulletin IT-524, "Trusts—Flow-through of taxable dividends to a beneficiary—After 1987"

"Rental Income Tax Guide"

Form T776, "Statement of real estate rentals"

If you are employed

- Arrange to get non-taxable benefits (7.1.1)
- Ask to have your source withholdings reduced where possible (7.2)
- Pay interest owing on loan from employer by January 30 of the following year (7.3)
- Encourage your employer to set up a stock option plan (7.4)
- Consider a stock purchase plan or phantom stock plan (7.4)
- Consider employees' profit-sharing plan for cash-flow purposes (7.6)
- Transfer retiring allowances to an RRSP (7.7)
- Keep track of, and maximize, business use of car (7.5, 7.10.1)
- Take steps to minimize the taxable benefit from car operating costs (7.5)
- Avoid employer-owned vehicles costing over $25,000 (7.5)
- Reduce time company car is available for personal use (7.5)
- Claim rebate for GST paid on expenses deductible from your employment income (7.11)
- Arrange to be a consultant rather than employed (8.1)

As a general principle, all **income** (including tips) and **benefits** from or related to your employment are taxed, except where the federal or Québec rules specifically provide otherwise. Also as a general principle, you cannot claim any deductions against employment income, except for those that are specifically allowed by the system. There are, however, many special rules, and we examine some of them in this chapter.

7.1 Employment benefits

7.1.1 Non-taxable employment benefits

Certain employment benefits are not taxable, even though many of them are deductible expenses to the employer. The government is therefore providing an incentive to employers to provide these benefits, since the after-tax returns are greater than straight salary. Non-taxable benefits include:

- Contributions to a registered pension plan (the pension is taxable when received—see 3.4.1).
- Contributions to a group sickness or accident insurance plan.

123

■ Contributions to a "private health services plan", such as those covering drugs, medical expenses and hospital charges not covered by public health insurance, and dental fees (except for Québec purposes—see 15.2.8).

■ All or a portion of the cost of free or subsidized school services for your children (for example, if the services are provided in a remote area).

■ Contributions to a supplementary unemployment benefit plan.

■ Contributions to a deferred profit-sharing plan.

■ Reimbursement of certain moving expenses on relocation.

■ Payment of club dues if your membership in the club may potentially benefit the employer's business (however, these dues are normally not deductible to the employer).

■ Employee discounts, where such discounts are commonly available to other employees (but not below the employer's cost).

■ One Christmas gift, wedding gift or similar gift of up to $100, where the employer does not deduct the cost for tax purposes.

■ Counselling services related to mental or physical health, employment termination, or retirement.

■ Subsidized meals, where you are required to pay a reasonable charge covering the cost of the food.

■ Uniforms or special clothing you need for your job.

■ Transportation to the job, if provided directly by the employer.

■ Board and lodging at, and transportation to, a "special work site" where you work temporarily or a "remote work site" that is remote from any established community.

■ Use of your employer's recreational facilities.

■ Transportation passes given to bus, rail and airline employees, except for airline employees travelling on a space-confirmed basis.

■ Transportation and parking costs, whether paid directly by the employer or reimbursed to you, if you are blind or are disabled due to a mobility impairment.

■ The cost of an attendant to assist you at work if you are disabled.

Note that where your employer deducts its contributions to a sickness or accident insurance plan, a disability insurance plan or an income maintenance insurance plan, any benefits you receive from the insurance will be taxable (but reduced by your own premium payments to the plan).

Arrange to get non-taxable benefits.

Ask your employer to make use of the non-taxable benefits outlined above as much as possible. If you have an employment benefit package where you and the employer share the costs, try to have the cost-sharing reallocated so your employer pays for all the non-taxable benefits and you pay for the benefits that are taxable if your employer pays them. In many cases, without changing the cost to your employer, you can reduce your tax burden this way.

One non-taxable benefit that is often overlooked is that of board and lodging at a "special work site" or "remote work site". A special work site need not be remote in the sense of isolated; as long as the duties you perform at that location are of a temporary nature, and you maintain another residence, the board (i.e., food) and lodging paid by your employer are a non-taxable benefit. This could apply, for example, if you spend several months in another city working on a project for your employer.

7.1.2 Taxable employment benefits

In general, employment benefits other than those listed above are taxed as though you had received an equivalent amount of income. Examples include:

- Tips (gratuities) that you receive from customers.
- Board, lodging, and rent-free or low-rent housing (with some exceptions for remote or special work sites).
- Travelling expenses for personal travel, including expenses for your spouse to travel on a business trip of yours, unless your spouse was engaged primarily in business activities on behalf of the employer during the trip.
- Personal use of employer's automobile (see 7.5 below).
- Gifts, except for $100 per year as noted above.
- Allowing you and/or your family to use a vacation property.
- Holiday trips, prizes and incentive awards.
- Use of frequent-flyer credits that you earn through employer-paid trips used for personal trips.
- Payment of provincial (public) health insurance premiums (note that many provinces no longer charge such premiums).
- Life insurance premiums.
- Reimbursement for the cost of tools used in employment duties.
- Most tuition fees, except where you are given time off with pay during working hours to attend the classes, in which case it's assumed the tuition is for the employer's benefit.
- Loans to employees (see 7.3 below).
- Stock option plans (taxed only when you exercise the option—see 7.4 below).
- Income tax return preparation and financial counselling (but not retirement or re-employment counselling).

In general, where the employer pays sales tax on goods or services, and then provides those goods or services to you as a taxable benefit, the calculation of the taxable benefit will require an additional 7% to account for the GST. This applies, for example, to automobiles. If you live in Nova Scotia, New Brunswick or Newfoundland, the 15% HST rate will apply (see 8.2.5); for Québec, the benefit is increased by the 7% GST and 6.5% QST (7.5% QST in 1998).

7.2 Reductions of source withholdings

As we'll see in 14.2.1, your employer and others are required to withhold tax at source and remit it to Revenue Canada. The same rules generally apply for Québec purposes.

Ask to have your source withholdings reduced where possible.

In any situation where you expect to receive a refund after filing your return (e.g., due to personal tax credits, RRSP contributions, medical expenses or charitable donations, alimony and maintenance payments), you should review the TD1 form (and MR-19 in Québec) you file with your employer and seek to have source withholdings reduced. You can ask your local Revenue Canada district office to permit your employer to reduce your source withholdings for deductions not normally provided for on the TD1 form, such as RRSP contributions and alimony and maintenance.

However, if your employer withholds from your remuneration RRSP contributions, union and professional dues and alimony and maintenance payments for direct remittance to the intended recipient, the employer can take these withholdings into account in calculating your tax withheld at source without requesting permission from Revenue Canada.

If you have a loan from your employer on which imputed interest is assessed as a taxable benefit (see 7.3 below), your source deductions of income tax will reflect that taxable benefit. If, however, you are using the funds for a purpose that allows you an offsetting deduction, you may write to Revenue Canada, setting out that fact, and request that your employer be permitted to reduce the source withholding. An example of this is where you use the loan proceeds for investment purposes.

Many people look forward to receiving a tax refund, but it's not good tax planning to get one. If you get a refund, that means Revenue Canada has been holding your money and not paying you interest on it for many months. Although fiscal responsibility is needed to make sure you can pay your tax when it is due, it is better to be required to send a cheque to Revenue Canada at filing time, since it means that you have had use of the funds (for investment or other purposes) in the meantime. However, you must pay instalments if the difference between your tax payable and amounts withheld at source is more than $2,000 ($1,200 in Québec—see 15.2.29) in both the current year and either of the two preceding years. (See 14.2.2.)

Note that interest is not paid on refunds for the first 45 days of processing after the filing deadline—i.e., until after June 14 for most employees. If you have a June 15 filing deadline because you have self-employment income (see 8.2.1), interest will not be paid until 45 days after April 30 or 45 days after the date that the return is actually filed, whichever is later. (See 14.1.1 and 14.3.)

7.3 Loans to employees

If you receive a low-interest or interest-free loan from your employer (or past or future employer), you are considered to have received a benefit from employment. The benefit is set at Revenue Canada's (and Revenu Québec's) current prescribed rate of interest, which varies quarterly, minus any interest you actually pay during the year or within 30 days after the end of the year. The prescribed rate is 4% lower (3% in Québec) than the rate charged on late payments of tax—see 14.3. (There may be an offsetting deemed interest deduction, as we shall see.)

Example:
Rebecca receives a loan of $10,000 from her employer on January 1, 1997. She is required to pay it back one year later, without interest. Assume the prescribed rate throughout the entire year is 4%.

Rebecca is considered to have an employment benefit of $400, and will be required to include this amount in her employment income.

But if instead the loan bore interest at 2%, and Rebecca made an interest payment before January 30, 1998, her taxable benefit would be calculated as 2% (the prescribed rate of 4% minus her employer's 2% rate) of $10,000, or $200.

Pay interest owing on loan from employer by January 30 of the following year.

If you have received an interest-bearing loan from your employer, consider deferring the payment of interest on the loan until January 30 of the next calendar year. This will provide you with a cash flow advantage. Make sure you do pay the interest by that date, however.

Exceptions

A **home purchase loan** is taxed on the same basis as other employee loans, but the rate applied in calculating the imputed interest for the first five years of the loan will not be greater than the prescribed rate in effect at the time the loan was made. At the end of the five-year period, it is considered a new loan, and the prescribed rate at that time will be the maximum for the next five years.

Example:
Keith receives an interest-free loan from his employer to help him buy a house. (He is not relocating, just moving from an apartment to a house.) At the time, the prescribed interest rate is 4%. Two years later, interest rates have gone up, and the prescribed rate increases to 8%.

Keith will still pay tax on the interest benefit calculated at only 4% of the amount of the loan. If the prescribed rate had gone below 4%, he would, however, pay tax on imputed interest at the lower rate as long as it stayed below 4%.

If you **relocate**, and receive a home purchase loan to acquire a residence at least 40 km closer to your new work location, then a special deduction in computing your taxable income is available to you for the first five years of the loan equal to the interest imputed on $25,000. Note that you must still report the entire interest amount as a taxable benefit, and claim this special deduction as a separate item on your tax return.

Where you use funds borrowed from your employer to purchase **investments** or to purchase an **automobile** (or aircraft) to be used for your employment, you can obtain an offsetting deduction. The amount of imputed interest that you include in your income as a taxable benefit is deemed to have been *interest paid by you*. As a result, if such interest would otherwise have been deductible, you can deduct it. (As we saw in 6.2.3, interest paid on loans to acquire investments is deductible, and as we'll see in 7.10.1, interest paid on loans to acquire a car is deductible if the car is required by your terms of employment.) The effect is to eliminate the tax cost of the taxable benefit.

If you are a **shareholder** of the company as well as an employee, or if a member of your family is a shareholder, you must be especially cautious. It is possible for the *entire* amount of the loan, rather than the imputed interest, to be included in your income for tax purposes, unless stringent conditions are met. In general, you can avoid this rule if the loan is made for certain specific purposes and with arrangements for repayment within a reasonable time. Alternatively, the entire loan must be repaid within one year, and not be part of a series of loans and repayments (see 9.2.6).

7.4 Stock option plans

A stock option plan is an arrangement whereby a corporation gives an employee the right (an option) to invest in its shares at a given price. The price may or may not be less than the market price at the time the option is granted. For example, suppose you work for a corporation whose stock trades at $20. In 1997, you are given an option to buy up to 1,000 shares at $20, good until 1999. If, in 1998, the stock is trading at $30, you can exercise the option, buy 1,000 shares for $20,000, and then, if you wish, turn around and sell the shares on the market for $30,000.

The general rule is that you are considered to receive a benefit from employment, not when the option is granted (1997 in the above example), but when you exercise it (1998). The taxable benefit is the difference between the price you pay ($20,000) and the value of the shares when you exercise the option ($30,000). You would, therefore, report a taxable benefit of $10,000 in your employment income for 1998. (The adjusted cost base of the shares to you will be $30,000, so you will not be doubly taxed when you subsequently sell them.)

An offsetting partial deduction is available if certain requirements are met. The first requirement is that the shares be normal common shares (not preferred shares). Second, the exercise price must be no less than the fair market value of the shares at the time the option was granted. (Otherwise you could simply exercise the option the day you received it, so the benefit would be just like cash.) Third, you must deal at arm's length with the corporation (meaning essentially that you or members of your family do not control it). If these conditions are met, you can claim a deduction from income of one-quarter of the amount of the taxable benefit. The effect of this deduction is to make the taxable benefit taxed at the same three-quarters rate as a capital gain.

Encourage your employer to set up a stock option plan.

You may wish to approach your employer about establishing a stock option plan as an employment benefit. It may cost your employer very little, and can even bring investment funds into the corporation to some extent. (The cost is the dilution of the existing shareholders' interests.)

If your employer is a Canadian-controlled private corporation ("CCPC") with which you deal at arm's length, stock options are particularly attractive since you do not record the taxable benefit until you *sell* the shares, rather than when you exercise the option and acquire them. And, if you have held them for at least two years at the date of sale, you can claim a deduction when computing your taxable income for one-quarter of the benefit realized in the year the shares were acquired without having to meet the first two requirements outlined above. This exception is designed to stimulate employee participation in ownership of small businesses. It also recognizes that valuation of shares in a private company at the time you exercise the option may be difficult.

Be cautious about relying on CCPC shares too much for your future, however; shares in private corporations are not liquid, and can become worthless very easily if the corporation runs into trouble.

If you receive shares in a CCPC through a stock option plan, consider contributing some of them to your RRSP if the shares qualify for that purpose (see 3.1.6).

Consider a stock purchase plan or a phantom stock plan.

A stock purchase plan is a possible alternative to a stock option plan. With a stock purchase plan, you would acquire the shares right away, rather than options. The acquisition might be assisted by a loan from your employer (see 7.3). Any increase in value of the shares will be a capital gain and only three-quarters taxed (see 5.2).

Needless to say, a stock purchase plan is not a good idea unless you are quite confident in the future prospects for the company's shares.

A **phantom stock plan** avoids the requirement that you acquire shares in the corporation, and thus may be more attractive to your employer's controlling shareholders. Under such a plan, you receive bonuses based on the increase in value of your employer's shares. Such bonuses are simply taxed as employment income. If they are not paid to you on an ongoing basis, you will need to determine whether they constitute a salary deferral arrangement (see 7.6), in which case they will be taxed in your hands even if not received.

7.5 Company automobiles

Special rules apply for determining the taxable benefit when your employer provides you with an automobile.

There are two elements to the benefit that must be reported for tax purposes: a **standby charge**, and the benefit in respect of **operating costs**. These will normally be reported together on your T4 (and Québec Relevé 1) statement from your employer as a single amount, and included in your total "income from employment" for tax purposes.

The standby charge is, essentially, 2% of the original cost of the car for each month that it is available to you—i.e., 24% per year. (For automobile sales persons, it can instead be 1.5% per month of the average cost of the dealer's cars acquired in the year.) You can have this amount reduced *only* if you can show both (a) that your business use of the car is 90% or more of the kilometres driven, and (b) that your personal use of the car is less than 12,000 km in the year.

Note that driving between your home and your place of employment is normally *not* considered business use (see 7.10.1). It can thus be very difficult to satisfy the above tests for a reduction in the standby charge.

Where the car is leased, the standby charge is two-thirds of the monthly leasing cost instead of 2% of the purchase price.

An extra 7% (15% in Nova Scotia, New Brunswick and Newfoundland) must be added to the employee's taxable benefit to reflect the GST or HST embedded in the value of the automobile to you [7% GST plus an extra 6.5% QST (7.5% in 1998) if you live in Québec]. Your employer may also be required to remit an equivalent amount of tax on the taxable benefit to Revenue Canada and Revenu Québec.

The taxable benefit for **operating costs** is 14¢/km of personal use for 1997. If your employer pays *any* operating costs during the year in respect of your personal use of an employer-provided car (and you don't fully reimburse your employer by the following February 14), the 14¢ rate applies. If you are employed principally in selling or leasing automobiles this rate is 11¢. (Again, your employer must remit part of this amount as though there was tax collected for GST and the provinces noted above.)

An alternative calculation is available for the operating expenses where your business use of the car exceeds 50%. If you notify your employer in writing *by December 31* that you wish this option, the operating costs benefit will be a flat **50% of the standby charge**. A benefit of one-half of the standby charge will be to your advantage where the cost of the car is relatively low (for a small car, or a car that was purchased used), and the number of personal kilometres is relatively high even though it is used personally less than 50% of the time.

If you receive a reasonable **allowance** for automobile expenses, the allowance will not be included in your income if it is based *solely* on the number of kilometres driven in the performance of your employment duties. If it is a flat amount not calculated in terms of your employment-related driving, it will be taxable (though you may be able to claim offsetting automobile expenses—see 7.10.1). For 1997, Revenue Canada and Revenue Québec accept as a "reasonable allowance" 35¢/km for the first 5,000 km and 29¢/km thereafter (4¢ more in the Yukon and Northwest Territories); in some cases you may be able to justify a higher amount as "reasonable".

Keep track of business use of your employer's or your own car.

Whether you drive your employer's car or your own, keep careful track of the distance you drive for purposes related to your employment. You may wish to keep a log book on the dashboard, or record your business driving in your daily appointment calendar.

Take steps to minimize taxable benefit from car operating costs.

If your employer pays only part of the operating costs of an employer-owned car that you use, the taxable benefit from operating costs can cost you more than the amount the employer pays. Sometimes the employer pays only the insurance and the employee pays for all gas and repairs, or the employer does not pay most operating expenses but might cover an occasional major repair bill.

For example, suppose you put 20,000 km on your company car over the year, all of which is personal use (including driving to work and back). Your employer pays the insurance ($500 per year) and you pay the rest of the operating expenses. Your taxable benefit for operating costs will be 14¢ per personal-use kilometre, or $2,800, which will typically cost you some $1,200 to $1,400 in tax. So having the employer pay for the insurance is very disadvantageous.

In such a case you should *repay* the $500 to the employer *by February 14* of the following year, so that the "14¢ per kilometre" rule will not apply. Of course, your employer can pay you additional salary of $500 which will simply be taxable as income, to offset your repayment of the insurance costs.

Avoid employer-owned vehicles costing over $25,000.

If you drive a company car that was purchased in 1997 and cost more than $25,000 ($20,000 or $24,000 for cars purchased in earlier years—see 7.10.1), there is an element of double taxation. Your taxable "standby charge" benefit is 2% per month of the *actual* cost of the car. However, only $25,000 can be written off (over time) as capital cost allowance by your employer. For cars purchased in 1997 and later, the purchase limit is increased by both the GST and PST paid on the first $25,000 ($24,000 if the car was bought in 1991through 1996). It may be more economical for you to purchase the car yourself and arrange for an appropriate increase in remuneration from your employer.

Reduce the amount of time your company car is available for personal use.

The standby charge discussed above is based on the number of 30-day periods in the year that a company car is "made available" to you or a member of your family. However, the actual calculation is based on the number of *days* during which the car is available. This number is divided by

30 and rounded to the nearest whole number, and rounded down if it is exactly in the middle.

If you can get the number of "available days" down to 345, which is 11.5 30-day periods, the standby charge will therefore be reduced to only 11 times 2% of the automobile cost instead of 12 times 2%.

If you take three weeks or more of vacations or business trips during the year, leave the car at the company's premises during those times. If the car cost $25,000 new in 1997, you can thus reduce your taxable income for the year by $500 (and save $200-$250 in tax) by getting the number of "available days" down to 345. Note, however, that Revenue Canada holds the view that the car is still made available to you during this time unless you are *required* to return the car and control over its use to your employer. You might wish to arrange for your employer to impose this requirement on you.

7.6 Deferred compensation

Various techniques have been tried over the years to avoid paying tax on employment income by having some of it held back in one way or another. (In general, employment income is taxed when received.)

Registered pension plans and **deferred profit-sharing plans** were discussed in 3.4 and 3.5. They are accepted mechanisms for deferring employment income.

Consider employees' profit-sharing plan for cash flow purposes.

Employee profit-sharing plans are not widely used. They do not defer the taxation of employment income. Contributions are made by the employer, based on profits for the year. Although the contributions are paid to the plan, the amounts contributed are treated as income of the employees for tax purposes. Such plans can therefore operate as forced savings plans for bonuses. Income (such as interest income) earned within the plan must be allocated to specific employees, who pay tax on it as it is allocated (even if it is not paid to them).

One tax advantage of employee profit-sharing plans is that there is no source withholding on the amounts paid into the plan, or on the amounts paid by the plan to you. Careful timing of the employer's contributions and the plan's disbursements can give you better cash flow than would a straight bonus payment.

The rules for **salary deferral arrangements** catch most arrangements for deferred compensation. For example, if you agree with your employer that your salary for 1997 will be $50,000, plus a further $10,000 to be paid in 2001, you will be taxed on the whole $60,000 in 1997. You can generally only escape this taxation if there is a substantial risk of forfeiting the future income.

The salary deferral arrangement rules allow certain exceptions. One is a self-funded leave of absence program, sometimes used by teachers, academics and others to fund sabbatical leaves. Provided you meet all of the conditions, you can arrange for your employer or a trustee to hold back a portion of your salary every year for up to six years, not recognize that portion as employment income each year, and receive it in the sabbatical year, paying tax on it then. Another exception is an arrangement whereby you have a right to receive a bonus to be paid within three years.

Retirement compensation arrangements are arrangements made outside the registered pension plan system, whereby a custodian will receive funds from an employer and make payments after the employee's retirement or termination. Since the employer receives a deduction for contributions to such plans, a 50% refundable tax applies to the payments made to the custodian (and which is refunded when the payments are made to the employee, at which point the employee reports the income for tax purposes).

7.7 Retiring allowances and severance pay

A "retiring allowance", as defined for tax purposes, includes what one would normally call severance pay or termination pay, as well as a court award or settlement for wrongful dismissal. It also includes, of course, a payment by an employer for long service on retirement.

Transfer retiring allowances to an RRSP.

A retiring allowance, like ordinary employment income, is included in your income. However, as we saw in 3.3.2, part or all of it can be transferred to an RRSP and thus sheltered from immediate tax.

The amount that can be transferred is $2,000 for each calendar year (or part year) of service before 1996, plus $1,500 for each year (or part year) before 1989 for which employer contributions to your pension plan have not "vested". ("Vested" pension rights are those that you can take with you on retirement or termination—see 3.4.1.)

Legal fees incurred in establishing your retiring allowance are deductible against the retiring allowance—see 7.10.6 below. Note that you should probably not transfer the maximum amount to an RRSP if you have incurred legal fees in obtaining your award (even if the case was settled without going to court). Legal fees can be carried forward for up to seven years and deducted against the "retiring allowance" income. If you transfer the entire retiring allowance into an RRSP, the legal fees will never become deductible. (When you take payments *out* of the RRSP, they are no longer considered a "retiring allowance".) However, if you intend to leave the funds to grow tax-free in the RRSP for many years, you may want to consider transferring the maximum anyway.

7.8 Death benefits

A death benefit is an amount paid in recognition of a deceased employee's service. It is usually paid to the deceased's spouse or children. Subject to the $10,000 exemption outlined below, it is taxable.

The first $10,000 of death benefits paid in respect of any one employee is exempt from tax. The employee's spouse gets the exemption; to the extent there is no spouse or the spouse receives less than $10,000 and other taxpayers receive such funds, any remaining amount of exemption can be split among the other recipients. "Spouse" includes a common-law spouse who meets the criteria outlined in 2.2.1.

Note that life insurance proceeds are completely different from death benefits, and are not taxed at all when received.

7.9 Overseas employment tax credit

If you are resident in Canada but you work outside Canada for a period of six months or more, a special tax credit may be available (if you live in Québec, see 15.2.23). To be eligible, you must be working for a Canadian employer (or its foreign affiliate) on certain kinds of projects, such as mining, oil and gas exploration or production, agriculture, construction or engineering.

The credit effectively allows you to offset the tax payable on up to $100,000 of overseas employment income per year, but is limited to 80% of that income. The details are very complicated—see the reference information in 7.12 below.

If you are self-employed, you used to be able to get this credit by incorporating your business and working as its employee. However, as of 1997, the credit cannot be claimed by individuals employed by corporations with fewer than five full-time employees and corporations of which the employee is a specified shareholder (i.e., generally, where the individual or related person(s) owns 10% of the corporation's shares).

7.10 Deductions from employment income

The only deductions allowed against employment income are those specifically provided for in the federal and Québec tax rules. We look at some of them below.

7.10.1 Using your own automobile for employment

If you are required by the terms of your employment to use your own automobile and are not receiving a (non-taxable) reasonable allowance based on the number of kilometres you drive for employment purposes (see 7.5), you can deduct a portion of your automobile expenses from your employment income. (You must file with your tax return the federal Form T2200 and Québec form TP-64.3-V on which your employer certifies that you were required to use your own vehicle.)

First, you can deduct **operating costs**, such as gas, repairs and car washes, to the extent they relate to your employment. As noted in 7.5, you will need to keep a detailed log of your driving, to track your employment-related use as opposed to your personal use. Second, you can deduct **capital cost allowance** (depreciation), or your monthly lease payments for the proportion of employment-related use. The allowable rate of capital cost allowance is 15% in the year of acquisition of the car, followed by 30% *on the remaining balance* in each subsequent year. However, there is a cap on the cost of the car for this purpose:

Date car purchased	Limit
Before June 18, 1987	none
June 18, 1987 to August 31, 1989	$20,000
September 1, 1989 to December 31, 1990	$24,000
January 1, 1991 to December 31, 1996	$24,000*
January 1, 1997 or later	$25,000*

*plus GST and PST on this amount

Example:

Michelle buys a new car in Ontario in January 1997 for $30,000 plus 7% GST and 8% Ontario sales tax. She is required to drive 10,000 km for employment-related purposes during the year. She also drives 10,000 km on personal trips.

Since half of her driving is employment-related, Michelle can claim half of the capital cost allowance normally allowed for a car. Although she spent $30,000, the cost is capped at $25,000, plus $2,000 Ontario sales tax and 7% GST (total of $28,750), for tax purposes. The maximum capital cost allowance for the year of acquisition is 15%. Fifteen per cent of $28,750 is $4,312.50. Michelle can therefore claim $2,156.25 as a deduction against her employment income for 1997.

Further, because she uses her car partly for business, Michelle can claim a GST rebate in 1997 from Revenue Canada equal to 7/107 of her capital cost allowance claim—see 7.11. (If she had purchased the car in Nova Scotia, New Brunswick and Newfoundland after April 1, 1997, the rebate would be equal to 15/105 of her capital cost allowance claim.)

If you **lease** the car, your deduction in respect of the lease payments is restricted to parallel the dollar limit on purchases:

Date lease entered into	Limit
Before June 18, 1987	none
June 18, 1987 to August 31, 1989	$600
September 1, 1989 to December 31, 1990	$650
January 1, 1991 to December 31, 1996	$650*
January 1, 1997 or later	$550*

*plus GST and PST

Third, you can deduct **interest** on any loan you have taken out to purchase the car (including financing on the purchase itself, where you make monthly payments that combine interest and capital). Your monthly interest is limited to:

Date car purchased	Limit
Before June 18, 1987	none
June 18, 1987 to August 31, 1989	$250
September 1, 1989 to December 31, 1996	$300
January 1, 1997 or later	$250

Example:
Michelle, who bought a new car in January 1997 for $30,000, is paying $700 per month on her car loan. She paid $2,000 down and the loan interest rate is 15%.

Calculations show that Michelle pays $350 per month in interest for the first month, and slightly less over the following months. Her interest for tax purposes over the year will be limited to $250 per month, or $3,000. Of this, she can deduct half, or $1,500, to reflect the proportion of her driving which was employment-related.

If you are **reimbursed** by your employer for employment-related use of your automobile, the reimbursement payments are not taxed. Of course, you cannot deduct your own expenses to the extent you have been reimbursed for them.

As noted in the example above, if you pay GST (or HST) on a car and you are entitled to deduct capital cost allowance (on the proportion of your employment-related use), you can receive a rebate of GST (or HST) related to the amount of your deduction—see 7.11. The amount of this rebate will reduce the capital cost of the car (and your base for further depreciation) in the year you receive it. (For Québec residents, similar QST rules apply.)

Maximize your employment-related use of your car.

Driving between home and work is normally considered personal use. If, however, you travel from your home to a business call (to visit a client or supplier, for example), that will constitute business use. You can maximize your employment-related travel by making all of your business calls at the beginning and end of your day, before you go to work and after you leave work. You can thus make your entire trip from home to work count as travel for employment purposes.

7.10.2 Travelling expenses

If you are required by your employment to spend funds on employment-related travel, as outlined in the case of automobile expenses above, the amounts you pay will normally be deductible. Examples might include parking, taxis and train fares.

If you travel for a transportation company (e.g., as a bus or truck driver or a flight attendant), you can also deduct costs of meals and lodging to the extent you are not entitled to be reimbursed. The deduction for meals will be further restricted to 50% of your cost (see 8.2.10).

7.10.3 Commission sales person's expenses

If you are employed as a sales person under a contract that requires you to pay your own expenses, and you earn commissions, you may be able to deduct the costs of your employment-related expenditures—the same kinds of costs as could be claimed if you were self-employed (see 8.2.2). To do so, you must be required by your contract of employment to pay your own expenses, and you must be ordinarily required to carry on your duties of employment away from your employer's place of business. The total expenses you claim this way cannot exceed your total commission income.

7.10.4 Supplies, assistant's salary and home office

If you are required by your contract of employment to pay for any supplies or to pay for an assistant or substitute, you can deduct the cost of the supplies or the assistant's salary.

You can also deduct expenses relating to a home office, in limited circumstances. First, you must be required by your employment contract to maintain the office, and your employer must sign a certificate (federal Form T2200 and Québec form TP-64.3-V) that you file with your return. Second, either the home office must be the place where you "principally perform the duties of employment", or you must use it on a regular and continuous basis for *meeting* people (such as your employer's customers) in the ordinary course of your employment. The second restriction is parallel to that which applies to self-employed people, as outlined in more detail in 8.2.11. The effect is that the deduction is rarely available to employed individuals. You will normally only be able to claim it if you spend more of your time working at home than at your employer's premises.

7.10.5 Union and professional dues

Union dues are deductible for federal tax purposes (see 15.2.20 if you live in Québec). These are normally withheld at source and reported on the T4 and Québec Relevé 1 you receive from your employer.

Dues required to maintain a legally recognized professional status are deductible, even if you do not need to maintain that status for your current job. Your status as a lawyer, engineer, accountant, physician, architect, nurse, dentist, etc., will qualify for this purpose. Dues to voluntary associations are not deductible, unless you are self-employed (see 8.2.2).

7.10.6 Legal fees

If you spend money on a lawyer to recover unpaid wages, you can deduct the legal fees.

Legal fees you incur to establish your right to a "retiring allowance" (which includes severance pay), or to private pension plan benefits, are deductible. However, you can only deduct the legal fees against the *income from the retiring allowance or pension benefits in that year*. To the extent you have not yet received that income, you can "carry forward" the expenses for up to seven years and claim them against such income in those later years. (See 7.7 if you transfer your retiring allowance to an RRSP.)

Example:
Lewis was fired from his job in 1995. He retained a lawyer and sued for wrongful dismissal, spending $3,000 in 1995 and $5,000 in 1996 in legal fees. In 1997, the case is settled and his former employer pays him $50,000.

Lewis can deduct his $8,000 in legal fees only in 1997 against his $50,000 "retiring allowance" income, thus recognizing only $42,000 as income in that year.

See also 2.9.2 regarding the deductibility of legal fees that are not related to employment.

7.10.7 Musicians' instruments

If you are employed as a musician and required to supply your own instrument, you may deduct any maintenance, rental and insurance costs. If you have purchased the instrument, you may claim capital cost allowance (depreciation), at a rate of 10% for the first year, and 20% of the remaining balance in each subsequent year. All of these deductions can only be used to offset your income from employment as a musician, not against other income.

7.10.8 Artists' expenses

If you are employed as an artist (including, for example, a painter, sculptor, playwright, literary author, composer, actor, dancer, singer or musician), you may deduct up to $1,000 of your actual expenses incurred in order to earn income from such activities. This deduction is limited to 20% of your income from artistic employment, and the $1,000 limit is reduced by any amounts you claim as automobile expenses (see 7.10.1) and musical instrument costs (7.10.7). (No parallel deduction is allowed for Québec tax purposes).

Of course, if you earn income from your artistic activities that is not employment income, you are self-employed, in which case *all* your expenses are normally deductible (see 8.2.2).

7.10.9 Northern employees

If your employer pays for you to take a vacation trip, with or without your family, the value of the taxable benefit is included in your income (see 7.1.2). If you live in northern Canada, a federal deduction is available to offset all or part of this benefit (a similar deduction is available for Québec purposes). Provided you meet certain residency requirements, the deduction can eliminate the taxable benefit associated with up to two trips per year, based on the cost of airfare to the nearest large Canadian city. (There is no limit to the number of such trips if they are taken to obtain medical services not available locally.)

See also 2.9.3, regarding the special deduction for residents of northern Canada, and 7.1.1, regarding the non-taxability of benefits relating to a remote work site.

7.11 GST rebate for employees

Claim rebate for GST paid on expenses deductible from your employment income.

In general, where you can deduct expenses from your employment income, such as those discussed in 7.10, you can also claim a rebate of GST or HST paid on those expenses. A QST rebate is available for Québec taxpayers. Documentation must be kept to support the claim for the rebate. The rebate claim is filed with your personal income tax return. That rebate will itself be considered income from employment in the year in which you receive it, except where it relates to capital cost allowance (see 7.10.1).

Example:

Continuing our example in 7.10.1, Michelle is required to drive 10,000 km for employment-related purposes during the year. She also drives 10,000 km on personal trips. She spends $2,140 (including GST) over the course of the year in gas and repairs for her car, and does not receive any reimbursement from her employer. All the expenses are paid in Ontario.

Since one-half of Michelle's expenses are required by her employment, she can claim $1,070 as a deduction from employment income. That figure, however, already includes $70 in GST that applied to the gas and repairs. Michelle can claim a rebate of the $70 on a form filed with her income tax return. The $70 rebate is taxable in the year she receives it.

Further, because she uses her car partly for business, Michelle can claim a GST rebate in 1997 from Revenue Canada equal to 7/107 of her capital cost allowance claim. That is, 7/107 of the $2,156.25 Michelle can deduct as capital cost allowance, or $141.06, is refunded to her. This $141.06 is deducted from the undepreciated capital cost of the car at the beginning of 1998.

Note that a rebate is only available where GST was paid on the purchase. Michelle cannot receive a rebate in respect of the deductible portion of her car insurance, since insurance is not taxable. Similarly, there is no rebate for GST paid on gas purchased in the United States, because there is no GST included in the price of such gas.

In the above example, we have assumed that Michelle's employer is a GST registrant and is not a financial institution. If, instead, she was employed by a financial institution or by a non-GST registrant, she would not be entitled to the employee GST rebate which, as shown, amounts to $211.06 in the first year.

We have also assumed that Michele did not receive a per kilometre allowance from her employer. If she had, she would not be able to claim a GST rebate on any of her automobile expenses unless her employer certified on her form GST 370 that the allowance was "unreasonable" and that her employer would not be claiming a GST tax credit with respect to her allowance. However, in the unlikely case that Michele's employer certifies that her per kilometre allowance *is* unreasonable, the amount will be included in her income and her employer must withhold income tax and other source deductions on the amount.

Finally, note also that if Michelle's expenses were incurred in Nova Scotia, New Brunswick or Newfoundland, she would have paid the 15% HST (instead of the 7% GST) and would be entitled to claim a rebate of 15/115 of her HST-included expenses.

7.12 References

The following publications can be obtained (in person or by telephone request) from your nearest Revenue Canada District Taxation Office. Forms and guides may also be available from Revenue Canada's Internet site at www.revcan.ca.

Interpretation Bulletin IT-63R5, "Benefits, including standby charge for an automobile, from the personal use of a motor vehicle supplied by an employer after 1992"

Interpretation Bulletin IT-113R4, "Benefits to employees—stock options"

Interpretation Bulletin IT-148R2, "Recreational properties and club dues"

Interpretation Bulletin IT-158R2, "Employees' professional membership dues"

Interpretation Bulletin IT-196R2, "Payments by Employer to employee"

Interpretation Bulletin IT-222R, "Advances to employees"

Interpretation Bulletin IT-337R2, "Retiring allowances"

Interpretation Bulletin IT-352R2, "Employees' expenses, including work space in home expenses"

Interpretation Bulletin IT-421R2, "Benefits to individuals, corporations and shareholders from loans or debt"

Interpretation Bulletin IT-470R, "Employees' fringe benefits"

Interpretation Bulletin IT-497R3, "Overseas employment tax credit"

Interpretation Bulletin IT-508R, "Death benefits—calculation"

Interpretation Bulletin IT-522R, "Vehicle, travel and sales expenses of employees"

Information Circular 73-21R7, "Away from home expenses"

Information Circular 77-1R4, "Deferred profit sharing plans"

"Completion Guide and Form for Employee and Partner GST Rebate"

"Employment Expenses Tax Guide"

Form TD1, "199__ Personal Tax Credit Return"

Form T626, "Overseas employment tax credit"

Form T777, "Statement of employment expenses"

Form T2200, "Declaration of conditions of employment applicable to expense claims"

Form GST 370, "Employee and partner GST rebate"

If you are self-employed

- Arrange to be a consultant rather than employed (8.1)
- Recover GST (or HST) and QST that you've paid by claiming input tax credits for your business (8.2.4)
- If you're a residential landlord, account for sales tax when setting rents (8.2.4)
- Be aware of your HST obligations for sales to customers in Nova Scotia, New Brunswick and Newfoundland (8.2.5)
- Simplify your paperwork by using the "Quick Method" for GST and QST reporting (8.2.6)
- Acquire depreciable assets before year-end (8.2.7)
- Consider claiming less CCA than the maximum (8.2.7)
- Keep track of, and maximize, the business use of your car (8.2.8)
- Deduct public transit fares, taxis and other business travel costs (8.2.9)
- Document and claim your business meals and entertainment expenses (8.2.10)
- Write off your eligible home office expenses (8.2.11)
- If you're a partner, claim sales tax rebates on your unreimbursed partnership expenses (8.3.7)
- Use your loss carryovers to maximum advantage (8.4)

In this chapter we highlight some of the major topics in the taxation of business income. If you are a professional, see Chapter 11 for additional planning ideas. If you are in a partnership, see also 11.2; if you are in Québec, see also Chapter 15. It goes without saying that anyone with a substantial amount of business income should obtain proper professional advice due to the large potential for planning legitimate deductions.

8.1 Employee or independent contractor?

As you will see in this chapter, people who are self-employed, carrying on business for themselves, generally have wider scope for tax planning than do employees.

Carrying on a business has nothing to do with setting up a corporation (which is discussed in Chapter 9). Any taxpayer can carry on business. If you set up a second-hand clothing-for-cash exchange in your basement, you are carrying on business. If you decide to put a name to your business (say, "XYZ Second-Hand Clothing"), that is just you carrying on business under that name. You have not created a new entity. You simply have a **proprietorship**, which means you are the proprietor of a business.

The distinction between employee and independent contractor (i.e., self-employed) is not always clear in cases where you receive most or all of your "work" income from one source. If you provide services to an organization, you can be classed in either group, depending on the facts.

Example:

Lisa is a computer programmer. She develops software for ABC Corporation, and is paid for each hour she works. She does a lot of her work at home, though she goes to ABC's offices for regular meetings.

Is Lisa an employee of ABC, or an independent consultant who carries on business and whose major (or only) client is ABC?

In cases like this, one must look at all the facts to determine the person's status. There are no hard and fast rules. In general, you are more likely to be considered an employee if you:

- work a set number of hours per day
- have to account for your time to the company
- are told what to do each step of the way
- are a member of the company's group life, drug, dental and pension plans and receive other "benefits"
- use the company's computer equipment and supplies and have an office at the company.

At the other extreme, you would likely be considered an independent contractor carrying on your own business as a proprietor if you:

- agree to get the job done, but you don't make a commitment for any particular number of hours on any particular day
- work on your own with no supervision, and simply report back to the company periodically on progress
- issue invoices and receive cheques (with no source deductions for income tax, EI or CPP/QPP) and receive no employee benefits
- use your own equipment and work at home, going to the company for planning meetings only
- provide services to more than one company.

These examples are fairly extreme. Between them is a large fuzzy area, where each case will depend on its facts. It doesn't matter very much what you and the company *call* your relationship; more specifically, calling it independent contracting doesn't make it independent contracting unless the facts support such a claim.

One case where Revenue Canada has a clear administrative policy is that of real estate agents. You will be considered self-employed if you are entitled to the full amount of commissions, and either (a) you pay only a fixed amount to your broker for administrative operating costs, or (b) you pay a percentage of your gross commissions to your broker to cover such costs, and you set your own commission rate for sales on your listings.

Arrange to be a consultant rather than employed.

If you are currently employed in a position where you maintain a fair amount of independence from your employer, investigate whether you can change your relationship so that you become an independent consultant rather than an employee. You will need to document the details of your relationship carefully, in case Revenue Canada or Revenu Québec challenges you in the future.

If you succeed in becoming independent, you will be able to take advantage of all of the planning tips throughout this chapter. You will lose certain advantages, however, including the right to Employment Insurance benefits, the employer's contribution to the Canada Pension Plan for you, and possibly all of the employment benefits you now have (pension plan, drug plan, etc.). You may wish to negotiate to have your cash compensation increased in exchange for any employment benefits you are giving up.

Revenue Canada has a questionnaire, Form CPT-1, through which your employer can supply the details of its relationship with you and ask for a ruling as to whether you are an employee or not for CPP purposes (and, by extension, for income tax purposes). However, there is no requirement to apply for such a ruling, and you and your employer/client are not bound by Revenue Canada's administrative decisions. If, after receiving professional advice, you believe that you are legally an independent contractor, then you are quite entitled to proceed on that basis. (Of course, your employer/client may not be willing to risk not withholding tax at source, if Revenue Canada has expressed the view that you are an employee.

8.2 Taxation of the business

In this section we review how your business income is taxed. If you are a professional, see also Chapter 11.

8.2.1 Business year-end

Until 1995, you could pick a year-end for any business when you started the business. The income was then taxed only in the taxation year in which the business year *ended*.

This rule allowed individuals and partnerships carrying on business to defer paying tax by up to a year. For example, if you had chosen to have the business year-end on January 31, you would not have to report—or pay tax on—the 11 months of income earned between February 1 and December 31 of the current calendar year until your tax return for the following calendar year was due.

This option has been eliminated by the 1995 federal and Québec budgets. As of 1995, all individuals, and all partnerships which have any individuals as members, **must use a calendar year** for reporting their income.

If you have been in business since before January 1, 1995 and were not already using a calendar year-end, you had to report two business "years" on your 1995 return: one ending on your normal year-end and the other ending on December 31. Since you probably would have ended up with much higher income for 1995, you are allowed to spread the "extra" income (for the "stub period" ending December 31, 1995) over 10 years, reporting at least 5% in 1995, 10% more by each of the next 8 years, and the final 15% in 2004.

> Example:
>
> Andy is a lawyer who earns $120,000 per year. His business year-end has always been January 31.
>
> For the 12-month year ending January 31, 1995, Andy's income was $120,000. As well, he had to recognize the income for the 11 months running from February 1 to December 31, 1995 (**$110,000**). For this "stub period", Andy reported 5% of the income, or $5,500, in 1995.
>
> In 1996, and for each year from 1997 through 2003, Andy must include a further 10% ($11,000) of his 1995 "stub period" income. The final 15% ($16,500) must be included by 2004.

In 1995, the income inclusion was done by reporting the full amount of the stub period income, and claiming a "reserve" (deduction) against that income of up to 95% in 1995. The amount of the reserve was then included in 1996 income, and a new reserve could be taken for 1996 of up to 85% of the original stub period income. You can claim up to 75% of your stub period income on your 1997 return.

You may choose to report (and pay tax on) more than the minimum in any given year. The real requirement is to pay tax cumulatively on 5% of the income in 1995, 15% by 1996, 25% by 1997, 35% by 1998, and so on.

If you are a proprietor or an individual who is a member of a partnership composed of individuals, you or your partnership may have elected to keep the off-calendar year-end by using an "**alternative method**" of eliminating the tax deferral. Under the alternative method, you or the partnership were required to add to the business income for the actual off-calendar fiscal period an estimate of income earned between the end of the 1995 fiscal period and December 31, 1995. The adjustment is determined by prorating the actual off-calendar fiscal period. For example, if your traditional fiscal year-end is January 31, 1995, the additional amount taxable in 1995 under the alternative method was 11/12 of your actual income for the fiscal period ended January 31, 1995. Similar adjustments need to be made for later years. You will be able to claim a reserve for the 1995 adjustment amount in the years 1996 through 2004 similar to the reserve described above.

If you had a non-calendar fiscal period and initially adopted the alternative method, you may later change to a December 31 year-end, but once you do, you will not be able to go back to an off-calendar year-end. The election to use this alternative method must have been made by June 15, 1996, the tax return due date for individuals for reporting of their 1995 business income.

8.2.2 Business income and expenses

As a general principle, business income for tax purposes is based on generally accepted accounting principles. (Among other things, this means operating on the **accrual** basis: you record your income when you have billed your clients, whether or not you have been paid.) However, there are many adjustments required for tax purposes. Some of them are discussed in the sections below.

When you earn business income, there is normally no withholding of tax at source. If you are providing services to a single organization, and are able to classify your relationship as one of independent consultant rather than employee (see 8.1), you can submit invoices that will be paid in full, without tax (or UIC premiums or CPP/QPP contributions) being taken off and remitted to Revenue Canada. You may, however, be required to pay instalments of income tax. Instalments are discussed in 14.2.2.

In general, expenses are deductible if they are laid out to earn income from the business and are in reasonable amounts. There are certainly exceptions, as we shall see in the following sections. However, the underlying principle is the reverse of that for employees. **Employees can only deduct expenses that are specifically permitted under the federal *Income Tax Act* and the *Québec Taxation Act*. Someone carrying on business can deduct any expenses that are not specifically prohibited by these statutes, provided such expenses relate to the earning of business income.**

8.2.3 EI, CPP and other payroll taxes

Employment insurance is available only to those who are employed. If you carry on business for yourself, you are neither required nor permitted to pay EI premiums. This will save you up to $2,714 in 1997 when taking into account both the employee and employer's portions; on the other hand, it means that if your consulting contracts terminate and you are left without work, you cannot benefit from EI.

Canada and Québec Pension Plan contributions are split equally between employees and their employers. If you are self-employed, you are required to pay the "employer's share" to make up what is not being paid for you, as well as your own share. Since you are not employed, no CPP/QPP contributions are withheld from your income. As a result, you will find yourself required to pay up to $1,890 for 1997 in mandatory CPP contributions or $1, 938 in QPP contributions when you file your return, offset by a 17% federal tax credit (worth about 27% of these amounts when provincial tax and surtax are factored in). If it's any consolation, you'll get your CPP/QPP contributions back in the form of a pension after you turn 65, or optionally as early as age 60 at a reduced amount.

Many provinces also have payroll taxes that apply to employment income. In some cases, they apply to self-employed income as well. For example, Ontario's Employer Health Tax ("EHT") currently applies to individuals with self-employment income, but will be phased out by 1999 (and replaced with a surtax increase). For self-employed individuals with incomes under $200,000, the tax no longer applies as of 1997. In 1998, income under $300,000 will be exempt. On income in excess of the 1997 and 1998 thresholds, the EHT applies at the rate of 1.95%, but the tax is reduced by a 22% credit.

8.2.4 Recovering GST by claiming input tax credits

Recover GST (or HST) and QST that you've paid by claiming input tax credits.

If you are self-employed (or the owner-manager of an incorporated business), the business can normally claim a full refund (an "input tax credit") of the 7% Goods and Services Tax ("GST") or 15% Harmonized Sales Tax ("HST"; see 8.2.5) paid on most purchases. To be eligible for input tax credits, you must **register with Revenue Canada** to collect GST even though you are not specifically obliged to unless your annual sales are more than $30,000. As is the case for income tax purposes, "personal or living expenses" are not eligible for input tax credits. Once you are registered, you must charge GST on all your taxable sales (or HST on taxable sales made to customers in Nova Scotia, New Brunswick and Newfoundland). You can build the tax into your prices if you wish.

Make sure to keep accurate records so you can claim credits where possible. Claims for input tax credits must generally be supported by receipts or other documentation, not submitted with the GST return but held on file in case of audit. All documentation must show the vendor's name, the date (or, for a contract, the date amounts are payable), and the total amount payable. Where the total (including all taxes) is $30 or over, the receipt must also show:

■ the amount of GST, or a statement that the total includes GST, and a clear indication of which items are taxable; and

■ the supplier's GST nine-digit registration number.

Where the total is $150 or over, the receipt must also show:

- the purchaser's name;
- the terms of payment; and
- a description sufficient to identify each item supplied.

Failure to have this documentation will normally lead to a disallowance of any input tax credit claim if the return is audited.

Input tax credits can only be claimed where the expenses were incurred in the course of providing "taxable supplies". A business engaged in providing supplies that are GST-exempt—such as a doctor, dentist or financial institution—cannot claim input tax credits in respect of the costs of making those supplies.

If you're a residential landlord, account for sales tax when setting rents.

If you rent out residential real estate (whether a house or an apartment building), no GST will apply to the rent since it is GST-exempt. As a result, you cannot use the input tax credit system to recover any of the GST that you pay on utilities, property management fees and other costs. You must set the rent high enough to cover your costs.

Rental of commercial real estate is subject to GST, unless your total revenue (including from any businesses you operate) is under $30,000 and you decide not to register for GST. If you are renting to a business that makes taxable supplies (that is, just about any business other than a financial institution, health care professional, school or day care), you are likely better off to register, collect GST (which your tenant will recover in the form of an input tax credit), and claim input tax credits for GST paid on your costs, such as utilities and property management fees.

In Québec, similar rules apply for QST purposes.

8.2.5 Harmonized Sales Tax

Be aware of your HST obligations for sales to customers in Nova Scotia, New Brunswick and Newfoundland.

No matter where in Canada your business is located, you should be aware of your obligations under the new Harmonized Sales Tax. On April 1, 1997, the the provincial sales taxes in Nova Scotia, New Brunswick and Newfoundland and Labrador were repealed and the GST rate that applies in those provinces increased to 15% (comprised of a 7% federal component and an 8% provincial component). The HST and the GST are the same tax and apply to the same goods and services. The only major difference is that the tax applies at the rate of 15% on goods and services supplied in the three

Atlantic provinces, instead of the 7% rate that applies in the rest of the country. As a general rule, our comments with respect to the GST throughout this book apply equally well to the HST, although there are some exceptions.

All GST registrants in Canada must collect HST on taxable supplies made to or in the above three Atlantic provinces. If you're registered for the GST, you are already in the HST system. Collection, reporting and remittance of the new tax is done through the existing GST system.

The HST could complicate your recordkeeping and sales tax reporting if you make taxable sales to customers both inside and outside Nova Scotia, New Brunswick and Newfoundland. Depending on the province to which the goods or services are delivered, you will have to determine whether you should charge GST only, HST only, or the GST and the appropriate provincial sales tax.

8.2.6   GST—the "Quick Method" and simplified accounting

Simplify your paperwork by using the "Quick Method" for GST and QST reporting.

Self-employed individuals and small businesses may elect to use the "Quick Method" to simplify record-keeping for GST. It can be used by any business with annual sales under $200,000 (excluding sales of basic groceries). This method can be particularly useful for certain consultants. However, the Quick Method may not be used by anyone providing legal, accounting, actuarial, bookkeeping, financial consulting, tax consulting or tax return preparation services.

Under the Quick Method, instead of remitting total GST collected minus total GST paid, the business remits to Revenue Canada a flat percentage of sales (including GST). The percentages vary depending on whether your business operates exclusively outside of Nova Scotia, New Brunswick and Newfoundland, exclusively in those provinces, or both in and out of those provinces. The rates also vary depending on whether your business is primarily selling goods (other than basic groceries) or services.

For businesses operating exclusively outside those provinces, where sales are mostly services rather than goods, the flat percentage is 5% (but only 4% on the first $30,000 of sales). For qualifying suppliers whose purchases of taxable personal property (other than basic groceries) for resale are at least 40% of sales (excluding basic groceries), the flat percentage is 2 1/2% (but only 1 1/2% on the first $30,000 of sales). Input tax credits can only be claimed for capital purchases.

For businesses operating exclusively in Nova Scotia, New Brunswick and/or Newfoundland and selling primarily services, the flat percentage is 10.7% (9.7% on the first $30,000 of sales). For businesses selling goods, the flat percentage is 5.4% (3.4% on the first $30,000 of sales). Special rules apply for businesses operating both inside and outside of these provinces.

Clearly, the Quick Method can be useful for businesses that have few taxable expenses. If the business' taxable expenses are high, however, the loss of the ability to claim input tax credits will offset the benefit of the Quick Method's reduced remittance rate.

As an alternative to the Quick Method, you can total up your GST-bearing purchases—including GST, provincial sales tax, late payment penalties and tips—and claim 7/107 of the total for input tax credit purposes (or 15/115 for expenditures on which HST was paid). Your business' annual sales must not exceed $500,000 for you to use this method. Not only does it make accounting for input tax credits simpler, but it gives you a slightly larger claim than you can make by totalling up individual amounts of GST paid.

For QST reporting in Québec, you can use a similar "Quick Method" and simplified accounting (however, the percentage rates under the QST system are somewhat different).

8.2.7 Capital cost allowance

The treatment of capital expenses is one of the major differences between business income based on accounting principles and income calculated for income tax purposes. In both cases, you cannot simply write off the cost of purchasing major capital assets (furniture, buildings, computers, automobiles, etc.). You must spread the cost over several years.

For accounting (not tax) purposes, a professional will make a judgment call as to the appropriate depreciation to claim. Various methods of depreciation can be used.

For tax purposes, depreciation is subject to strict rules and limitations, since it reduces your income (and thus the tax you pay). The income tax system of depreciation is called **capital cost allowance** ("CCA"); the rules are numerous and complex.

In very general terms, your capital assets are grouped into **classes**, and capital cost allowance can be claimed annually against each class. The "declining balance" method is used for most classes; the maximum you can claim against each class is a fixed percentage of the "**undepreciated capital cost**". What you claim then reduces that balance for next year's claim.

Some common CCA rates	
Buildings acquired after 1987 (class 1)	4%
Buildings acquired 1979-1987 (class 3)	5%
Furniture and fixtures (class 8)	20%
Computer hardware (class 10)	30%
Automobiles (class 10 or 10.1)	30%
Most computer software (class 12)	100%
Tools costing less than $200 (class 12)	100%

Acquire depreciable assets before year-end.

For most acquisitions, only one-half of the CCA you could otherwise claim for the asset will be allowed in the year of acquisition. As a result, acquiring an asset just before your year-end will accelerate the timing of your tax write-off, while acquiring the asset at the beginning of the year will delay your CCA claim. Assets are normally required to be **available for use** and not simply "on the books" to be eligible for CCA, unless you have owned them for at least two years. (The term "available for use" has a specific and complex definition, and professional advice should be sought if you are unsure as to how it applies in your case.)

Consider claiming less CCA than the maximum.

Note that you are never required to claim the maximum CCA. You may in any year choose to claim less than the maximum, or nothing at all, for any given class of assets. The undepreciated capital cost for that class will remain intact, so you can make claims in later years based on that carried forward balance.

In some circumstances you may wish to claim less CCA than you are entitled to. For example, if you have old non-capital losses or investment tax credits that will otherwise expire, you are better off to not claim CCA, use up the losses or credits, and save your "undepreciated capital cost" balances for CCA claims in future years.

You might also choose not to claim CCA if you are in a low-income year and expect your income to be much higher (and thus taxed at higher marginal rates) in subsequent years. Such a decision should only be made after careful analysis of the present value of the future tax savings, including the impact on your ability to make an RRSP contribution in the subsequent year.

8.2.8 **Automobiles**

As a general principle, you can deduct the proportion of your automobile expenses that represents your business use of the vehicle, normally based on kilometres driven.

Keep track of, and maximize, the business use of your car.

If half of your driving is done for your business (excluding driving from your home to your own place of business) and half is personal use, you can deduct one-half of the expenses of the car for that year. The expenses would include gas, washes, repairs, insurance, interest on financing the vehicle, leasing costs if the car is leased, and capital cost allowance if you own it.

However, there are limits to how expensive a vehicle you can write off. Your claims for CCA and leasing costs will be based on a maximum cost:

Date car acquired	Purchase limit	Lease limit
Before June 18, 1987	none	none
June 18, 1987 to August 31, 1989	$20,000	$600
September 1, 1989 to December 31, 1990	$24,000	$650
January 1, 1991 to December 31, 1996	$24,000*	$650*
January 1, 1997 or later	$25,000*	$550*

*before GST and PST

For most businesses, since you get back all GST paid as an input tax credit (see 8.2.4), "before GST and PST" effectively means "plus PST". (However, if you are a sole proprietor, you can only claim an input tax credit for the GST portion of your CCA. For other businesses, no input tax credits are available if the vehicle is driven 90% or more of the time for personal use.)

In addition, where you have financed the purchase of a car, your monthly interest expense before determining the business portion will be limited to:

Date car purchased	Deductible interest limit
Before June 18, 1987	none
June 18, 1987 to August 31, 1989	$250
September 1, 1989 to December 31, 1996	$300
January 1, 1997 or later	$250

These rules are identical to those for employees' use of a vehicle for employment purposes (see 7.10.1).

The $25,000 limit also applies for purposes of calculating your GST input tax credit (see 8.2.4) and Québec input tax refund.

See the planning tips suggested for employees in 7.10.1—the same considerations apply to business use of your own car.

8.2.9   Other transportation expenses

Deduct public transit fares, taxis and other business-related travel costs.

If you rely on modes of travel other than an automobile for your business travel, you can generally deduct the related expenses. Keep records of all such business trips, and deduct the appropriate costs of public transit, taxicabs, etc.

You cannot consider transportation from your home to your own office as a business expense. However, if you have an office in your home, and you travel from there to your major client (who might happen to provide you with an office on its premises), you are engaging in business travel.

8.2.10   Meals and entertainment

Document and claim your business meals and entertainment expenses.

If you take a client or potential client (or a group of such people) to lunch or dinner, you can normally consider the cost of the meal as a business expense. The tax rules restrict the amount you can claim to **50%** of the amount paid; the restriction is designed to deny a deduction for some of the personal benefit you receive (since you would need to eat anyway). The same 50% limitation applies to entertainment expenses, such as taking a client to a sports event. (If you pay Québec tax, see 15.2.25.)

Similarly, if you are registered for GST purposes, you can only claim input tax credits for half of the GST paid on such expenses (see 8.2.4).

Make sure you claim all lunches and dinners that you can justifiably relate to your business. For audit purposes, you should make a notation on your receipt of the individual(s) treated and the reason for the meeting.

8.2.11 Home office expenses

If you have an office in your home, you can claim a portion of your ongoing home expenses as business expenses, subject to the restrictions discussed below. The portion will normally be based on the fraction of the home that is used for your office (you can usually exclude common areas, such as hallways, kitchen and washrooms, when making the calculation).

Example:
Mary is a computer programmer and works as a consultant to various companies. She works in her home, where her office is a room that is . 200 square feet. The total area of the rooms in her house (bedrooms, living room, dining room and the office) is 2,000 square feet.

Provided her home office qualifies (see below), Mary can claim 10% of her mortgage interest, property taxes, house insurance, utilities, etc., as expenses for tax purposes.

Write off your eligible home office expenses.

The expenses you can claim include:

- rent, if you are a tenant
- mortgage interest (but not the principal portion of blended mortgage payments)
- property taxes
- utilities: electricity, heat, water, gas
- telephone (if you have a separate business telephone which is fully deductible, consider whether you also use your personal phone for business calls)
- home insurance.

Also make sure to claim your business portion of some of the less obvious expenses, such as garden service, driveway snowplowing, and minor repairs. You will need to keep receipts on file; do not simply estimate your expenses.

You may also claim capital cost allowance on the appropriate fraction of your home, but this is often not advisable. If you claim CCA, Revenue Canada will take the position that that fraction of your home is not part of your principal residence, and will disallow your claim for the principal residence exemption (see 5.5.2) in respect of that portion of the home. Any

CCA you claimed can also be "recaptured" into income when you sell your home. (If you bought your home at the top of the housing market and do not expect to recover your costs when you sell, claiming CCA may be a good idea, however.)

The home office expenses are subject to restrictions. First, you can only claim the expenses **against your income** from the business. You therefore cannot use home office expenses to produce an overall business loss that is applied against other income. However, losses disallowed because of this rule can be carried forward and used in any later year against income generated from the same business.

Second, the home office will only be allowed if you fall into one of these two categories:

(a) your home is your **principal place of business**—that is, you do not have an office elsewhere. Note that if you have one major client and that client provides you with an office on its premises, it is still the client's premises and it will not disentitle you to your claim for a home office; or

(b) the home office is used exclusively for your business, and is used "on a **regular and continuous basis** for meeting clients, customers or patients".

Example:

Les is a chiropractor and has an office outside his home. He also has an office in his basement, where he does a lot of his business' paperwork and occasionally sees patients (usually neighbours who come over for treatment in the evening).

Les will not be able to claim any expenses in respect of his home office unless he can show that he uses it "on a regular and continuous basis" to see patients.

Of course, *supplies* that relate exclusively to your home office are fully deductible and not subject to the above restrictions. Fully deductible expenses would normally include a separate business phone line; fax and printer paper; laser printer or photocopier toner cartridges; computer repairs (assuming your computer is used only for your business); and so on.

If you pay Québec tax, see also 15.2.26.

8.2.12 Capital gains

Any capital gains that you realize are accounted for directly, through the capital gains system discussed in Chapter 5. They are not counted within the business' income.

8.2.13 Investment tax credits

Federal investment tax credits ("ITCs") are available for investment in certain regions of the country (e.g., the Maritimes) and for investment in scientific research and experimental development.

ITCs are claimed in the return for the calendar year in which they are generated. Unused ITCs can be carried back three years or carried forward for up to ten years.

8.3 Partnerships

If you join together to carry on business with one or more other people—which could include your spouse—you will be in **partnership**. You are still, for tax purposes, carrying on business. (As well as the discussion below, see 11.2, where some special rules applying to partnerships are discussed.)

8.3.1 How partnership income is taxed

Partnerships do not pay tax. Partnerships with more than five partners are required to file "information returns" with Revenue Canada, reporting partnership income, but these are not tax returns. The individual partners must each report their share of the partnership's income (or loss) as their own, *whether or not they have taken any of the profits out of the partnership.* Effective 1995, the partnership is required to report income on a December 31 year-end basis (see 8.2.1). Resource allowances and various other resource-related expenses (see 6.3.5) are claimed by the individual partner rather than at the partnership level.

Note that a partnership cannot pay a "salary" to a partner. Even if you, as a partner, receive something called a "salary", it is really partnership drawings (withdrawal of profits or capital from the partnership). You are *not* taxed on your partnership drawings, but on your **share of the partnership's income**, which may be very different.

If the partnership suffers losses, you can normally claim your share of those losses against your other sources of income. (This may not be the case where the partnership is a limited partnership—see 6.3.2.)

8.3.2 Adjustment of partnership allocation

The allocation of partnership income (or losses) among the partners is normally left up to the partners to resolve. If you set up an unreasonable allocation for income-splitting purposes, however, Revenue Canada may disallow your allocation and substitute a reasonable one.

For example, if you supply all of the capital and do almost all of the work in your business, and your spouse does almost nothing, Revenue Canada could be expected to disallow a 50/50 allocation of the business's income between the two of you.

8.3.3 Capital gains

Capital gains or losses realized by a partnership are allocated to the individual partners at the end of the partnership's taxation year. This will continue to be the case where the partnership has elected to follow the alternative method and keeps its off-calendar year-end (see 8.2.1). However, effective 1995, for partnerships that must use a December 31 year-end, such gains or losses will always be reported by the individual partners in the calendar year in which they are realized.

8.3.4 Allocation of investment tax credits

Investment tax credits (see 8.2.13 above) earned by a partnership are allocated to the individual partners and claimed in the year in which the partnership's year ends.

8.3.5 Gain or loss on partnership interest

When you are a member of a partnership you own a "partnership interest", which has an adjusted cost base for capital gains calculation purposes (see 5.2). If you sell your interest in the partnership (or are deemed to dispose of it at fair market value on death or emigration—see 5.5.3 and 5.5.4), the adjusted cost base will determine whether you have a capital gain or capital loss.

Your initial cost base is the capital you put into the partnership. Each year, when you report your share of the partnership's **income**, that amount is **added** to your cost base (since you have already been taxed on it, it should not be taxed again if you sell your interest without withdrawing the profits). When you **withdraw** profits from the partnership (see 8.3.1 above), the amount you withdraw **reduces** your adjusted cost base. Thus, in simplified terms, your adjusted cost base is your contributions, plus all partnership profits, minus all partnership losses and your withdrawals. (The details are much more complicated and there are many special rules, but that is the essence of it.)

A partnership is a "flow-through entity" for purposes of the 1994 capital gain election, so you may have an "exempt capital gain balance" that you can use until the year 2004 against the capital gain on a partnership interest (see 5.4.4).

8.3.6 Assessment of partnership

Under new rules announced in 1995 but not yet enacted, Revenue Canada will be able to issue a "determination" of a **partnership's income or loss**. This "determination" will be much like an assessment of a taxpayer's tax (see 14.4.1), in that it will be binding on the partners unless a Notice of Objection is filed. One partner will have to be designated by the partnership to file any such Notice of Objection, and the other partners will not be able to object directly to the determination. These new rules will take effect only after the legislation implementing them is passed (which is likely to happen by the end of 1997). The Québec government has said it will be adopting similar rules.

If you're a partner, claim sales tax rebates on your unreimbursed partnership expenses.

Like employees, partners who are not registered for GST purposes and who have unreimbursed expenses such as automobile expenses that are deductible for income tax purposes can generally claim a rebate for the GST, HST or QST paid on those expenses (see 7.11 for an example).

Make sure to keep records through the year and obtain invoices that indicate the amount of tax paid. The rebate is claimed with your individual income tax return.

8.4 Business losses

If your business expenses claimed for tax purposes exceed the revenues from the business, you have a loss. You also have a loss for tax purposes if you share in a portion of a partnership's loss.

You can only claim a business loss against other income if your business has a **"reasonable expectation of profit"**. As well, if your loss arises from a limited partnership, you may not be able to claim it (see 6.3.2).

A business loss must first be used in the year in which it arises, to offset income from other businesses and other types of income, such as employment income, interest, (grossed-up) dividends and taxable capital gains. You do not have any choice in this matter; even if, for example, the tax on your dividend income could be offset by the dividend tax credit anyway, you must apply your business losses against any income you have in that year.

Use your loss carryovers to maximum advantage.

Business losses not deductible in the year they arise are called **non-capital losses**. They can be applied to other years' income. They can be carried **back for up to three years** and **forward for up to seven years**. They can be applied against any source of income in those years. All such claims are optional.

Example:
Judy earned $40,000 in 1995 and $50,000 in 1996 as an employee. In 1997 she goes into business for herself. Her business year-end is December 31, and for her 1997 business year she suffers a loss for tax purposes of $100,000.

Judy can file a form requesting that her non-capital loss from 1997 be applied against any amount of her 1995 and 1996 income. She will then receive a refund for the tax she paid in those years. If she wipes out all of her 1995 and 1996 income, she will still have a $10,000 non-capital loss, which can be carried forward to future years.

Judy should not, however, use up $90,000 of her loss. She only needs to use enough to bring her 1995 and 1996 income so low that she pays no tax at all ($6,500 or so). If she wishes, she may choose to use even less, and leave some of the 1995 and 1996 income taxed at relatively low rates.

The above example shows the need to use any non-capital losses carefully. When using non-capital losses against income for any given year, consider whether you want to keep some of the income taxed at a low rate. For example, if you have a loss in 1997 and are carrying it back to 1996 any taxable income below $29,590 was taxed at only about 27%. If you (confidently) expect to have a large income within the next few years, so that you can apply the loss against income which will otherwise be taxed at approximately 50%, you are probably better off not to bring your 1996 taxable income below the $29,590 level.

Of course, you should never use loss carryovers to reduce your taxable income below the level (about $6,500, or more depending on the credits you can claim—see Chapter 2) where no tax is payable anyway.

8.5 References

The following publications can be obtained (in person or by telephone request) from your nearest Revenue Canada District Taxation Office. Forms and guides may also be available from Revenue Canada's Internet site at www.revcan.ca.

Interpretation Bulletin IT-79R3, "Capital cost allowance—Buildings or other Structures"

Interpretation Bulletin IT-131R2, "Convention expenses"

Interpretation Bulletin IT-232R2, "Non-capital losses, net capital losses, restricted farm losses, farm losses and limited partnership losses—Their composition and deductibility in computing taxable income"

Interpretation Bulletin IT-514, "Work space in home expenses"

Interpretation Bulletin IT-518R, "Food, beverages and entertainment expenses"

Interpretation Bulletin IT-521, "Motor vehicle expenses claimed by self-employed individuals"

Interpretation Bulletin IT-525R, "Performing artists"

"Business and Professional Income Tax Guide"

"Guide to the Partnership Information Return"

"Guide to the GST Return for Registrants"
"Completion Guide and Form for General GST Rebate Application"
"Completion Guide and Form for Employee and Partner GST Rebate"
"The Quick Method of Accounting Guide and Election Form"
Brochure, "Paying Your Tax by Instalments"
Brochure, "Canada Pension Plan—Information for the Self-employed"
Brochure, "Simplifying the GST for Small Businesses"
Brochure, "The Simplified Methods for Claiming Input Tax Credits and GST Rebates"
Form CPT1, "Request for a Ruling as to the Status of a Worker"
Form T1A, "Request for Loss Carry-Back"
Form T2038, "Investment tax credit (Individuals)"

If you have your own corporation

- Keep the corporation a small business corporation at all times (9.1)
- Consider crystallizing your capital gains exemption (9.1)
- Multiply your access to the $500,000 capital gains exemption (9.1)
- Defer income to the next calendar year by accruing bonuses (9.2.2)
- Maximize capital dividend payments (9.2.4)
- Consider a tax-free repayment of capital (9.2.5)
- Crunch the numbers to calculate your optimum salary/dividend mix (9.3)
- Consider the tax benefits of setting up a holding corporation (9.3)
- Look into the potential advantages of a corporate partnership (9.3.1)
- Be cautious about having investment income in your corporation (9.6)

In this chapter we suggest some tax planning techniques that are available if you are an owner/manager—that is, you carry on your business through a corporation. We will not discuss tax planning for the corporation itself, except in relation to how to most effectively get its profits into your hands. Note that the tax rules in this area are substantially the same for both federal and Québec tax purposes.

9.1 Taxation of the corporation

A corporation is a distinct legal entity, and if you have an incorporated business, the corporation's profits are not yours simply to take. You, as a director of the corporation (even if you are the sole director), act in a different capacity from yourself as a shareholder of the corporation. Legally, as a shareholder your only right is to elect the board of directors, who then cause the corporation to take specific actions.

To extract funds from the corporation you must follow one of the "correct" methods we discuss in 9.2 below. If you do not, the tax system will penalize you.

For tax purposes, the corporation's business and investment income will be calculated in much the same way as your own. (See 8.2 regarding the calculation of business income.) As with individuals, certain deductions (such as loss carryforwards) are available in computing taxable income. The corporation then pays federal tax and provincial tax on its taxable income.

The federal corporate tax rate (including federal surtax) is currently 29.12%, and 22.12% for income from manufacturing and processing. However, for small "Canadian-controlled private corporations", the federal rate on the first $200,000 of "active business income" is 13.12%. (A Canadian-controlled private corporation is a corporation that is resident in Canada and is not controlled in any manner by any combination of non-residents or public corporations.) The small business rate is not available for large corporations. It begins to be phased out once the corporation's capital exceeds $10 million.

Provincial tax varies, but is typically around 16% of taxable income. All provinces have reduced rates for the first $200,000 of business income; they range from 5-10%. The combined tax burden is thus about **23%** on the first $200,000 of a small business corporation's income, and about **45%** on the remainder.

Keep the corporation a small business corporation at all times.

If possible, ensure that your corporation remains a "small business corporation" (see 5.3.2) and that your shares are "qualified small business corporation shares" (see 5.4.1) at all times. This will preserve, respectively, your ability to claim allowable business investment losses in respect of any loss on the corporation's shares, and the $500,000 capital gains exemption on any gain.

Note that you cannot always predict when the sale of the shares will be triggered for tax purposes. On the death of any shareholder, there will be a deemed disposition of that shareholder's shares at their fair market value unless the shares are transferred to a spouse or a qualifying "spousal trust" (see 13.3.2).

Consider crystallizing your capital gains exemption.

As an alternative, you may wish to "crystallize" your capital gains exemption. "Crystallizing" means triggering a capital gain on your shares of a qualified small business corporation, while continuing to own (or at least control) the corporation. This will permanently increase your adjusted cost base of the shares and possibly eliminate the need for the corporation to retain its qualified small business corporation status. Several techniques (such as selling shares to a family member) can be used to crystallize an exemption; professional advice should be sought. Crystallization may be a good idea given that the federal and Québec governments could eliminate the $500,000 exemption at some point in the future.

Multiply your access to the $500,000 capital gains exemption.

If you arrange for your spouse to invest in common shares of your corporation, you can effectively double the available exemption by each claiming $500,000. Your spouse's own funds must be used for the investment, to avoid the attribution rules discussed in 4.2.2. You may also be able to multiply the exemption by transferring shares to your children.

On death, it is possible to double the available capital gains exemption by leaving shares to your spouse or to a trust for your spouse. See 13.1.2 and 13.3.2.

9.2 Ways of extracting funds from the corporation

Since the corporation is legally a separate "person", you must follow one of the methods described below to get your hands on the corporation's income.

9.2.1 Dividends

Dividends are the distribution of a corporation's profits to its shareholders. They are **not deductible** to the corporation. In your hands, dividends will be grossed up by one-quarter and eligible for a dividend tax credit worth approximately the same amount (one-quarter of the actual dividend). See 6.1.2 for details.

If the corporation earns income, pays tax on it and pays what is left to you as a dividend, the combined effect of the corporation's tax and your personal tax will be about the same as if you had earned the income directly, if the corporation's tax rate is 20%. This is called "integration".

Where the corporate rate (federal plus provincial) is more than 20%, the combined effect of the two levels of tax will normally be that more tax is paid than if you had earned the same income directly. Conversely, where the corporate tax rate is less than 20%, paying dividends results in less tax than if you were to pay tax directly on the business income.

Example:

Ken owns all the shares of Ken Ltd. Ken Ltd. earns $100,000 in small business income, which is taxed at a combined federal/provincial rate of 20%. Ken Ltd. then pays the remaining $80,000 as a dividend to Ken.

Ken will "gross up" the $80,000 dividend by one-quarter, or $20,000, and will pay tax on $100,000, which conceptually represents the corporation's original income. He will then receive a combined federal/provincial dividend tax credit worth about $20,000, equal to the amount of tax the corporation paid. So Ken and the corporation will together be taxed as if Ken had earned the $100,000 on his own.

Note that Ken's gross-up and dividend tax credit will be 25% of the dividend regardless of the rate of tax that Ken Ltd. actually paid.

9.2.2 Salary

Where the corporation pays you a salary, the amount paid is deductible to the corporation and taxable to you as employment income. If the corporation pays all of its profits to you as salary, you are therefore in much the same position as you would be if you earned the income directly, without having a corporation.

Although your salary may become quite high in such situations, Revenue Canada's general policy is not to consider it an unreasonable deduction (for the corporation) where you are the owner/manager of the corporation. It is usually acceptable to consider the corporation's income is due to your efforts, and therefore that a salary equal to that income is a reasonable one. Of course, you are paying tax on the salary anyway.

You may decide on a base salary followed by a bonus, to be paid to you after the corporation has calculated its income at the end of the year. In general, you are taxed on employment income only when you receive it, while the corporation can accrue salary or bonus, counting it as deductible in the year even though it is paid after year-end.

However, any salary or bonus that is deducted by the corporation must actually be *paid* to you no later than 179 days after the end of the year. (As an administrative concession, Revenue Canada actually allows you 180 days instead of 179.) Otherwise, it is not deductible by the corporation until the year in which it is actually paid.

Defer income into the next calendar year by accruing bonuses.

If the corporation's year-end occurs after early July, it can declare a bonus to you as of its year-end, but pay the bonus within 180 days which will be after December 31. The corporation can thus get a deduction from its income, but you do not have to recognize the income personally for tax purposes until the next calendar year.

9.2.3 Payments on loans from shareholders

If you lend funds to the corporation (or if you did so when originally setting up the business), the corporation can **repay any amount of the loan** without tax consequences. Such a repayment is neither deductible to the corporation nor taxable to you.

You could arrange to have the corporation pay you interest on your loan. The interest paid will normally be taxable to you as investment income. The tax effect would be about the same as if the corporation paid you that amount in salary. However, if your loan to the corporation does not *require* that interest be paid or there is no formal loan document, there is a danger that the interest will not be deductible to the corporation since it has not been paid pursuant to a legal obligation to pay interest. (Conversely, if you arrange for documentation requiring that interest be paid, the annual interest accrual rule discussed in 6.2.1 may require you to include interest in your income even in years when it is not paid!)

9.2.4 Capital dividends

We mentioned capital dividends in 4.3.8 and 6.1.4. As you will recall from Chapter 5, only three-quarters of capital gains are taxed. When a "private" (i.e., non-public) corporation realizes a capital gain, the untaxed portion is added to its "capital dividend account". Similarly, one-quarter of capital losses reduce the capital dividend account.

Maximize capital dividend payments.

Any amount in the corporation's capital dividend account may be paid out entirely tax-free to its shareholders. This preserves the non-taxability of the appropriate fraction of the capital gain. So if the corporation has realized any capital gains, you should cause it to pay out capital dividends as your first choice for extracting funds.

> Example:
> Tod owns all the shares of Todcorp Inc. In 1997, Todcorp Inc. sells some land for a capital gain of $120,000, three-quarters of which is brought into Todcorp's income and taxed as a taxable capital gain.
>
> Todcorp can pay a dividend of up to $30,000 (one-quarter of the capital gain) to Tod in 1997 or any later year, provided he elects beforehand to make the dividend a "capital dividend." The capital dividend will then be completely tax-free to Tod. (Of course, because it is a dividend, it is not deductible to Todcorp.)

Note also that if you allow a capital dividend account to build up in the corporation without paying capital dividends, the account can be reduced or wiped out by future capital losses. Once you have paid out capital dividends, however, they are safely out of the corporation, and subsequent capital losses will have no effect on them.

9.2.5 Repayment of capital

Consider a tax-free repayment of capital.

Any amount that is less than the corporation's "paid-up capital" may be paid out to the shareholders as a repayment of capital, generally with no tax consequences, if the paid-up capital is reduced by that amount.

Paid-up capital is essentially the amount of capital contributed to the corporation in exchange for its shares. However, the figure can be adjusted in various ways for tax purposes, as a result of transactions involving the corporation.

Example:

ABC Corp. was capitalized with $50,000, the amount that the original shareholders contributed when subscribing for 1,000 common shares.

If the directors of ABC approve a reduction in paid-up capital to $20,000 and a simultaneous repayment of $30,000 in capital to the shareholders, there will be no adverse tax consequences for either ABC or its shareholders. The $30,000 simply comes out tax-free. ABC then has 1,000 common shares issued with a paid-up capital of $20,000.

Similarly, if shares are redeemed or cancelled by the corporation, any amount paid on the redemption or cancellation, as long as it does not exceed the paid-up capital of the shares, will ordinarily come out free of tax.

If the corporation was originally funded with a substantial amount of capital, consider extracting funds by a reduction of the paid-up capital of the corporation. Make sure the corporation remains sufficiently capitalized to satisfy any requirements of its creditors or bankers.

9.2.6 Loan to shareholder

All of the mechanisms we have looked at so far—dividend, salary, repayment of a shareholder loan, capital dividend and repayment of capital—are legitimate ways to get your hands on the corporation's income or funds. We now turn to some of the rules designed to prevent you from doing so without following the normal routes.

Suppose the corporation simply lends you its funds? If you do not fit within certain exceptions, the entire amount of the loan will simply be included in your income. This is a very serious penalty, because the corporation receives no deduction for the amount of the loan, and you do not benefit from the dividend tax credit. The same rule applies if you become indebted to the corporation in some other way (e.g., you buy property from it, but pay for the property with a promissory note rather than cash.) However, where a loan has been included in your income and you subsequently repay it, you will be allowed a deduction from your income.

To avoid this provision, bona fide repayment arrangements must be made at the time the loan is made and the loan must fall into one of the following exceptions:

■ a loan to an employee who (along with family members) does not own 10% of the shares of any class of the corporation, where the reason for the loan is the individual's employment rather than the shareholding (this exception was introduced in draft legislation released in 1995, but will be retroactive to 1991 once enacted)

■ a loan to an employee, where the reason for the loan is the individual's employment rather than the shareholding, to help the employee

purchase (a) a home, (b) shares in the employer or a related corporation, or (c) a car to be used in employment duties

▪ a loan that is repaid within one year of the end of the corporation's
taxation year in which the loan was made, and which is not part of a
series of loans and repayments.

If the loan falls into one of the above exceptions, but is made at no interest or
at a low rate of interest, you will be considered to be receiving a taxable
benefit from the corporation based on the difference between Revenue
Canada's current "low rate" prescribed rate of interest (see 14.3) and the rate
that you are paying. This rule is exactly the same as for loans to employees,
which we saw in 7.3. As in the case of employees, you may be allowed an
offsetting deduction as a notional interest expense (which affects your
entitlement to the capital gains exemption—see 5.4.3) if such expense would
otherwise meet the rules concerning the deductibility of interest.

9.2.7 Deemed dividends

Certain types of actions that involve changes to a corporation's capital
structure will deem you to have received a dividend from the corporation.
Generally, this happens when the corporation takes actions that would
otherwise allow you to extract profits as a repayment of capital.

For example, if the corporation redeems shares that you own, any amount
paid by the corporation in excess of the paid-up capital of the shares is
deemed to be a dividend (and not part of your proceeds of disposition for
capital gains purposes).

9.2.8 Shareholder appropriations

We have covered all of the "proper" mechanisms for extracting funds from a
corporation. Suppose you don't follow any of the legalities and you simply
take the corporation's funds or property, and use them as your own? If you
are the sole shareholder, there will be no one to object to you doing this.

In such cases, the *Income Tax Act* deems that any benefit the corporation
confers on you will be brought into your income for tax purposes. So, for
example, if you simply take $10,000 out of the corporation's bank account
without declaring a dividend, that $10,000 will be added to your income
(without you benefitting from the dividend tax credit).

Clearly, it is to your advantage to follow the more conventional mechanisms
for extracting funds. In the next section, we explore some of the
considerations that will affect your decision as to the appropriate mix
between salary, dividend and other forms of remuneration for yourself.

Determining your salary/dividend mix

Crunch the numbers to calculate your optimum salary/dividend mix.

Careful analysis will be needed to calculate the best mix of salary and dividends for your case. It will depend on your cash flow needs, your income level, the corporation's income level, the corporation's status for tax purposes, and many other factors. Computer spreadsheets and planning tools are available to assist in this task.

In many cases, the best strategy for a small business corporation is to pay enough salary to reduce the corporation's income to $200,000. This maximizes the amount of income that is taxed at the low small business rate, without having corporate income taxed at the high rate that applies to income beyond $200,000.

However, you will usually want to pay yourself enough salary to allow the maximum possible contribution to an RRSP (see 3.1.3). The same goes for any family members you've employed for income splitting purposes (see 4.3.2).

Note also that if you are in a business that can suffer a downturn, paying out a large salary can prevent you from carrying back a later year's loss. Suppose, for example, your business earns $1 million in 1997, and you pay out $800,000 to yourself as a salary, leaving $200,000 as the business' income. If in 1998 the business loses $1 million, you will have no way of carrying back the loss against your personal income. If you had left the funds as business income and paid out dividends, you would be able to carry back the 1998 loss to 1997 retroactively wiping out the business' 1997 corporate tax, and obtain a refund of that tax from Revenue Canada.

9.3 Effect of having a holding company

Consider the tax benefits of setting up a holding corporation.

You may choose to interpose a holding company between yourself and your corporation for various reasons. One reason for doing this is to pay out dividends from the operating business to make the funds harder for creditors to reach, while keeping the income subject to a lower level of taxation than would apply if it were paid out to you personally.

For example, you own 100% of the shares of Yourname Holdings Ltd., which owns 100% of the shares of Yourname Manufacturing Ltd. In general, dividends can be paid from the manufacturing company to the holding company without any tax effects.

If your children do not have any ownership in the business, you can consider bringing them in as shareholders at the time you set up the holding corporation. (See the estate planning example in 13.5.2 for one way of doing this.) This may be desirable for several reasons including income splitting as well as planning for your succession. However, if your children are under 18 you must be particularly careful about the attribution rules (see 4.2.3).

A holding company is often appropriate where you have family members involved in ownership of your share of the business (perhaps for income-splitting purposes), and there are other shareholders not related to you. If you and your family members own shares in the holding corporation, and the holding corporation owns all of your family's interest in the operating company, the other shareholders of the operating company need not be concerned with your internal family arrangements.

You should be cautious about accumulating funds in a holding company, however. If you intend to treat the holding corporation as qualifying for the $500,000 capital gains exemption (see 5.4.1), you can run into trouble if the corporation begins to have a substantial amount of funds that are used for generating investment income, rather than owning only the shares in the operating corporation. You may also be caught by the attribution rules (see Chapter 4), depending on when and how you introduced family members as shareholders of the corporation. Note also that investment income in a corporation is subject to an extra refundable tax that makes the up-front cost of earning the income very high (see 9.6).

9.3.1 Corporate partnerships

Look into the potential advantages of a corporate partnership.

An alternative to the use of holding companies is a corporate partnership. This is a partnership between your corporation and one or more other corporations (owned by other people).

There are a number of advantages to this form of corporate structure, including the deferral of tax in the initial years and increased flexibility concerning remuneration. Professional advice should be obtained to determine whether this structure is appropriate.

9.4 Shareholders' agreements

Where you share the ownership of a private corporation, it is usually wise to have a shareholders' agreement. Such an agreement can set out rights and obligations of the shareholders that go beyond the basic ownership of shares.

Typically, a shareholders' agreement will provide for the orderly termination of the relationship between the shareholders if there is a future disagreement, or death or disability of one of the key shareholders.

Example:
George and Alan start a small manufacturing business together. Each owns 50% of the shares of the corporation. Over the years, the business becomes very successful, but George and Alan cannot get along and decide that one of them must leave.

George and Alan signed a shareholders' agreement that contains a "shotgun" clause. George now offers Alan $500,000 for Alan's shares in the corporation. If Alan refuses to sell, the agreement provides that Alan must buy George's shares for the price George is offering ($500,000).

The "shotgun" clause is just one example of a provision that can resolve (or prevent) major disputes between key shareholders. Typical provisions in a shareholders' agreement deal with:

- desire of a shareholder to sell his or her shares
- dissension among shareholders
- death or disability of a shareholder
- agreement as to who the directors and/or officers of the corporation will be
- agreement to vote the shares in a particular way on certain issues
- what will happen if the corporation's shares are awarded to a key shareholder's spouse on separation or divorce.

Tax considerations play a major part of planning for shareholder agreements. The tax treatment of life insurance payments, the availability of the $500,000 capital gains exemption, the valuation of shares, and many other issues must be considered. Clearly, shareholder agreements should always be drafted with proper professional advice as to both the legal and the tax issues.

9.5 Pension plans for small business owners

Registered pension plans were discussed in 3.4.1. Both "money-purchase" and "defined-benefit" pension plans can be used to accrue benefits for major shareholders (see also 3.4.2, regarding individual pension plans). As an alternative to saving for retirement exclusively through an RRSP, consider having your company establish an individual pension plan, which we discussed in 3.4.2. However, this is a complex area and professional advice is essential.

If you are a small business owner and you don't want the trouble of administering a pension plan, you may simply want to set up an RRSP for yourself and ensure that you have sufficient "earned income" (i.e., salary from the corporation) to be able to make adequate contributions (see 3.1.3).

9.6 Investment income earned in a corporation

Until June 1995, it was generally advantageous to have investment income earned in a corporation, if you did not need to extract the funds. Although investment income (such as interest) is not eligible for the low "small business" rate of corporate tax, the regular corporate tax rate (combined federal/provincial) is about 44%, which is substantially lower than the rate that applies to high levels of personal income. Therefore, if you were able to leave the funds in the corporation, incorporating your investment portfolio was often a good idea.

Effective July 1995, a new federal 6 2/3% refundable tax applies to interest and other investment income in a Canadian-controlled private corporation. Most dividends received by a private corporation from public companies are also subject to a refundable tax (Part IV tax), which increased to 33 1/3% effective July 1995. These refundable taxes are paid back to the corporation only when it has paid out sufficient dividends (resulting in tax being paid by the shareholders).

Be cautious about keeping investments in a corporation.

As a result of these changes, there is generally no tax advantage to earning investment income in a corporation. In some cases there is a definite disadvantage. The precise calculation depends on your province of residence, your level of personal income, the extent to which you need to extract the funds from the corporation, and the way in which you extract those funds. It may well be cheaper to hold them personally.

Be particularly wary of moving investments into a corporation carrying on an active business. You will likely jeopardize the status of the corporation's shares from being eligible for the $500,000 capital gains exemption (see 5.4.1 and 9.1). In addition, the creditors of the active business will have access to the investments.

9.7 Selling the business

If you decide to sell your incorporated business, there are two general approaches that can be taken. One is for the corporation to sell the **assets** of the business. The other is for you to sell the **shares** of the corporation.

If your shares are "qualified small business corporation shares" (see 5.4.1), you may be able to claim an exemption for up to $500,000 of your gain on the sale. Even if they are not, you may have elected with respect to the accrued gain on the shares to February 22, 1994 (see 5.4.4), so that you can now sell the shares with a reduced or no tax cost. No capital gains exemption is available to the corporation if it sells the assets. From your point of view, it may therefore be preferable to sell the shares.

The buyer of your business, however, will often prefer to purchase the assets. One reason is that this will normally allow the buyer to claim higher capital cost allowance on the cost of depreciable assets (see 8.2.7).

No GST or other sales tax applies on a sale of shares. On a sale of assets, GST (or HST) and QST will usually apply, but can almost always be recovered by the purchaser in the form of an input tax credit (see 8.2.4). Also, in many cases on the sale of part or all of a business an election can be made to have no sales tax apply to the sale.

Needless to say, any purchase and sale of a business must be done with detailed professional advice.

If your business goes public without you selling the shares, you can make a special election to "crystallize" part or all of your accrued capital gain, and get the $500,000 exemption as if you had sold the shares (see 5.4).

9.8 References

The following publications can be obtained (in person or by telephone request) from your nearest Revenue Canada District Taxation Office. Forms and guides may also be available from Revenue Canada's Internet site at www.revcan.ca

Interpretation Bulletin IT-66R6, "Capital dividends"

Interpretation Bulletin IT-67R3, "Taxable dividends from corporations resident in Canada"

Interpretation Bulletin IT-109R2, "Unpaid amounts"

Interpretation Bulletin IT-119R3, "Debts of shareholders, certain persons connected with shareholders, etc."

Interpretation Bulletin IT-432R2, "Benefits conferred on shareholders"

Farming

- Establish that your farming business has a "reasonable expectation of profit" (10.1)
- Classify farming as your chief source of income (10.1)
- Claim deductions available for the self-employed (10.2)
- Consider using the "cash method" of accounting to defer taxes (10.2.1)
- Make the most of the $500,000 capital gains exemption for qualified farm property (10.5.1)
- Take advantage of intergenerational transfer rules (10.5.2)
- Claim alternative principal residence exemption where appropriate (10.5.3)

The income tax system has a number of special rules to deal with farming. We outline them in this chapter.

10.1 Farming—a business or not?

No matter what kind of activity you undertake, you are only allowed to write off losses for tax purposes if you are engaged in a business "with a reasonable expectation of profit" (see 8.4). This issue comes up repeatedly in the case of part-time farmers.

"Farming", for tax purposes, includes a number of activities ranging from growing crops to raising poultry, fur farming, fruit growing, keeping bees and training horses for racing. The *Income Tax Act* classifies people engaged in farming into three groups. The principal difference among the groups is the extent to which they can deduct expenses relating to their farming activities.

At one extreme are the full-time farmers, for whom farming is **a chief source of income**. Such people are allowed to treat their farming business like any other business, and can therefore claim losses against other income for tax purposes if they suffer losses in any given year (see 10.3.1 below).

Establish that your farming business has a "reasonable expectation of profit".

At the other extreme are people who do not have a **"reasonable expectation of profit"** from their farming activity. Such people are sometimes called "hobby farmers", as farming is considered to be their hobby rather than something they are doing in order to make money. Hobby farmers may not deduct any losses from their farming activity. You will need to keep records that establish that your farming business is carried on with a "reasonable expectation of profit" on an objective basis. If your activities never actually turn a profit over many years, a claim that you had a reasonable expectation of profit will be hard to sustain in court.

In the middle are the people who *do* have a reasonable expectation of profit, but whose "chief source of income is neither farming nor a combination of farming and some other source of income", to quote the *Income Tax Act*. Such people are allowed only "**restricted farm losses**", limited to certain dollar amounts (see 10.3.2).

Example 1:

Darryl lives on his farm and raises dairy cattle. Almost all his income comes from selling the cows' milk. In 1997, Darryl's cows have a bad year and he loses $30,000.

Darryl will be able to deduct his $30,000 against any other income he has (such as investment income) and carry it over to be used in other years (see 10.3.1). His farming loss is very much like a loss from any other kind of business, such as manufacturing or retailing.

Example 2:

Bob is a jeweller who lives and works in Toronto. He spends his weekends on his ranch, where he keeps a stable of racehorses. In past years, Bob's horses have won a fair amount of prize money. In 1997, Bob has a bad year and spends $30,000 on maintaining his horses without winning any prize money at all.

Bob's loss will likely be considered a "restricted farm loss", and only a portion of it (see 10.3.2) will be deductible against his jewellery business income. Although his horse-racing business (which for income tax purposes is considered farming) does have a reasonable expectation of profit, it is not a chief source of income to him and therefore falls into the "restricted" category.

Classify farming as your chief source of income.

A large number of reported court cases have considered the question of whether farming, or farming in combination with some other source, constitutes a taxpayer's "chief source of income". You may wish to consult a tax professional to determine what facts will best establish a claim that will entitle you to a full deduction for farm losses, rather than the more limited deduction for "restricted farm losses".

10.2 Computing farming income

If you are engaged in a farming business—whether or not your losses will be "restricted" as we saw in 10.1—you may take advantage of a number of special rules when calculating income for tax purposes.

Claim deductions available for the self-employed.

In addition to the specific rules for farmers discussed in this chapter, see 8.2 for ideas as to deductions that can be claimed by the self-employed. If you successfully establish that you are carrying on a farming business with a reasonable expectation of profit, such deductions will be available to you.

10.2.1 The cash method

Businesses are generally required to follow the accrual method of accounting for income. That is, you take your sales for the year into income, even though you may not have been paid for some of those sales until after your business year-end. You claim expenses the same way (see 8.2.2).

Consider using the "cash method" of accounting to defer taxes.

For a farming business, you may choose to use the "**cash method**" instead. In general, this means you will count payments received, rather than your sales—and only deduct amounts that you have paid, but not still-unpaid expenses that you have incurred. This usually provides a certain amount of deferral of income, and may result in lower tax payable. Once you have chosen the cash method, you are normally required to continue to use that method for the farming business for all subsequent years.

When you are using the cash method, you may, if you wish, include into income any amount up to the fair market value of your inventories on hand at year-end. The amount you include will then be deductible in the following year. You might wish to do this for 1997, for example, if you had very low income in 1997 and can see by April 1998 (when you file your return) that your 1998 income will be substantially higher, enough to put you into a higher tax bracket.

10.2.2 Purchases of inventory

If you are using the cash method of accounting, it is clearly possible to generate a loss for tax purposes by purchasing large amounts of inventory. Special rules have been introduced to deal with this possibility and to limit the loss you can claim.

Example:
Darryl, from the first example in 10.1, purchased dairy cows for $5,000 just before his year-end on December 31, 1997. This purchase has been included as an expense in arriving at his farming loss of $30,000. He did not purchase any other items of inventory at the end of the year. For income tax purposes, he will be required to include $5,000 as a mandatory inventory adjustment to his 1997 income, reducing his farm loss to $25,000. In 1998, this $5,000 mandatory inventory will be treated as a farm expense.

In general, you will be denied a loss that is attributable to purchases of inventory. However, for horses and certain registered bovine animals, you can deduct a portion of the loss. Professional advice should be obtained when dealing with these complex rules.

10.2.3 Cost of improving land for farming

Normally, when calculating income from a business, the cost of work done to improve land is considered a capital expense and is not deductible. However, for a farming business, amounts paid for clearing land, levelling land or installing a land drainage system are deductible.

10.2.4 Sales of livestock in a drought region

If you are farming in a region designated for the year as a "drought region", special relief is available if you sold a significant portion of your breeding herd. This rule is designed to allow you to defer paying tax where you are forced to sell off part or all of your herd because of drought. The list of regions designated for the year is determined by Agriculture Canada's Prairie Farm Rehabilitation Administration in Saskatoon each September.

The rule only applies where, by the end of the year, you have sold off (and not replaced) at least 15% of your "breeding herd". When it applies, some or all of your sales of the breeding animals are not counted into your income, but are deferred until a later year when your area is no longer designated as a drought region.

10.2.5 Forced destruction of livestock

If you have livestock that is diseased, you can be forced by the government to destroy the livestock under the *Animal Contagious Diseases Act* or similar legislation. If you receive compensation for the destruction, the compensation is included in your income. However, a special rule allows you to deduct all or part of this compensation and include it in your income in the next year. This allows you to defer paying tax on the compensation by one year.

10.2.6 Net Income Stabilization Account ("NISA")

The NISA program has created a number of tax issues including certain planning opportunities. You should consult your tax advisor to ensure that you are taking maximum advantage of the program from an income tax perspective.

Western Grain Transition Payments Program ("WGTPP")

If you own farm land in Western Canada, you may qualify for a one-time transition payment to partially offset the drop in land values that is expected to result from the elimination of the Crow Rate freight subsidy.

For income tax purposes, if you receive a transition payment in respect of farmland that is capital property, the "adjusted cost base" of the farmland is reduced by the amount of the transition payment. As we saw in 5.2, your adjusted cost base is the cost of your property, with certain adjustments, for purposes of calculating your capital gain on the property's disposition.

10.3 Farming losses

10.3.1 Ordinary farm losses

As we saw in 10.1, if your chief source of income is farming, or your chief source of income is "a combination of farming and some other source of income", you may deduct your farm losses as though they were ordinary business losses.

The carryover available for such losses is somewhat more generous than that for normal business losses (non-capital losses), which we saw in 8.4. Like normal losses, farm losses can be carried back and used against income of the past three years. They can also be carried forward, and used against income in any of the next ten years (rather than seven).

10.3.2 Restricted farm losses

As noted in 10.1, a loss from farming cannot all be used if you do not meet the "chief source of income" test. In this case, the loss you claim is limited to the first $2,500, plus one-half of the next $12,500 (that is, up to an additional $6,250).

> Example:
> Bob the jeweller, whom we met in 10.1 above, loses $30,000 on his racehorses in 1997.
>
> Bob's "restricted farm loss" will be $2,500, plus one-half of the next $12,500. Since his total loss is more than $15,000, he reaches the maximum, and he can only deduct $8,750 against the income from his jewellery business for 1997.

Any amount of loss that cannot be used because of the "restricted farm loss" rules can be carried back for three years and forward for ten years, but can be used only against farming income. So, in our example, Bob has $21,250 that can be used to offset income from his horse operations during the years 1994 to 1996 and 1998 to 2007.

10.4 Investment tax credits

Investment tax credits (see 8.2.13) are available for investment in agricultural equipment in the Maritimes and the Gaspé region of Québec. The amount of the credit is generally 10%. Unused credits may be carried back three years and forward for ten.

10.5 Transfers of farming assets

A number of special rules, as outlined below, are available to alleviate the tax burden of selling or transferring a farm and the assets of a farming business.

10.5.1 The $500,000 capital gains exemption

Make the most of the $500,000 capital gains exemption for qualified farm property.

As discussed in 5.4.2, a $500,000 exemption from capital gains is available on the disposition of "qualified farm property"—if you are disposing of farm property, investigate whether it qualifies. In some circumstances you may be able to take action, such as delaying the sale, so you can gain time to reorganize your affairs in order to take advantage of the exemption. You also may be able to take steps to increase the cost base of your qualifying farm property to reduce the tax liability that will arise in the future on the property's sale. The tax rules in this area are quite complex so you should seek professional tax advice if you own farm property that qualifies for the exemption.

10.5.2 Transferring farm property to children or grandchildren

Normally, if you sell or give property to members of your family other than your spouse, you are deemed to have sold the property for its "fair market value", and will thus have to recognize as a capital gain the difference between your original cost (or the value on February 22, 1994 if you elected to use your capital gains exemption on the farm property) and the property's current value. (See 5.5.5 and 5.4.4.)

Take advantage of the intergenerational transfer rules.

If you transfer property used in a farming business to a child, grandchild or great-grandchild (including a spouse of your child, a child of your spouse, etc., where "spouse" includes a common-law spouse as outlined in 2.2.1), you can avoid this rule. If you simply give the property, it will be deemed to be transferred at your cost (adjusted cost base [see 5.2] for capital property, or undepreciated capital cost [see 8.2.7] for depreciable property). If you sell it for something in between your cost and the current market value, that amount will be accepted for tax purposes. Any gain on the property will thus be deferred.

For this "rollover" rule to apply, you or your spouse or one of your children must have used the property "principally" in a farming business in which you, your spouse or children were actively engaged on a regular and continuous basis.

When the rollover applies, the recipient (your child, grandchild, etc.) will be deemed to have acquired the farm property for the amount at which you are deemed to have sold it. This means that the gain will eventually be taxed, if the child sells the property at some later time.

Example:

Florence operates a wheat farm in Saskatchewan. In 1997, Florence decides to retire and gives the farm to her grandson Daniel. The farmland cost her $10,000 in 1975 and is now worth $150,000.

Florence is deemed to receive $10,000 for the land, and so has no capital gain. Daniel is deemed to have acquired the land for $10,000; if he ever sells the land, the $10,000 figure will be used as his cost for capital gains calculation purposes. (Of course, if Daniel transfers the farm one day to his child, a further rollover will be available, assuming the rules have not changed.)

If you are transferring farm property to a child, grandchild, etc., you may wish to realize a partial capital gain, in order to use up your $500,000 capital gains exemption and give your child a higher cost base in the property. In such a case, you will need to sell the property to your child for an amount greater than your cost. (Where land is being transferred, don't forget to consider the possible cost of provincial land transfer tax. GST, HST or QST may apply as well, depending on the circumstances.)

10.5.3 Principal residence exemption

As we saw in 5.5.2, the exemption in respect of the gain on the sale of a principal residence normally applies to the house itself plus one-half hectare of surrounding land. The gain on any land beyond one-half hectare is subject to the normal rules for capital gains.

Claim alternative principal residence exemption where appropriate.

For land used in a farming business, another option is available. Instead of the ordinary principal residence exemption, you may elect to claim a special exemption of $1,000 plus $1,000 for each year since 1972 during which the house was your principal residence. You subtract this amount from your total gain on both house and land.

This election can be useful where you have occupied the property for many years and the value of the house is small relative to the land. Alternatively, consider whether you might claim more than the one-half hectare under the principal residence exemption if you can substantiate that such additional land was necessary for your personal use and enjoyment of the property.

10.5.4 Capital gains reserve on sale of farm to child

We discussed capital gains reserves briefly in 5.5.1. It was noted there that the capital gain must be recognized at a cumulative rate of one-fifth each year, so that no reserve can last for more than four years after the year of sale.

Where you sell property used in a farming business (including land) to your child, grandchild or great-grandchild, the allowable reserve is 10 years rather than five. As with the rules discussed in 10.5.2, a spouse of your child, grandchild or great-grandchild, and a child, grandchild or great-grandchild of your spouse also qualify. (For this purpose, "spouse" includes a common-law spouse as outlined in 2.2.1.)

10.6 References

The following publications can be obtained (in person or by telephone request) from your nearest Revenue Canada District Taxation Office. Forms and guides may also be available from Revenue Canada's Internet site at www.revcan.ca.

Interpretation Bulletin IT-156R, "Feedlot operators"

Interpretation Bulletin IT-232R2, "Non-capital losses, net capital losses, restricted farm losses, farm losses and limited partnership losses— Their composition and deductibility in computing taxable income"

Interpretation Bulletin IT-268R4, "Inter vivos transfer of farm property to a child"

Interpretation Bulletin IT-322R, "Farm losses"

Interpretation Bulletin IT-349R3, "Intergenerational transfer of farm property on death"

Interpretation Bulletin IT-373R, "Farm woodlots and tree farms"

Interpretation Bulletin IT-425, "Miscellaneous farm income"

Interpretation Bulletin IT-427R, "Livestock of farmers"

Interpretation Bulletin IT-433R, "Farming or fishing—Use of cash method"

Interpretation Bulletin IT-485, "Cost of clearing or levelling land"

Interpretation Bulletin IT-526, "Farming—Cash method inventory adjustments"

"Farming Income Tax Guide"

Form T2042, "Statement of farming income and expenses"

Professionals

- Defer tax by electing to follow the modified accrual method for computing income (11.1.1)
- Adjust billings and drawings to maximize your 1971 receivables (11.1.2)
- Maximize your deductible interest (11.2.1)
- Pay retiring partners income or capital as appropriate (11.2.2)
- Consider paying club dues at partnership level (11.2.3)

Most of income tax planning for professionals is the same as that for other self-employed people (see Chapter 8). Self-employed professionals are, after all, carrying on business. However, a number of special rules exist which we consider in 11.1. Since many professionals carry on their practice in partnership, we also look at some rules that apply to partnerships in 11.2.

11.1 Specific rules for professionals

11.1.1 The modified accrual method of accounting for income

As we noted in 8.2.2 and 10.2.1, businesses other than farming businesses are generally required to report income on the accrual basis. That is, you take your sales into income even though you may not be paid until after your year-end.

Most businesses must also account for **work in progress**— work that has been done but not yet billed. However, there is an exception for the professional practice of an accountant, dentist, lawyer, medical doctor, veterinarian or chiropractor. If you are practising one of these professions, you may elect to exclude work in progress from your income.

Defer tax by electing to follow the "modified accrual" method.

This method of accounting is sometimes called the "modified accrual" method. It is not the cash method, since once an amount has been billed, it must be reported as income even if not yet paid. But excluding work in progress is a step away from the full accrual method.

Example:

Dianne is a lawyer who is in sole practice. Her business year-end is December 31. She spends almost the entire month of December 1997 preparing for a major trial, which takes place in January. She does not bill the client until the conclusion of the trial, in January 1998.

If Dianne elects to exclude work in progress from her income for 1997 she will not have to recognize as income any amount in respect of her work in preparing for the trial until her business year ending December 31, 1998.

As you can see, electing to exclude work in progress from your income can create a substantial deferral of tax. If you are practising one of the eligible professions, you will almost certainly want to follow this method. The only reason not to do so might be if you are in your first year or two of practice, with relatively low income, and you wish to recognize income earlier while it can be taxed at relatively low rates.

Once you choose to exclude work in progress, you must normally continue to do so for all future years.

Upon retirement or withdrawal from the business, the remaining work in progress is brought into your income. Such income is considered to be "earned income" for RRSP contribution limit purposes (see 3.1.3).

11.1.2   1971 receivables

If you have been in practice continuously since before 1972, you may still have a "1971 receivables" balance.

Before 1972, professionals were allowed to use the cash method of accounting, much as farmers still are. In your 1971 taxation year, therefore, you would exclude from income your billings which had not yet been paid.

With the change to the accrual (or modified accrual) method, a special allowance was provided as a transitional rule, to preserve the deferral of taxation of these receivables and avoid taxing the professional too heavily in any one year. The allowance takes the form of a deduction for "1971 receivables".

Each year, you can deduct your original 1971 receivables, up to a limit of your receivables at the end of the current year. (For a partnership, however, the limit is the adjusted cost base of your interest in the partnership.) However, whenever the amount you claim goes down in any year, that lower amount will be your maximum for future years. As your receivables fluctuate from year to year, therefore, your 1971 receivables deduction may eventually become very small.

Example:
Norm is an architect who has been in practice since 1969. At the end of 1971, his receivables totalled $10,000. Since then, he has claimed a deduction for his 1971 receivables of $10,000 every year. Most years he has had substantial amounts outstanding at the end of the year, but in 1985 he was ill in November and December, and his year-end

receivables were only $3,000. In 1997 Norm earns $200,000 from his practice, and his year-end receivables are $30,000.

The maximum deduction Norm can claim in 1997 is $3,000. That has been the limit for his 1971 receivables deduction since 1985 (when he had to bring $7,000 of his 1971 receivables into income).

Adjust billings and drawings to maximize your 1971 receivables.

If you have been in sole practice since before 1972, and you still have an untaxed "1971 receivables" balance, you will want to make sure your receivables are high enough at the end of each year that your deduction is not reduced at all. This can be done by issuing billings towards the end of the year.

If you are a member of a partnership and you have a 1971 receivables balance, you need to keep the adjusted cost base of your interest in the partnership at a high enough level to preserve the 1971 receivables. This can be done by delaying drawings towards the end of the year, or even by investing additional capital in the partnership before the year-end.

11.1.3 Professional corporations

Some provinces allow certain professionals to incorporate their professional practices. For example, lawyers in Alberta and physicians in Nova Scotia can be incorporated.

For tax purposes, a professional corporation is generally treated like any other small business corporation. See Chapter 9.

As of 1995, professional corporations which are members of partnerships must use a December 31 business year-end. This is the same rule as applies to individuals carrying on business (see 8.2.1). A professional corporation which is not a member of a partnership, however, retains its normal year-end.

11.2 Specific rules that apply to partnerships

In 8.3 we discussed the taxation of partnerships in general. In this section we shall look at two rules applicable to partnerships that are of particular relevance to professionals.

11.2.1 Deductibility of interest paid by the partnership

As we saw in 6.2.3, interest paid is normally deductible as long as the funds borrowed are used to earn income from business or property. Where a partnership borrows funds for working capital, the interest is therefore clearly deductible.

Maximize your deductible interest.

As a member of a partnership, consider whether you can accelerate your drawings or have the partnership repay a portion of your capital contribution. You could then use the funds to pay off non-deductible debt (such as a home mortgage), while the partnership can borrow funds to replace the lost working capital. The interest would then become deductible. Alternatively, you yourself could borrow funds to inject back into the partnership. However, Revenue Canada could challenge such an arrangement under the general anti-avoidance rule (discussed in 4.2.5) if it considers this type of refinancing technique to be a misuse or abuse of the *Income Tax Act*.

If the partnership borrows funds in order to make a distribution of profits and/or capital to the partners, the interest paid on such borrowings is normally deductible, but only up to the amount of the partnership's "net equity" as determined under generally acceptable accounting principles.

11.2.2 Income payments to retired partners

Normally, if you withdraw from a partnership, and you receive a payment to compensate for your interest in the partnership, the payment will be considered capital. That is, any excess over your adjusted cost base in the partnership will be a capital gain, and taxed as discussed in Chapter 5. (Your adjusted cost base is essentially the amount you contributed to the partnership, plus your share of the profits on which you have been taxed, minus your drawings. See 8.3.5.)

Another option is available under the *Income Tax Act*, however. If your partners agree to pay you a share of the income from the partnership, and to treat it explicitly as an income payment, you will be considered as still being a partner for tax purposes. You will therefore be taxed on that income, but your former partners will effectively pay less tax, since their partnership income will in part be allocated to you.

Example:

Joel, an accountant, retires from his firm at the beginning of 1997. There are three other partners, who share equally in profits. The firm's income for 1997 is $300,000. The partners agree to pay Joel $60,000 upon his retirement, and declare the $60,000 to be a share of the income from the partnership (rather than as a repayment of his capital interest).

Joel will be required to report the $60,000 as income. However, each of the partners will effectively get a deduction of $20,000, since after Joel's allocation, there is only $240,000 to be divided three ways. Each partner will thus report $80,000 in income instead of $100,000.

Note that the continuing income payments to a retired partner are not included in "earned income" for purposes of calculating the retired partner's RRSP contribution limit.

Pay retiring partners income or capital as appropriate.

When you (or a partner of yours) decide to withdraw from a partnership, you will need to calculate the best way of paying out the retiring partner's interest.

On the one hand, if you are retiring and have a high cost base in your partnership (perhaps as a result of electing to apply your capital gains exemption to your partnership interest as of February 22, 1994—see 5.4.4), it may be best to receive a capital payment. This amount could be entirely exempted from tax, or, if there is a gain, only three-quarters of the gain will be taxed. However, it will effectively be paid in after-tax dollars by the other partners.

On the other hand, if your partners choose the option of an income payment, you will be fully taxed on it (possibly at lower rates than the continuing partners, if your income is going down substantially). However, your partners will effectively receive a deduction for the amount paid to you.

If you have a **10-year reserve** in respect of your 1995 "stub period" income due to the 1995 budget's calendar-year reporting rules for unincorporated business income discussed in 8.2.1, you are entitled to claim the appropriate amount of the reserve in the year that you retire. However, you will only be able to continue claiming the reserve in later years if you retain an income interest in the partnership. Otherwise, you will have to bring your remaining reserve amount into income in the year after the year in which you retire.

11.2.3   Club dues

As you may know, most club dues are not allowed as business expenses. Many professional partnership agreements therefore provide that such dues should be paid by the partners personally (since they are not deductible in computing the partnership's income anyway).

Consider paying club dues at the partnership level.

You should consider having the partnership pay such dues even though they are not deductible. The reason is that the individual partners' adjusted cost bases in the partnership are not reduced by such disallowed expenses, even though the assets of the partnership are reduced by making the payments. (As noted above, your adjusted cost base is essentially the amount you contributed to the partnership, plus your share of your after-tax profits, minus your drawings. See 8.3.5.) As a result, having the partnership pay the club dues can reduce the capital gain (or increase the capital loss) on an eventual sale of the partnership interest.

11.3 References

The following publications can be obtained (in person or by telephone request) from your nearest Revenue Canada District Taxation Office. Forms and guides may also be available from Revenue Canada's Internet site at www.revcan.ca.

Interpretation Bulletin IT-90, "What is a partnership?"

Interpretation Bulletin IT-135R, "Investment interest in a professional business" [for 1971 receivables]

Interpretation Bulletin IT-138R, "Computation and flow-through of partnership income"

Interpretation Bulletin IT-242R, "Retired partners"

Interpretation Bulletin IT-358, "Partnerships—Deferment of fiscal year-end"

Interpretation Bulletin IT-457R, "Election by professionals to exclude work in progress from income"

Information Circular 89-5R, "Partnership information return"

"Business and Professional Income Tax Guide"

"Guide to the Partnership Information Return"

Form T2032, "Statement of professional activities"

Form GST 370, "Employee and partner GST rebate"

Form T5013, "Partnership Information Return"

Minimum tax

- Have 35¢ regular income for each $1 in exempt capital gains (12.4.1)
- Continue generating interest expense and business losses (12.4.2)
- Watch out for RRSP deductions (12.4.3)
- Limit your "tainted" tax shelter deductions (12.4.4)

12.1 What is the minimum tax?

The minimum tax was enacted as a political solution to the perception that many high-income taxpayers were paying little tax through the use of tax shelters and other so-called tax preferences. It is relatively narrow in focus, concentrating on specific shelters and credits.

The minimum tax is an alternative tax calculation. You must calculate your tax both normally and under the minimum tax rules, and pay the higher of the two.

In simplest terms, you calculate minimum tax by taking your taxable income, adding back "tainted shelter" deductions (such as resource write-offs, tax shelters and RRSP/RPP contributions) and the untaxed one-quarter of capital gains, taking a $40,000 exemption and then calculating federal tax at 17%. Most personal credits, but not the dividend tax credit or investment tax credits, are then allowed as with regular tax. Once federal surtax and provincial tax are added in, the minimum tax rate comes to about 27%, varying slightly depending on the province. If you live in Québec, see 15.2.28 regarding the Québec minimum tax.

Minimum tax paid can be recovered in later years to the extent your regular tax exceeds your minimum tax. Minimum tax does not apply to the year of death.

12.2 Calculating the tax

Somewhat simplified, the calculation is as follows:

1. Start with your **taxable income** (after all deductions allowed for regular tax purposes).
2. **Add back the deductions** that you are not allowed to claim for minimum tax purposes:
   - losses from any investment that requires a tax shelter identification number (see 6.3.1)

- losses from a partnership where you are a limited partner or passive partner (see 6.3.2)

- resource write-offs (see 6.3.4)

- carrying charges, such as interest expense, relating to any of the above (see 6.3)

- RRSP contributions and transfers of retiring allowances (see 3.1.3 and 7.7)

- RPP contributions (see 3.4.1)

- employee home relocation deduction (see 7.3)

- employee stock option deduction (see 7.4)

(These are sometimes called "tainted" deductions, since you cannot claim them for minimum tax purposes.)

3. Add **one-quarter of all capital gains**, whether the other three-quarters was eligible for the capital gains exemption or not. (Note that you don't add back the exemption; that is still allowed for minimum tax purposes. It's the one-quarter which is *never* taxed that you add back no matter what.)

4. **Deduct the gross-up** on dividends (see 6.1.2). Since the dividend tax credit will not be allowed for minimum tax purposes, you are only taxed on the actual dividend received, rather than on the grossed-up amount.

5. **Deduct $40,000** as your basic minimum tax exemption. This gives you your "adjusted taxable income".

6. Calculate federal tax at **17%**.

7. Deduct **personal credits** (see Chapter 2), such as your basic credit, other dependants, old age, disability (for self or spouse only), CPP/QPP contributions, UI premiums, tuition, education, medical and charitable. Do not deduct investment tax credits (8.2.13), political contribution credits (2.8.3), pension tax credits (2.5.2), transfer of unused tax credits from spouse (2.1.3), tuition and education credits transferred from a child (2.4), dividend tax credits (6.1.2) or labour-sponsored venture capital credits (6.3.8).

8. If the resulting tax is higher than your federal tax calculated normally, you must pay the minimum tax. **Federal surtax and provincial tax** (other than Québec tax) will be calculated on this figure rather than your regular federal tax figure.

12.3 Minimum tax carryover

If you find that you have to pay minimum tax in any given year, the excess of your minimum tax over your regular tax becomes a "minimum tax carryover", which can be used in any of the next **seven years**.

In a future year, you can use the carryover to the extent your regular tax exceeds your minimum tax.

Example:
Your 1997 regular federal tax is $30,000. Your 1997 minimum tax (federal) is $35,000.

You must pay the $35,000 tax, plus surtax and provincial taxes (total about $56,000). However, you have a $5,000 federal minimum tax carryover. If, in 1998, your regular federal tax is $32,000 and your minimum (federal) tax is $22,000, you can deduct the carryover from your regular federal tax and pay only $27,000 basic federal tax (before calculating provincial tax and surtaxes).

12.4 Tips for minimizing minimum tax

12.4.1 Exempt capital gains

The minimum tax can have a serious impact on capital gains, particularly where the $500,000 capital gains exemption would otherwise enable you to avoid regular tax entirely.

Example:
Max sells the shares of his small business corporation for a $480,000 capital gain, which is fully exempt under the enhanced capital gains exemption (see 5.4.1). Max has no other income in 1998.

Max will pay no regular tax. For minimum tax purposes, however, his adjusted taxable income will be $120,000 (one-quarter of the gain), minus the basic $40,000 exemption. His federal minimum tax will therefore be 17% of $80,000, or $13,600, minus personal credits. Max's total tax for 1997, including surtax and provincial tax, will be about $20,000. This federal minimum tax of $13,600 (net of personal credits) may be carried forward for seven years and applied against regular federal tax payable in those years.

Have 35¢ regular income for every $1 in exempt capital gains.

As a general rule of thumb, minimum tax will not apply if you have at least 35¢ of "regular" income for each $1 in capital gains which are fully exempt due to the capital gains exemption. If your gains are relatively small, they may be shielded by the $40,000 minimum tax exemption anyway.

12.4.2 Interest expense and business losses

Continue generating interest expense and business losses.

Two important deductions are not affected by the minimum tax. The first is deductible interest paid (see 6.2.3) on loans not used for tax shelter purposes.

The second is business losses and loss carryforwards (see 8.4) other than loss carryforwards that are attributable to "tainted" shelters (see 12.4.4). Where it otherwise makes sense from a business perspective, you can generate such deductions without triggering any minimum tax liability. Keep in mind, however, that high interest expense may give you a high cumulative net investment loss (see 5.4.3) and thus make the capital gains exemption unavailable to you, to the extent you would otherwise want to use it (see 5.4.1 and 5.4.2).

12.4.3 RRSP deductions

Watch out for RRSP deductions.

As noted in 12.2, contributions to an RRSP are normally added back for minimum tax purposes. The $13,500 for 1997 maximum normal RRSP contribution (see 3.1.3) will not normally create much of a problem in this respect. However, if you are transferring a large retiring allowance (see 3.3.2) to an RRSP, you may inadvertently trigger a minimum tax liability.

12.4.4 Tax shelter deductions

Limit your "tainted" tax shelter deductions.

Be aware of possible minimum tax implications when planning for large tax shelter claims, particularly on resource funds (see 6.3.4) such as drilling funds and flow-through shares. Resource expenses that exceed your total income from such funds (and are therefore claimed as losses) must be added back for minimum tax purposes.

To the extent you have loss carryforwards from previous years that are attributable to "tainted" shelters, they must also be added back to your taxable income for minimum tax purposes.

As a general rule of thumb, you can have "tainted" tax shelter losses equal to about 41% of your other income without being affected by minimum tax.

12.5 References

Form T691, "Calculation of minimum tax" can be obtained (in person or by telephone request) from your nearest Revenue Canada District Taxation Office. It is also available from Revenue Canada's Internet site at www.revcan.ca.

Estate planning

- Make a will or review your existing will (13.2)
- Take steps to minimize probate fees (13.1.3)
- Consider the advantages of establishing one or more family trusts (13.3.4)
- Look into the potential benefits of an "estate freeze" (13.5)
- Make sure you have sufficient insurance (13.6)
- Consider planned charitable gifts and bequests (13.7)
- Think about donating publicly traded securities instead of cash (13.7.4)
- Plan for the succession of your business (13.8)
- Watch out for the effects of foreign estate taxes (13.9)
- Consider a pre-paid plan to finance your funeral and cemetery arrangements (13.10)

In this chapter we provide an overview of the rules that apply on death and some estate planning strategies you can use to minimize the taxes arising on death and to leave as much as possible to your beneficiaries. Estate planning can be extremely complicated, and depends very much on your personal situation and goals. Professional advice is highly recommended.

13.1 Taxes on death

13.1.1 Tax payable by the estate

When a person dies, the executor or administrator of the estate (called the "estate trustee") must file a "terminal return" for the deceased to report income up to the date of death. Although the regular T1 and Québec TP1 return forms are used, there are a number of special rules for these returns. For example:

- charitable donations, which can normally be claimed for the year of donation or carried forward to future years (see 2.8.1 and 13.7.1), can be carried back and claimed in the year before (subject to the limits discussed in 13.7.1)
- medical expenses paid, which can normally be claimed for a 12-month period ending in the year (see 2.8.2), can be pooled for any 24-month period that includes the day of death
- the full amount of the deceased's RRSP (see 3.1) is brought into income for the year of death, unless the

beneficiary of the RRSP is the deceased's spouse or certain dependants (see 3.3.3); if the RRSP funds are not transferred to the spouse's own RRSP, the spouse must report the funds as income for tax purposes

▪ any balance borrowed by the deceased from an RRSP under the Home Buyers' Plan (See 3.3.6) and not yet repaid may be included in income

▪ minimum tax (see 12.1) does not apply to the year of death

▪ capital property is generally deemed disposed of at its fair market value, resulting in either a capital gain or a capital loss (see 13.1.2)

▪ capital losses, which are normally only allowed to offset capital gains (as discussed in 5.2), may be deducted from other income (unless you have previously claimed the capital gains exemption)

▪ certain kinds of income earned but not received by the deceased before death can be reported on a separate return (against which the deceased's personal credits can be claimed a second time).

The terminal return for the deceased, along with any tax payable, is due by the usual deadline (see 14.1.1) or six months after death, whichever is later. For example, if Lee dies on March 10, 1998, his 1998 return is due by April 30, 1999.

A similar extension is allowed for filing of the return for the year before the year of death if the individual dies before the return's normal due date. As a result, Lee's 1997 tax return would be due by September 10, 1998 instead of the usual April 30, 1998 deadline.

Any income earned after death will be subject to tax as part of the estate. The estate is treated as a separate person which must file a return as a **trust** each year until all of the assets are distributed. (Sometimes this can take several years, but normally an estate can be wound up within one year.) Any income paid to beneficiaries of the estate may be taxed in their hands directly, instead of in the estate.

Note that life insurance proceeds received as a result of an individual's death are not subject to income tax. Life insurance is discussed in more detail in 13.6 below.

13.1.2   Deemed disposition of capital property

Canada has no estate tax or inheritance tax, nor do any of the provinces. To the extent you simply have cash in the bank and you leave it to your family, there will be no tax to pay at all (other than probate fees, discussed in 13.1.3 below).

Many people, however, have capital assets such as stocks, real estate and jewellery. As a general rule, capital assets are deemed for tax purposes to have been sold at their fair market value immediately before death. This results in the realization of any accrued capital gains or losses at that time.

This rule was discussed in 5.5.3 as well. If you own depreciable property, recaptured depreciation or a terminal loss may also be triggered.

Example:
Agnes dies in 1997. Her only capital assets are her house, which has a cost base of $50,000 and is now worth $600,000; a diamond ring, which has a cost base of $5,000 and is now worth $10,000; and a stock portfolio, which has a cost base of $10,000 and is now worth $17,000.

The house will be deemed sold at fair market value just before Agnes' death, but there will be no capital gain because it is Agnes' principal residence (see 5.5.2). The ring and the stocks will also be deemed sold at their current values, for a total gain of $12,000. Three-quarters of the capital gain, or $9,000, will be taxed as a taxable capital gain on Agnes' terminal return.

As you can see, the normal capital gains rules apply, including the availability of any exemptions.

The main exception to the "deemed disposition" rule is the case where you leave assets to your **spouse**, or to a **spousal trust** (a trust that meets certain requirements, as outlined in 13.3.2 below). In such a case, you are deemed to have sold your assets immediately before your death at their cost, so no capital gain results, as long as your spouse or a spousal trust obtains an enforceable right to the property within 36 months of your death. Your spouse (or the trust) then inherits that cost for tax purposes along with the assets. When your spouse (or the trust) sells the assets, or on your spouse's death, the full capital gain or loss from your original purchase price will be taxed.

There is, however, a special rule under which your estate trustee may elect to realize a capital gain or loss on a property-by-property basis when assets are left to your spouse on your death. This election may be beneficial if your estate trustee elects to trigger a capital gain in order to use loss carryforwards or a capital gains exemption. Alternatively, triggering a capital loss may recover tax in the year prior to death, since capital losses in the year of death may be carried back to the immediately preceding year and used against any income, except to the extent that the deceased previously claimed the capital gains exemption (see 5.4).

13.1.3 **Probate fees**

Probate fees are charged by the courts in each province except Québec for granting "probate" of a will, or for approving the administration of an estate where there is no will. In theory they are administrative fees, but in most provinces they are really disguised taxes.

In some cases, the assets of the deceased can be distributed and the estate wound up without going to the court for probate. Generally, however, probate is required before third parties (e.g., banks) will release property to the estate trustee.

Probate fees are highest in Ontario and British Columbia, where they are 1.5% and 1.4% respectively of the value of the estate in excess of $50,000. In other provinces the top rates are typically 0.4% to 0.7% of the value of the estate. Alberta has progressive flat rates to a maximum of $6,000; the probate fees for large estates in other provinces can be substantial as there is no maximum.

The fee generally applies to the total value of the assets of the estate, without any deduction for debts other than those encumbering real property. Property held by two people as "joint tenants" with right of survivorship (rather than as "tenants in common") is not subject to probate, since on the death of one joint tenant the property does not form part of the estate but simply becomes wholly owned by the other.

Example:
Jonah, who lives in Ontario, dies in 1997. His estate consists of a house worth $500,000, with a $200,000 mortgage on it, $100,000 in personal effects, and the shares of his business, worth $1 million. He also owes $80,000 on a personal line of credit to the bank at the time of his death.

The value of Jonah's estate for probate purposes is $1,400,000. The house is counted as $300,000 (i.e., minus the mortgage), and his other assets are $1,100,000. The $80,000 debt is not deducted. The fee for probating Jonah's will is $20,500.

Take steps to minimize probate fees.

Some of the following techniques can reduce the cost of probating your estate. Note, however, that any planning to reduce probate fees must take numerous other issues (such as family law, income tax effects, land transfer tax, GST and other sales taxes) into account—professional advice is strongly recommended.

- If you are leaving property to your spouse (or another person), consider holding the property as joint tenants with your spouse (or that other person). On your death, the property will pass automatically to the other joint tenant and will not form part of your estate. Note that there may be immediate adverse tax consequences if you transfer the property to a joint tenant who is someone other than your spouse (for example, your child). Also, there are some situations where a joint tenancy will be severed on death by provincial legislation.

- Try to keep certain assets out of the estate. This is quite practical in the case of life insurance and RRSPs issued by life insurance companies, where beneficiaries (other than the estate) can be designated in the RRSP plan documents or in the life insurance policy. Also consider transferring property during your lifetime, either directly to your intended beneficiaries or to a trust.

■ Change the situs of property to a different jurisdiction where probate fees are low or fixed (for example, Alberta) through the use of a corporation.

■ If you own real estate with no mortgage, and you also owe money (perhaps on a personal line of credit or on a debt secured by other assets), consider having the debt converted to a mortgage or charge on the real estate. It may then reduce the value of the real estate for probate purposes.

13.1.4 Death benefits

Death benefits may be paid by the deceased's employer to the surviving spouse or other family members. Up to $10,000 of such benefits may be received tax-free (see 7.8).

13.2 The will

13.2.1 Purpose of a will

The will is a key element of estate planning. It allows you to provide for an orderly distribution of your assets in accordance with your desires and in a way that minimizes the tax burden on your estate and on your beneficiaries.

Make a will, or review your existing will.

Your will's primary function, of course, is to specify where and when your assets are to be distributed. You may want to leave specific properties (e.g., jewellery, furniture or shares in your business) to specific beneficiaries. You may want to leave a stated sum of money to certain people or to named charities (make sure you get the correct legal name of the charity). You will also want to specify a "residual" beneficiary, who will get everything left in the estate after your specific bequests are satisfied.

For example, you may wish to simply leave everything to your spouse. Alternatively, you may want to make use of a "spousal trust" which, as we'll see in 13.3.2, can offer certain tax advantages and a measure of protection from potential creditors without any loss in flexibility for your surviving spouse. As discussed in 13.1.2, there will be no tax on the accrued capital gains on your property when the property is transferred to your spouse or the spousal trust, provided the assets vest with your spouse or spousal trust within 36 months of your death.

If you do not make a will, the provincial law will determine how your assets are distributed. The result can vary significantly, depending on where you reside at the time of death. In Ontario, for example, the law provides that the surviving spouse gets the first $200,000 of the estate and divides any additional amounts with the deceased's children in accordance with a formula. However, in British Columbia, the surviving spouse is only entitled to the first $65,000, with the balance of the estate divided among the surviving spouse and the deceased's children under a formula.

Note also that, in some provinces, family law can effectively override the instructions in your will. In Ontario, for example, your spouse can elect to ignore the will and take the amount of money due to him or her under the "net family property" rules (see 13.4). If this is done, your estate may lose the benefit of the capital gains rollover described above.

If you have specific desires as to who should have custody of or guardianship over your children after your death and while they are under 18, you can put these desires into your will for consideration by the courts. However, in some provinces, this designation is not binding.

While in some provinces an entirely handwritten will may be valid, it is strongly advisable to have your will prepared or reviewed with the assistance of a lawyer or a notary in Québec and a tax advisor to ensure it meets your wishes and takes tax and family law considerations into account.

Periodic **reviews** of your will are necessary to ensure that your estate plan is consistent with changes in the tax law, which occur regularly, as well as any changes in provincial family law and succession law. In addition, changes in your own personal circumstances such as the birth of a child could necessitate a change to your will.

Note also that in many jurisdictions, a will becomes void if you marry after making the will, unless it was made in contemplation of the marriage.

If you do not make a will or if your will is invalid, the process of obtaining court approval for distribution of your assets may be more cumbersome and expensive. Your representative or heirs must apply to the court to appoint an **administrator** (also called an "estate trustee") to administer and distribute the estate in accordance with a formula set out in legislation.

As discussed in 1.2.4, consider also executing **powers of attorney** in the event you become unable to act by reason of disability or mental incompetence—one for decisions related to your finances and one for decisions related to your personal care. If, for example, you become mentally disabled, the continuing powers of attorney would enable the named "attorney" to act in your stead. You may wish to give the powers of attorney to the same person you name as your executor, such as your spouse.

13.2.2 **Your executor and estate trustee**

In your will, you should designate one or more persons as your executor and estate trustee. The person should be someone you can trust to take charge of your affairs and distribute your assets in accordance with your desires as set out in your will. The executor and estate trustee will normally apply to the court for "letters probate" (see 13.1.3), which will give the executor the right to take over your property, manage it and distribute it to your beneficiaries.

The responsibilities of your executor and estate trustee include determining the assets and liabilities of the estate, filing all income tax returns for the deceased and the estate (including any foreign succession duty or tax returns) and paying the debts (including all taxes) of the deceased.

Ideally, you should choose an executor and estate trustee who is familiar with your personal situation. Often the executor will be your principal beneficiary (such as your spouse). Sometimes this may not be appropriate, however, because of a possible conflict of interest with other beneficiaries.

You should consider naming an alternate executor and estate trustee should your executor die before you do. Otherwise your estate may be handled by the executor of your executor's estate. Naming an alternate executor and estate trustee is also important in case the named executor is either unable to or chooses not to act. This can avoid costly court proceedings.

If you are an executor and estate trustee yourself, you should seek advice with respect to how to minimize the tax burden on the estate which has been left under your care. If you do not, you can be sued by the beneficiaries. The courts have found executors liable for failing to take active steps to structure the estate's affairs to minimize income tax.

13.2.3 Will planning to minimize your estate's tax liability

There are many tax-oriented clauses that can be included in a will to help minimize the tax liability. The will should include a provision granting executors and trustees broad authority to make or join in any election, designation or allocation under tax legislation. This will ensure that your executor can use benefits such as the principal residence designations and capital gains exemptions. The following clauses should also be considered:

- forgiveness of certain loans made to family members
- a discretionary power permitting trustees to determine which assets are to form the trust property of a spousal trust
- a reminder to your executors that if you have not made your maximum RRSP contribution at the time of your death, one should be made by your estate to your spouse's RRSP before the required deadline

In your will, you can name the beneficiary of your RRSP, deferred profit-sharing plan, death benefits and life insurance proceeds. Alternatively, these plans and policies may allow for naming a direct beneficiary within the plan documents. While designating beneficiaries directly in the plan documents may reduce probate costs, there may also be implications for spousal rights under family law.

If you designate someone other than your spouse as the beneficiary of your RRSP, your estate may have to pay tax on the full value of your RRSP on your death (see 3.3.3).

13.3 Trusts

13.3.1 What is a trust?

A trust is an arrangement whereby one or more persons (the trustees) hold legal title to property (the trust property) for the benefit of other persons (the beneficiaries). The person who creates the trust and puts ("settles") property into it is called the settlor.

> Example:
>
> Brian is leaving the country to work in Africa for several years. He gives Paul $80,000 to hold in trust for Brian's two teenagers, Dianne and Darryl. Brian draws up a trust agreement that allows Paul to use the trust funds to pay for Brian's children's education, to invest the funds not yet used, and to pay half of the capital of the trust to each child when he or she turns 23.
>
> In this example, Brian is the settlor, Paul is the trustee and Dianne and Darryl are the beneficiaries. Paul will have legal ownership of the $80,000, but he is required to use it only for Dianne and Darryl's benefit and not for his personal use. If the trust document permits, he can pay himself a fee for his services as trustee.

There is no legal requirement that the settlor and the trustee be different people. (In the example above, Brian could simply declare and document that he is holding funds in trust for his children, and a trust would be created.) Similarly, the settlor and the beneficiary can be the same person. (This is what happens when you put funds into a self-directed RRSP, for example. You are the settlor and beneficiary, and a trust company is the trustee of your assets—see 3.1.6.) However, the choice of settlor, trustee and beneficiaries will affect the taxation of the trust and its beneficiaries. For example, there are a number of attribution rules that apply to trusts, including those outlined in Chapter 4. Careful planning is required.

Note that the mechanics and terminology of trusts are different in Québec, which is governed by the province's *Civil Code* rather than by the common law which governs the rest of Canada.

13.3.2 What kinds of trusts are there?

A trust can be set up during the settlor's lifetime (as in the example above). Such a trust is called an *inter vivos* (Latin for "among the living") **trust**.

A trust can also be created by the settlor's will, in which case it is called a **testamentary trust**.

A trust for the settlor's spouse that meets certain conditions is a **spousal trust**. The principal conditions are, first, that all of the income of the trust must be paid to the spouse during the spouse's lifetime, and second, that none of the capital can be distributed to anyone other than the spouse during the spouse's lifetime. (After the spouse's death, however, the capital can be distributed to someone else, such as the settlor's children.) Such a trust can be either testamentary or *inter vivos*. A transfer of property from the settlor to a spousal trust does not trigger tax on any accrued capital gain; instead the property passes at the settlor's cost, and any capital gain is taxed only when the trust eventually disposes of the property or the spouse dies (see 5.5.3 and 13.1.2).

Note that if your will creates a trust, that trust will be separate from your estate. The estate is taxed as a trust for as long as it takes to wind up your affairs and distribute your assets. A trust set up in your will, on the other hand, can be designed to continue for many years beyond your death.

13.3.3 How is a trust taxed?

A trust is a **separate person** for income tax purposes. The trustee(s) must file a T3 trust tax return and pay tax on the trust's income (a TP-646 trust return is filed for Québec purposes). A trust is generally taxed as an individual, but is not eligible for the personal credits (see Chapter 2). A testamentary trust pays tax at the same marginal rates as individuals (see 4.1), but an *inter vivos* trust pays tax at a flat rate—the top rate of combined federal and provincial tax for individuals (about 50%).

The trust's income includes its income from carrying on business (see Chapter 8), from taxable capital gains (see Chapter 5) and from investments (interest, dividends, rent, etc.—see Chapter 6). Amounts that are payable or paid to beneficiaries are deducted, and the beneficiaries report such income on their tax returns.

Certain kinds of income, such as capital gains and dividends, preserve their character when flowed through to a beneficiary. Thus, such income can be treated as capital gains (see Chapter 5) or as dividends (see 6.1.2) on the beneficiary's tax return.

Trusts that meet certain conditions can use special rules in the *Income Tax Act* to treat amounts as paid to beneficiaries even if the amounts are not actually paid or payable to the beneficiary in that year. This can be useful where a beneficiary has no other income and can receive a certain amount of income tax-free. For example, if a trust entitles a beneficiary who is under 21 years of age to a set amount or share of income, the trust may allocate that share to the beneficiary for income tax purposes. The beneficiary will pay tax (if any) on that income even though the funds will not be paid out by the trust until a later time.

A special election called the "**preferred beneficiary election**" allows the trust and a certain kind of beneficiary to agree that the trust's income will be taxed in the beneficiary's hands so that, in a later year, the income can be paid out by the trust to the beneficiary free of tax. As of 1996, this election is only available where a beneficiary is disabled (as defined for tax purposes in 2.6.1).

Other special tax rules allow income and capital gains to be taxed in the trust even if these amounts have been paid out to the beneficiary during the year. This can be beneficial if the trust has unused losses from previous years which can offset this income. For certain testamentary trusts, this election may also save taxes if the beneficiary would otherwise be subject to tax at a higher rate than the trust.

Every 21 years a trust is deemed to dispose of all of its property, so that accrued capital gains are taxed. Under recent tax law changes, this deemed disposition can be deferred in many cases to January 1, 1999 by older family trusts which make an appropriate election. Certain planning steps can be taken to minimize the tax cost arising from this rule.

If you are considering a family trust, advice from a qualified tax professional will be essential.

13.3.4   The benefits of setting up a family trust

A trust offers tremendous flexibility in structuring your affairs and controlling the future use of your property. The powers of the trustees can be strictly limited and defined; or they can be given full discretion as to when and whether to pay income or distribute capital to the beneficiaries, how to manage the trust property and when to wind up the trust.

Consider the advantages of establishing one or more family trusts.

In your will, you can provide a separate testamentary trust for each beneficiary. This will allow each trust to benefit from lower graduated rates of tax for the income retained in such a trust.

Setting up the trust while you are alive can also provide several advantages:

- by making yourself a trustee, you can keep control of the trust assets (such as shares of your business)

- by getting the assets out of your estate, you can reduce probate fees (see 13.1.3)

- because the assets will not be in your estate, they will not form part of the public record that anyone can examine in the court office

- income splitting may be possible, depending on the application of the attribution rules (see Chapter 4)

A trust can also be useful as part of an estate freeze plan (see 13.5). In many cases, you may not know at the time you set up the freeze how you will want the growth allocated among your children. You may also not yet want to give them direct ownership in the business. In such an event you should consider setting up a family trust and having the trust subscribe for the "growth" common shares (or, preferably, have them gifted to the trust). If you are the trustee and have discretion as to how to allocate the income and capital of the trust, you can decide several years later (or even in your will) which of your children should inherit the business. This may also provide some protection for your children against family law legislation (see 13.4).

13.4 Family law

Provincial family law can have a significant impact on your estate planning. Every province has legislation to protect the interests of spouses on marriage breakdown. This legislation may apply on death as well (although in some provinces, such as British Columbia, it does not apply). We shall use Ontario family law for purposes of this description. The laws of each of the ten provinces are different, however, and professional advice should be obtained.

On marriage breakdown, Ontario's *Family Law Act* provides for an equal division of "net family property", which includes almost all property acquired during the marriage and the increase in the value of property owned at the time of the marriage. Business assets, shares in a privately-held or public corporation and investments are typically all included in "net family property". Each spouse's assets are totalled and an equalizing payment is required, so that each spouse ends up with half of the value of the net family property.

The above provisions apply on death as well. The surviving spouse may elect to take an equalizing payment for one-half of the difference in net family property rather than whatever has been left to him or her under the deceased's will. Clearly, such rules can interfere with one's estate planning, and should be considered when making a will.

Spouses can agree to have these provisions of the *Family Law Act* not apply by signing a "domestic contract". Separate independent legal advice for each spouse is required before signing such a contract.

13.5 Estate freezing

13.5.1 What is an estate freeze?

Estate freezing is the term used to describe steps taken to fix the value of your estate (or some particular asset) at its present value, so that future growth will accrue to your children (or to a trust for your children) and not be taxed on your death. Several provisions of the *Income Tax Act* are designed to facilitate this type of planning.

Estate freezing is most often used when you own a business that you expect will increase in value in future years. Your children may be involved in running the business. Even if they are not, you may want them to own it after your death.

13.5.2 How does one freeze an estate?

There are many different types of estate freeze, some of them very complex. The following example is one of the simplest types:

Example:

You own all of the common shares of X Corp. (your business). Your original share investment in X Corp. was $100, and it is now worth $400,000. You expect it to increase in value significantly over the next several years. You have two children, both in their early 20s, who work in the business.

First, you exchange your common shares of X Corp. for 400 new preferred shares (a step that can be taken without triggering any income tax). The preferred shares are voting shares. They are also retractable at any time, at your option, for $1,000 per share. In other words, you can demand that the corporation pay you $400,000 for your shares at any time.

Each of your children then subscribes for 50 new common shares in X Corp., paying $1 per share. Since X Corp. is worth $400,000, and your preferred shares are retractable for $400,000, the common shares have negligible value at the moment.

Over the next few years, the value of X Corp. rises to $900,000. Now your preferred shares are still worth only $400,000, but the common shares are worth $500,000. You have thus transferred the post-freeze "growth" in the corporation to your children at no tax cost to you.

Note also that since your preferred shares are voting shares, you have kept control of the corporation. You have 400 votes and your children together have only 100.

The mechanics of an estate freeze are complex, and there are numerous income tax rules that have to be considered. The basic concept, however, is generally as outlined above. Often you will set up a holding company and a family trust (see 13.3.4) as part of the freeze, rather than having your children subscribe directly for shares in the operating company.

Look into the potential benefits of an "estate freeze".

An estate freeze can significantly reduce the tax payable on your death, if the value of your business is "frozen" sufficiently early. The lower cost base will effectively be transferred to your children, and so the tax on the subsequent capital gain will be deferred until they sell the business (or until their deaths). You can also multiply the availability of the capital gains exemption for certain small business shares (see 5.4.1), if it is still available when your children eventually dispose of the shares. At the same time, you do not need to give up control of the business.

You can also continue to receive income from the corporation, either by declaring dividends on the preferred shares, or by drawing a salary if you continue to work in the business.

If you use a trust to acquire the common shares, you can retain flexibility with respect to allocating the shares of the business among your children later.

At the time you set up the freeze, you can trigger part or all of the accrued capital gain on your shares to date. This may allow you to use your $500,000 capital gains exemption (see 5.4.1), for example. Be aware of the various restrictions on claiming the exemption (see 5.4.3).

Depending on how the freeze is structured, you can achieve income splitting (see Chapter 4) by directing income into the hands of your children for tax purposes. Note that certain attribution rules do not apply if your corporation qualifies as a "small business corporation" (see 5.3.2) or your children have reached the age of 18 (see 4.2.5).

Whether an estate freeze is useful to you will depend very much on your business, your financial position, your future plans and your goals. Qualified professional advice should be obtained before this type of planning is undertaken.

13.6 Life insurance

Life insurance plays many roles in estate planning. For example, it can

- provide replacement income for your dependants
- provide a fund for emergency expenses or children's education in future years
- pay for final expenses such as funeral costs
- assist in funding the succession of a business in a closely-held corporation
- fund capital gains tax liability that arises on death (see 13.1.2)
- allow you to accumulate funds on a tax-sheltered basis to supplement retirement income

Insurance proceeds received on the death of the life insured are not taxable. Similarly, the premiums you pay for your life insurance are generally not tax deductible.

If your corporation is the beneficiary of a policy on your life, the corporation may be able to transfer the life insurance proceeds to other shareholders without any tax applying.

Make sure you have sufficient insurance.

Your need for insurance will change as factors such as your income, investment portfolio and dependants change. Therefore, a regular review of your coverage is important.

There are many different life insurance products available. These products can generally be divided into two types: term insurance and permanent insurance.

Term (or "pure") insurance policies usually have lower premiums at younger ages. You are paying the cost of insuring against the risk of your death in the current year, and nothing more. As long as you continue to pay the premiums, your coverage will continue; many policies guarantee renewal without additional medical evidence as long as you remain in the plan. However, the cost of premiums can increase dramatically in later years. Most term policies terminate at age 70 to 75, which is lower than the current average life expectancy.

A **permanent insurance** policy (often called "**whole life**" or "**universal life**") combines pure insurance coverage with an investment fund. As a result, the cost of premiums when you are young is often much higher than term insurance. However, many permanent insurance policies offer fixed premiums for guaranteed maximum terms (say, 10 or 20 years); at the end of the term, the policy is fully paid for. The policy can be designed so that the investment fund or cash surrender value accumulates tax-free. Such a fund can be borrowed against or "cashed out" in later years. However, doing so may have a tax cost.

Permanent insurance products are usually desirable for the following purposes:

- capital gains tax funding
- estate equalization (to allow for an even distribution of your estate, such as where you wish to leave business assets to beneficiaries active in a family business and non-business assets to those family members not active in the business)
- business succession planning
- tax-sheltered, long-term investment strategies

When buying insurance, consider who should be the beneficiary. If your estate is the beneficiary, the insurance proceeds will form part of your estate on your death, and will be subject to any claims that creditors have on your estate. The proceeds will also be subject to probate fees (see 13.1.3 above). You may therefore want to have the insurance proceeds payable directly to your spouse or another beneficiary, so that they bypass the estate. The investment fund or cash surrender value of a policy can also be protected from creditors during your lifetime where certain beneficiaries are named.

13.7 Charitable gifts and bequests

In this section we look at some ways you can structure charitable gifts, both during your life and through your will, to further your estate planning goals and make the most of the available tax credits. The options are much broader than simply leaving a sum of money to a charity in your will.

Consider planned charitable donations and gifts.

There are many ways in which gifts may be made to charitable organizations—including gifts of property (such as securities, artwork, real estate), life insurance and annuities—with significant tax benefits. These benefits depend on the type of gift, the timing of the donation and the nature of the charitable organization.

A gift made today can provide a current tax saving and, in addition, a charitable gift annuity (see 13.7.7) or a gift of a remainder interest in a trust or property (see 13.7.9) will also allow you the continued use of, or income from, the property itself.

Proper will planning can help ensure that your bequest will be made as you intend and provide significant tax savings for your estate.

Careful planning together with an informed advisor can ensure your philanthropic goals are met and the tax benefits are available when you need them most.

13.7.1 The tax credit for charitable donations

As discussed in 2.8.1, the federal government has enriched the federal tax credit for charitable donations for 1997 and later years (the Québec credit is discussed at 15.2.9). To the extent your total donations exceed $200 per year, you receive a credit worth about 50% of the donation in most cases. As of 1997, the limit of donations you can claim each year is 75% of your "net income" plus 25% of the taxable capital gains arising from donations of capital property (see 13.7.3). Any donations you do not claim can be carried forward for up to five years.

Charitable gifts can be made through your will. A bequest in your will is treated as if the gift was made in your final year and is claimed for credit on your final tax return. For 1996 and later years, the charitable donations limit in the year of death and the immediately preceding year is 100% of the deceased's "net income" (20% of net income for Québec purposes).

It is possible that large bequests in your will (or large donations during your lifetime) may become unusable for tax purposes, if they far exceed the allowable threshold. You may therefore want to consider other options, so as to maximize both the tax credits and the funds available to your beneficiaries—both family members and charities.

Note that recent federal government measures affecting charitable donations have not yet been enacted and that aspects of the proposals may change before they become law. If you are thinking about taking any tax planning steps involving charitable donations, be sure to check with a professional advisor on the status of these changes.

13.7.2 Gifts to the Crown

Before 1997, gifts to the federal or a provincial government ("Crown gifts") were not subject to the charitable donations limits. You could claim up to 100% of your net income for Crown gifts, including gifts to Crown agency foundations set up for the benefit of universities, colleges, hospitals and museums. The advantage of the pre-1997 higher income limit allowed on Crown gifts often made it more attractive for donors to make large gifts to the Crown rather than to other charities. To level the playing field for all charities, the 1997 budget proposed to reduce the federal limit for claiming Crown donations to 75% of net income, the same limit that now applies to gifts made to other charities.

13.7.3 Gifts in kind

Both during your lifetime and on your death, you can donate property to a charity as an alternative to money. A gift of property is called a **gift in kind**. Examples include artwork, shares and real estate, as well as some more esoteric gifts we discuss below, such as life insurance or a residual interest in real property. (You cannot "give" services, however—only property.)

A gift in kind is normally valued at its **fair market value**. For purposes of determining the tax credit for your donation, it will be the same as a gift of cash. Thus, the tax credit will generally be worth about 50% of the value of the property. However, at the time of the donation you are deemed to have disposed of the property at its fair market value—meaning that you must recognize any capital gain or income that would apply had you sold the property for that price.

For purposes of the tax credit, the 75% net income limit is effectively increased to 100% of net income for:

- donations of capital property resulting in taxable capital gains (as of 1996)

- donations of depreciable property in 1997 and later that trigger recapture of capital cost allowance (see 8.2.7)

- gifts of ecologically sensitive lands to municipalities and certain charities

- gifts of "certified cultural property" (and capital gains on such property may not be taxable—see 13.7.5)

However, if you have large capital gains in a year from other dispositions, gifts that trigger significant gains could result in a liability for alternative minimum tax ("AMT"—see Chapter 12). Before you make such a donation, be sure to run the numbers to ensure that AMT will not result.

As a result of the 1997 federal budget, individuals and corporations who donate securities listed on prescribed stock exchanges to charities (other than private foundations) will only have to include in their taxable income 37.5% of the capital gain (instead of the usual 75%) that arises on the securities' disposition. This change applies to such donations made between February 18, 1997 and the end of 2001 (after which the government will review this measure's effectiveness in encouraging donations). (If you live Québec, see 15.2.9.)

Example:

David lives in Prince George and owns shares in a mining company traded on the Vancouver Stock Exchange that have a cost base to him of $10,000. In 1997, the shares are worth $70,000, and on April 15, 1997 David donates them to a hospital foundation. David's employment income in 1997 is $75,000.

David is deemed to have disposed of the shares for $70,000, and so must recognize a $60,000 capital gain, 37.5% of which is brought into his income as a $22,500 taxable capital gain (see 5.2). His total income for tax purposes is thus $75,000 + $22,500, or $97,500.

David gets a receipt from the hospital foundation for $70,000. David's charitable donation limit for 1997 is $78,750—25% of the amount of the taxable capital gain of $22,500 (or $5,625) plus 75% of his net income of $97,500 ($73,125). As a result, David will be allowed to claim the entire $70,000 as a charitable donation on his 1997 tax return. This will entitle him to a credit worth about $35,000.

If you make a gift of capital property, you can file an election with your tax return to use a lower amount than the fair market value, for purposes of determining both your proceeds of disposition of the property and the value of your donation. You can elect any amount between the adjusted cost base (see 5.2) and the actual fair market value.

Whether the election is useful depends on a number of factors, including your tax bracket, your other sources of income and deductions, and your prospects for income in future years against which to use up the charitable donation carryforward.

The election described above can also be used by artists for gifts of work they have created (which is inventory rather than capital property).

13.7.4 Cash vs. shares—which should you donate?

Think about donating publicly traded securities instead of cash.

Say you want to make a $2,000 donation to a favourite cause and you have publicly traded securities that originally cost you $1,000 and that are now worth $2,000. Should you sell the securities and donate the proceeds or should you simply donate the securities? Assuming your income is taxed at the top marginal rate of about 50% and you have already donated $200 in the year, the tax effects of both choices are as follows:

- If you sell the shares and donate the before-tax proceeds, a $1,000 capital gain will arise on the securities' sale ($2,000 proceeds – $1,000 original cost). You would then have to pay $375 in tax on the taxable portion of your gain (75% of $1,000 × 50% tax rate). Your $2,000 donation will give you a tax credit of $1,000 (50% × $2,000). In the end, the donation will result in net tax savings of $625 ($1,000 tax credit – $375 capital gains tax.

- If you donate the shares directly, the charity will still get the full $2,000 value of the shares. The taxable portion of the $1,000 capital gain will only be 37.5%, so your tax payable will only be $187.50 (37.5% of $1,000 × 50%). You will also get a tax credit of $1,000 for the donation (50% of $2,000). The net tax savings resulting from your donation will be $812.50 ($1,000 tax credit – $187.50 capital gains tax).

As you can see, under the new rules in effect for the period between February 18, 1997 and the end of 2001, you will come out ahead if you donate the securities directly. In the above example, you give up property of the same value but your after-tax cost is $187.50 less than had you sold the securities and donated the proceeds. (If you live in Québec, your savings would be about half this amount since the province has not adopted these changes — see 15.2.9.)

13.7.5   Gifts of cultural property

Gifts of "cultural property" to certain public authorities or institutions (such as museums) are not subject to the general 75% limitation. In addition, if the cultural property is certified by the government as a national treasure with cultural significance to Canada, the donation will be equal to the property's fair market value for purposes of the credit but no taxable capital gain will result.

13.7.6   Gifts of life insurance

If you have a "permanent" life insurance policy (see 13.6), such as whole life or universal life, you can donate it to a charity by transferring the ownership of the policy to the charity and having the charity become the beneficiary of the policy. For tax purposes, the value of your donation will be the policy's cash surrender value, plus any accumulated dividends and interest that are also assigned, minus any policy loan outstanding. However, to the extent that value exceeds the tax cost of the policy to you, you must recognize the excess as income, as if you had cashed in the policy.

Once you have donated the policy to the charity, if you continue to pay the premiums on the policy, each such payment will be considered to be an additional charitable donation entitling you to a tax credit.

Note that if you simply make the charity a beneficiary of a life insurance policy that you continue to own, there will be no tax benefits available to you or your estate.

13.7.7 Purchasing an annuity from a charity

You can purchase an annuity from a charity, whereby you give the charity a sum of money up front and receive a fixed annual payment for the rest of your life.

While the "cost" of this type of annuity is usually more than the market price to purchase an annuity from a life insurance company offering the same annual income, the annuity purchased from a charity may actually provide you with more annual disposable income and allow you to make a sizable gift to the charity at the same time. If the total payments that you expect to receive from the charity during your lifetime are less than the original sum you gave to the charity, the annual payments to you will be tax-free. You will also be entitled to a tax credit on the difference according to the usual rules as outlined above.

Revenue Canada has published a table outlining the number of annual payments that donors can expect to receive based on their age at the time the annuity is purchased.

If the total payments that you expect to receive are more than the original sum given to the charity, the excess amount will be taxable on an annualized basis.

13.7.8 Charitable insured annuity

Another strategy is to set up a "charitable insured annuity". You buy an annuity from a life insurance company, and use part of the monthly payments to pay the premiums on a life insurance policy with a charity as the owner and beneficiary. Thus, you receive an income stream over your lifetime (from the annuity), and tax credits for the insurance premiums you pay. On your death, the charity receives the insurance proceeds.

13.7.9 Charitable remainder trusts

If you have property that you would like to donate to a charity, but you need the income from the property during your lifetime, consider donating a "residual" interest in the property—that is, the capital that will remain on your death. One way to do this is to set up a "charitable remainder trust". This is a trust (see 13.3) whose conditions are that the income be paid to you during your lifetime, while the *capital* will go to the charity on your death. In some cases, you can transfer the residual interest in property (e.g., real estate) directly, without setting up a trust.

The value of a gift of the residual interest in a property is its discounted present value. This value will depend on factors such as the current fair market value of the property, current interest rates, and your life expectancy.

The gift entitles you to the normal tax credit for charitable donations. If you arrange to receive less income from the trust (or property) than you might otherwise be entitled to, the value of your donation may be higher.

Such a gift has several attractions. First, the charity gets a vested interest in the property right away, and need not worry about whether you will leave the property to it in your will (or whether your will might be contested). Second, you get an immediate tax credit based on the amount of your donation (the residual value). Third, you continue to receive the income from (or use of) the property for the rest of your life.

Aside from the cost of professional fees in structuring a charitable remainder trust, you will be deemed to have disposed of the remainder interest for its fair market value. This may lead to a capital gain and an income inclusion for tax purposes, with an enhanced tax credit as illustrated in the example in 13.7.3 above. In addition, the trust will have to file an annual tax return (see 13.3.3), though it will normally not pay any tax since all of its income will be paid out to you.

13.8 Business succession

Plan for the succession of your business.

If you own and manage a business, it could well be your family's largest asset. After your death, the business may be crucial for meeting your family's financial needs. Taking steps to ensure your business' ongoing profitability and management can be just as important as considering the planning opportunities available to minimize taxes on your death.

One of the first issues you must resolve is what will happen to the business when you die. You could plan for the business to be kept in the family, sold to a buyer outside the family, or liquidated. The option you choose will depend on things such as the nature of the business, the likelihood of its continued success after your death, and the abilities of your family members and/or key employees to run the business' operations.

If the family is not capable or does not want to run the business, it may be in everyone's best interests to sell or liquidate the business on or before your retirement. If some family members are quite active in managing the business while others are not, dividing ownership equally among your family might seem fair but it could disrupt the business and create tension in the family. Often in these cases, you could use other family assets or life insurance to ensure fairness for all family members.

If you decide to keep the business in the family, you should seek professional advice to help you decide whether to transfer ownership during your lifetime or on death, who will receive the business' shares and in what proportion, whether the shares will be gifted or sold, and the most tax-effective way to structure the transfer.

If you do not own 100% of your company's shares, the transfer of its legal control may be smoothed by a carefully drafted shareholders' agreement (see 9.4).

Life insurance owned by you or your company can facilitate the sale of your shares of the company and help to fund any tax liability arising on death. Due to proposed income tax changes, you may be able to secure certain tax advantages if your company was the beneficiary of a life insurance policy held for this purpose or held before April 26, 1995.

13.9 Foreign estate taxes

Watch out for the effects of foreign estate taxes.

If you own assets in other countries, investigate the possibility of estate, inheritance or succession taxes of those countries (or their states or provinces) applying on your death.

Note that estate taxes and succession duties imposed by other jurisdictions are not normally eligible for a foreign tax credit in Canada, even though you may have a Canadian income tax liability as a result of the deemed disposition described in 13.1.2. Double taxation can result. You may need to plan for this ahead of time.

If you are a U.S. citizen, see our discussion of U.S. estate tax in 16.8.1.

If you are not a U.S. citizen but own assets legally located in the U.S., including real estate, debts owed to you by U.S. citizens or shares in U.S. corporations, see the planning techniques discussed in 17.4.

13.10 Pre-paid funeral and cemetery arrangements

Planning and paying for your funeral and cemetery arrangements in advance can go a long way toward easing the stress on your survivors at a difficult time. Many funeral and cemetery service providers offer plans through which you can deposit funds as pre-payment for their services.

Consider a pre-paid plan to finance your funeral and cemetery arrangements.

To help Canadians finance these arrangements, the tax rules provide a special tax exemption for the interest earned on eligible pre-paid amounts. Like the deferred income plans discussed in Chapter 3, the sooner you contribute to a pre-paid funeral or cemetery arrangement, the longer your funds will benefit from the effect of tax-free compounding of interest.

Under proposed rules effective for 1993 and later years (once enacted), you can contribute up to $35,000 to an arrangement that covers both funeral and cemetery services. If the funeral and cemetery services will be provided by separate businesses, you can contribute up to $15,000 to an arrangement that covers only funeral services and up to $20,000 to an arrangement that covers only cemetery services. The funds in your account can be used to cover your own funeral and cemetery arrangements or those of anyone you choose; the limits only restrict the amount that any one person can contribute to such plans over his or her lifetime.

Although the amounts of your lump-sum or periodic contributions are not tax-deductible, any interest income earned on the deposited amounts will not be subject to tax while they are in the plan. If you withdraw the funds and use them for other purposes, any amounts in excess of your total contributions will be taxable in the year of withdrawal.

Any amounts left over after the funeral and cemetery expenses have been paid for will be refunded to the contributor or the contributor's estate. The tax payable on the refund is calculated with a formula that ensures that only the fund's investment income is subject to tax.

13.11 References

There is little published information on estate planning that is easily understood by the layperson. As well, every individual's case is different. Consult a qualified tax professional for advice.

Revenue Canada publishes the following, which are available (in person or by telephone request) from your nearest District Taxation Office. Forms and guides may also be available from Revenue Canada's Internet site at www.revcan.ca.

> Interpretation Bulletin IT-111R2, "Annuities purchased from charitable organizations"
>
> Interpretation Bulletin IT-210R2, "Income of deceased persons—periodic payments"
>
> Interpretation Bulletin IT-212R3, "Income of deceased persons—rights or things"
>
> Interpretation Bulletin IT-226R, "Gift to a charity of a residential interest in real property or an equitable interest in a trust"
>
> Interpretation Bulletin IT-234, "Income of deceased persons—farm crops"
>
> Interpretation Bulletin IT-244R3, "Gifts by individuals of life insurance policies as charitable donations"

Interpretation Bulletin IT-278R2, "Death of a partner or retired partner"

Interpretation Bulletin IT-288R2, "Gift of capital properties to a charity and others"

Interpretation Bulletin IT-297R2, "Gifts in kind to charity and others"

Interpretation Bulletin IT-305R4, "Testamentary spousal trusts"

Interpretation Bulletin IT-313R2, "Eligible capital property—rules where a taxpayer has ceased carrying on business or has died"

Interpretation Bulletin IT-349R3, "Intergenerational transfers of farm property on death"

Interpretation Bulletin IT-407R4, "Disposition of cultural property to designated Canadian institutions"

Interpretation Bulletin IT-427R, "Livestock of farmers"

Interpretation Bulletin IT-508R, "Death benefits"

Interpretation Bulletin IT-510, "Transfers and loans of property made after May 22, 1985 to a related minor"

Interpretation Bulletin IT-511R, "Interspousal and certain other transfers and loans of property made after May 22, 1985"

Brochure, "When You Retire"

"Preparing Returns for Deceased Persons"

"T3 Trust Income Tax and Information Return"

Dealing with Revenue Canada and Revenu Québec

■ File your return on time even if you can't pay your taxes owing (14.1.1)

■ Pay your taxes owing by April 30 even if you're filing later (14.1.1)

■ EFILE your return for a quicker refund (14.1.2)

■ Consider prepaying instalments to reduce deficient instalment charges (14.2.2)

■ Be aware of rates and compounding of interest (14.3)

■ If you know you owe interest on late or deficient instalments, think about paying an estimate with your final payment (14.3)

■ Sign a waiver only if necessary (14.4.3)

■ File a Notice of Objection to preserve your right to appeal (14.5.1)

■ When your return is reopened on reassessment, consider requesting other adjustments (14.5.1)

■ Be sure you understand the legal issues when appealing (14.5.2)

■ Consider paying the amount owing even if you are going to file an objection (14.5.4)

In this chapter we deal with the administrative side of the tax system—how tax is collected, how your return is assessed and what you can do if you disagree with Revenue Canada or Revenu Québec as to the amount of tax you owe.

14.1 Tax returns

14.1.1 General

Most individuals are required to file their federal and Québec tax returns by **April 30** each year. The deadline for individuals who have business income and their spouses (including common-law spouses) is **June 15** because of the 1995 change requiring individuals and partnerships to use a calendar year for business purposes (see 8.2.1). Even though the return may not be due until June 15, any balance of tax owing for the year is due on April 30.

If you have no tax to pay for the year (as distinguished from no balance owing in April), no return is required unless Revenue Canada or Revenu Québec requests one.

In all provinces except Québec, you file a single return with Revenue
Canada to cover both federal and provincial tax. Québec residents and
taxpayers with business income from operations in Québec must file a
Québec provincial tax return as well (see Chapter 15).

The return must be postmarked (or transmitted electronically) by the due
date. If the return is late, an automatic penalty of 5% of any tax still owing
applies. This penalty is increased by 1% of the unpaid tax for each full
month that the return is late, to a maximum of 12 months. Repeated failures
to file a return on time results in higher penalties.

File your return on time even if you can't pay your taxes owing.

To avoid the 5% penalty, you should file your return on time even if you are
not able to pay your balance owing. Interest will accrue on the unpaid
balance, but the penalty will not apply.

Pay your balance by April 30 even if you're filing later.

Conversely, if you are unable to get your return completed (or your return is
not due until June 15), but you do have a rough idea of how much tax you
owe, it is a good idea to pay that amount to Revenue Canada or Revenu
Québec by April 30. Make sure to have it credited to the correct taxation
year (and not as an instalment for the subsequent year, for example).

14.1.2 Electronic filing of tax returns (EFILE)

Revenue Canada permits most taxpayers to file their returns in electronic
form using a personal computer. The system, dubbed **EFILE**, is available
across the country, and allows authorized tax return preparers or transmitters
to file returns directly to Revenue Canada using tax return preparation and
transmission software. The Québec government has also implemented
electronic filing for Québec provincial tax returns.

Due to the technical requirements and start-up costs involved, most
individuals cannot yet file returns on their own using EFILE. However, most
professional tax return preparers now offer this service in addition to
preparing the actual tax returns. If you prepare your own return, most EFILE
preparers will charge a small fee to transmit your return.

EFILE your return for a quicker refund.

The main benefit of EFILE to a taxpayer is the ability to have the return
assessed and a refund paid in as little as two to three weeks, as opposed to a
somewhat longer wait using the conventional filing method. If you are

expecting a refund, EFILE will significantly speed up the processing of your return and the delivery of your refund cheque.

Further, no paper returns or receipts need be filed with the return. (However, receipts and other supporting documentation still must be retained for any subsequent review by Revenue Canada.) This reduces the paper burden on you, your EFILE preparer and the tax authorities.

If you are concerned about reassessment of your return down the road, filing with EFILE will normally get your return assessed sooner and start the three-year reassessment period (see 14.4.3) earlier.

14.2 Payment of tax

14.2.1 Source withholdings

Tax is withheld at source and remitted to Revenue Canada and Revenu Québec by employers and others. Tax withheld from a payment to you is considered to have been paid by you to the tax authorities, even if your employer never remits it. It is also considered to have been paid to you in the sense that it forms part of your income.

Source withholding applies to the following kinds of payments, among others:

- employment income
- pension benefits
- unemployment insurance benefits
- withdrawals from an RRSP
- annuity payments
- Old Age Security benefits
- payments of passive income to non-residents (interest, dividends, rent, royalties, etc.)
- purchase of real estate from a non-resident (unless the non-resident has a certificate from Revenue Canada and Revenu Québec, where applicable)

Note that there is no withholding of tax on interest, dividends, rent or royalties paid to Canadian residents. Self-employment income such as consulting fees (see 8.1) is also paid without source deductions.

14.2.2 Instalments

You must pay instalments if the difference between your tax payable (including provincial tax) and amounts withheld at source is more than $2,000 in both the current year and either of the two preceding years. For Québec residents, since provincial tax is not collected by Revenue Canada, the threshold is $1,200 of federal tax instead of $2,000—see 15.2.29.

Quarterly instalments are due on the 15th of March, June, September and December.

There are three possible ways to calculate your instalment obligations.

The first method is for your total instalments, paid in four equal payments, to equal the **tax owing for the year** on your sources of income from which tax is not withheld. In other words, your instalments should equal the balance owing at the end of the year.

The second method is for your quarterly instalments to equal the **tax owing on your previous year's** sources of income for which tax was not withheld. In other words, take the balance you had to pay last year after accounting for source withholdings, and pay that amount over the year in instalments.

The first method requires you to estimate your current year's income. If you guess low, you will end up not paying enough. The second method lets you use the previous year's income, but on March 15, when the first instalment is due, you might not yet have calculated your previous year's total tax. For this reason the third method was introduced.

Under the third method, your March and June instalments are each one-quarter of the total tax owing on income from which tax was not withheld for **two years ago**. Your *total* instalments for the year must still equal the total amount for one year ago, as with the second method. Therefore, the September and December instalments must be enough to reach this total. Revenue Canada and Revenu Québec will mail you a statement twice a year advising you of your quarterly instalment obligations under the third method.

Example:

Chris is self-employed as a consultant. Her 1996 tax payable (combined federal/provincial) was $20,000. Her 1997 tax payable was $24,000. She expects her total 1998 tax bill to be $27,000.

Chris should pay quarterly instalments on March 15, June 15, September 15 and December 15, 1998, totalling $24,000, her tax payable for the previous year. If she wishes, she may pay four instalments of $6,000 each.

Revenue Canada will advise Chris in February 1998, however, that her March and June payments should be $5,000 each—one-quarter of her 1996 tax payable, since her 1997 figures aren't yet available. If she makes these payments, and then pays $7,000 on each of September 15 and December 15, she will have paid the required $24,000 and met her instalment obligations under the "third method".

The $3,000 balance (assuming Chris' estimate of income for 1998 turns out to be correct) will then be due on April 30, 1999, although her return need not be filed until June 15.

Consider prepaying instalments to reduce deficient instalment charges.

If instalments are made on time and in the correct amount as per any of the three methods, no interest is payable. If instalments are not made when required or are deficient, interest is assessed at Revenue Canada's and Revenue Québec's current high "prescribed rate" (see 14.3), compounded daily.

You cannot *earn* interest by paying instalments early, but you can earn "contra-interest" at the same rate as applies to late payments, to offset interest that would otherwise be assessed on late instalments. If you've fallen behind in your instalments, consider making an extra or early payment to offset the (non-deductible) interest that will otherwise be assessed.

Example:
Chris, from the above example, does not make any instalment payments until June 15, 1998. On that day she makes a single payment of $15,000. She then makes a $2,000 payment on September 15, 1998 and a $7,000 payment on December 15, 1998.

Chris should not owe any interest on instalments, assuming the prescribed interest rate stays constant through 1998. Her June 15 payment can be thought of as three parts: $5,000 due in March, paid three months late; $5,000 paid on time; and $5,000 of the $7,000 not due until September, paid three months early. The payment that is early will generate "contra-interest" to offset the interest that Chris would otherwise have to pay due to her being late with her March payment.

For federal purposes, if the interest owing on late instalments is greater than $1,000, you may be subject to an additional penalty of up to 50% of the interest.

14.2.3 "Direct Deposit" of refunds

The federal government offers a "Direct Deposit" service whereby tax refunds, GST Credits and Child Tax Benefit payments can be deposited directly into your account at any financial institution in Canada. To take advantage of this service, which saves the time it takes to print and mail the cheques and avoids the problem of cheques lost in the mail, complete form T1-DD if you are filing a paper return or form T183 if you are filing electronically. For other government payments, such as monthly Old Age Security or Canada Pension Plan payments, contact your financial institution for the appropriate forms.

14.3 Interest

Interest that you owe on late payments of federal tax and instalments and on refunds is calculated at a prescribed rate, which varies quarterly based on the Bank of Canada rate. The new rate for each quarter is announced by Revenue Canada in a news release about three weeks before the quarter begins.

Be aware of rates and compounding of interest.

There are three different "prescribed" interest rates each quarter. The lowest rate, which is roughly the Bank of Canada rate for the previous quarter, applies for purposes of applying the **attribution rules** (see 4.2.2) and the **employee and shareholder loan** rules (see 7.3 and 9.2.6). The middle rate, which is two percentage points higher, applies to **refunds** paid by Revenue Canada. The highest rate, which is a further two points higher, applies to **late payments of tax and instalments** owing by taxpayers.

Although the rate is expressed as an annual rate, it is in fact **compounded daily**, so the effective rate is somewhat higher than shown. A 10% interest rate, for example, is equivalent to a rate of about 10.52% in simple annual interest.

Interest that you owe on late payments runs from when the payment was due. Interest on refunds generally runs from 45 days after the due date for the return, or from the day on which you file your return, whichever is later. However, if you have a June 15 filing deadline because you have self-employment income (see 8.2.1), interest will not be paid until 45 days after April 30 or 45 days after the date that the return is actually filed, whichever is later.

Interest that you are required to pay to Revenue Canada, such as on late payments of tax or instalments, is not deductible.

Interest paid to you on a refund is taxable in the year in which you receive it. Thus, if you file your 1997 return when it is due in April 1998 and receive a refund in August, the interest from June 14 included in that cheque must be reported on your 1998 return.

If you know you owe interest on late or deficient instalments, think about paying an estimate with your final payment.

Since interest paid to Revenue Canada is not deductible, but interest you receive is taxable, the interest you pay costs up to twice as much. For example, if you receive $200 in interest on your 1996 refund, but are assessed $200 in interest owing on your 1997 return, and are in a 41% tax bracket, you are out of pocket $82, which is the tax owing on the refund.

If you have tax owing at April 30 and you know interest will be charged because of late or deficient instalment payments, consider paying an estimate of the interest with your April 30 payment to stop any further interest from accruing.

The federal prescribed interest rates for the last few quarters to time of writing are as follows:

Quarter	Low Rate	Middle Rate	High Rate
Oct.-Dec. 1996	5%	7%	9%
Jan.-March 1997	4%	6%	8%
April-June 1997	3%	5%	7%
July-Sept. 1997	4%	6%	8%

As mentioned above, the high rate applies to late tax and instalment payments and the middle rate to refunds. The low rate applies for the purposes of the attribution rules and shareholder and employee loans.

For Québec purposes, the low rate is the same as the federal rate and the middle rate is slightly lower (so less interest is paid to you on refunds). For late taxes, the Québec high rate is set 1% higher than the federal rate, but a whopping 10% higher for late Québec tax instalments.

14.4 Assessment, audit and reassessment

14.4.1 "Quick" assessment

When you file a conventional (paper) return, it is processed over a period of typically three to six weeks, after which you receive a "Notice of Assessment" and any refund owing to you. The processing includes a review of the numbers on your return to make sure they are consistent (e.g., that your arithmetic is correct and that any numbers that need to be supported by receipts or information slips are consistent with them).

Most EFILE users can expect their returns to be assessed in two to three weeks.

The assessment (whether the return is filed on paper or with EFILE) is normally not based on any investigation beyond what is on your return. It is sometimes referred to as a "quick assessment". The fact that a particular claim is allowed at this point does not mean that Revenue Canada or Revenu Québec is "letting" you claim it; it merely means that Revenue Canada has not addressed the issue in any detail.

For a partnership, the tax authorities may issue a **determination** of the partnership's income or loss, which is effectively an assessment of each partner's portion of the income or loss. See 8.3.6.

14.4.2 Audit

Some time after the initial assessment, your return may be selected for **audit**. Most audits of individual taxpayers (as opposed to corporations) are "desk audits", in which the auditor will ask you to supply supporting material for claims you have made. Some audits are "field audits", in which the auditor will come to your place of business to look at your records.

If you use EFILE, you will not have to file any receipts with your return. However, Revenue Canada or Revenu Québec may later "spot-check" your return to verify certain claims, such as donations, RRSP contributions or tuition fees. This is normally just a formality, designed to maintain the integrity of the EFILE system.

You should be aware of your rights on an audit. The auditor is not entitled to go on a "fishing expedition" through your books. He or she may request specific information, and you may ask why that information is needed. You may wish assistance from your professional advisors in dealing with the auditor, if you anticipate problems.

If you have not engaged in tax evasion, an audit should not normally be cause for concern.

14.4.3 Reassessment

If the audit (or an audit of another taxpayer) turns up an indication that your tax payable should be other than what was initially assessed, Revenue Canada will issue a **reassessment**. If the reassessment results in more tax payable by you, this will not normally be done without you first being consulted and given an opportunity to explain your position.

A reassessment cannot normally be issued more than three years after the date of the original assessment. However, in cases of fraud, or misrepresentation attributable to "neglect, carelessness or wilful default", the reassessment may be issued at any time.

Sign a waiver only if necessary.

There are several other situations where the three-year limitation does not apply. The most important is where you have filed a **waiver**. The waiver, which is directed to a specific issue that is in dispute, will allow Revenue Canada to reassess you on that issue at any time. You can revoke a waiver on six months' notice to Revenue Canada. If you are asked by a Revenue Canada auditor to sign a waiver, consider the request carefully and obtain professional advice before agreeing.

First, consider the auditor's alternative if you do not sign the waiver. You are under no obligation to file a waiver simply to be "nice". If the three-year reassessment period is about to expire, and the auditor does not yet have enough information to justify a reassessment, it may be to your advantage not to sign the waiver. Bear in mind that a reassessment normally takes some time to work its way through Revenue Canada's internal system, although it can be rushed through in a couple of days in extreme cases.

Second, make sure that the waiver is very specific and waives the three-year period only in respect of the specific issues that are under investigation or dispute. A waiver covering your entire return in respect of a given taxation year would not be appropriate.

Similar rules apply for Québec tax purposes.

14.5 Objections and appeals

14.5.1 Notice of Objection

If you cannot come to an understanding with the auditor and a reassessment is issued, or if you disagree with the original assessment, you may file a **Notice of Objection**. This is done by writing to the Chief of Appeals of your local district taxation office. It begins the formal administrative appeal process. The notice should set out the specific issue(s) that you are objecting to.

When you file a Notice of Objection, your objection is reviewed by an Appeals Officer within Revenue Canada. The Appeals Officer is independent of the Audit Branch, and he or she should conduct the review impartially and objectively.

File a Notice of Objection to preserve your right to appeal.

To be valid, a Notice of Objection must be filed either within 90 days of the date of the assessment or reassessment to which you are objecting, or within one year of the original due date for the return. For example, an objection to an assessment of your 1996 return would have to be filed by April 30, 1998 or 90 days after the (re)assessment you are objecting to, whichever is later. The same deadlines apply for Québec purposes.

Filing your Notice of Objection before the deadline is vital—even if you are in the midst of discussions with Revenue Canada authorities, and even if you have been assured that a reassessment in your favour will be issued. Otherwise your right to appeal vanishes, and any reassessment will be entirely up to Revenue Canada.

If the period for objecting has expired, you may request a reassessment of your return. In this case, you have no legal right to force a reassessment, but in many cases the reassessment will be issued anyway. Revenue Canada will allow a reassessment of a return for any year back to 1985, if the request meets the guidelines issued under the government's "Fairness Package".

In some cases you can also apply to Revenue Canada or the Tax Court of Canada for extension of the time for filing a Notice of Objection.

When your return is reopened on reassessment, consider requesting other adjustments.

If Revenue Canada issues you a routine reassessment for some reason after your own right to force a reconsideration of your return has expired, bear in mind that the reassessment reopens your return for 90 days. If this happens and there are other issues that you want to contest or change, you can raise them within the 90-day period and file a Notice of Objection to preserve your rights of appeal. However, you cannot do this where the return was reopened for any of a number of special reasons (such as a carryback of losses from a later year).

Similar rules and deadlines apply for Québec tax purposes.

14.5.2 **Appeal to the Tax Court**

The Appeals Officer is normally your last level of appeal within Revenue Canada. A further appeal is available to the **Tax Court of Canada** (or the Court of Québec if Québec taxes are in dispute).

You have a choice between the Court's "informal" and "general" procedures for making an appeal.

The **general procedure** normally requires you to retain a lawyer. It is similar to higher court proceedings in provincial courts. If the amount of tax in dispute for any one taxation year is more than $12,000 of federal tax (about $19,000 including provincial tax other than Québec tax), you must follow the general procedure. In certain "test cases", Revenue Canada may also force a case below the threshold into the general procedure, in which case Revenue Canada will be required to reimburse you for most or all of your legal fees.

The **informal procedure**, as its name suggests, is much less complicated. You may appear on your own, or have someone else (such as a lawyer, accountant, consultant or friend) there to assist you. No specific form needs to be filed to launch the appeal. The formal rules of evidence that normally apply to court proceedings will not necessarily apply. Under the informal procedure, your case will normally be heard fairly quickly, and a judgment given within a year of when you first file the appeal. The decision given is not binding as a precedent for future cases, whether yours or another taxpayer's.

Be sure you understand the legal issues when appealing.

If you are taking an appeal to the Tax Court of Canada, make sure you understand the legal issues involved. Even if you wish to represent yourself or be represented by a friend or relative, consult with a qualified tax professional before the appeal. Many issues in tax law have answers on which all the experts (and the judge!) will agree, yet which will not be obvious to the non-expert.

14.5.3 Appeal beyond the Tax Court

A decision of the Tax Court of Canada under its informal procedure can be appealed, on a question of law only, in the form of a "judicial review" by the **Federal Court of Appeal**. A decision under the general procedure can be appealed directly to the Federal Court of Appeal. In either case you would need a lawyer for such an appeal, which would typically take about two years from time of filing until judgment is given. Court of Québec decisions may be appealed to the Québec Court of Appeal.

Once a decision is given by the federal or Québec appeals courts, either you or the tax authority may seek "leave to appeal" from the Supreme Court of Canada. Only if a panel of three justices of the Supreme Court grant the application for leave to appeal can an appeal be made. The Supreme Court rarely grants leave to appeal in tax cases; typically only three or four tax cases a year reach the Supreme Court.

14.5.4 Amounts in dispute—should you pay up?

Suppose you are contesting an amount of $5,000, but you are not sure whether you will win or not. Although you have filed a Notice of Objection or perhaps an appeal, you are receiving notices from Revenue Canada Collections asking you to pay even though Revenue Canada cannot start collection action as long as you have an objection or appeal outstanding.

Consider paying the amount owing even if you're filing an objection.

It may be a good idea to pay the balance anyway. The interest rate charged on late payments (see 14.3) is likely higher than the rate you would otherwise earn with your money, or higher than the rate at which you must borrow from the bank. If you ultimately succeed in your appeal, you will recover all the funds you paid, plus interest (at the middle rate shown in 14.3).

Note also that when you receive a statement from Revenue Canada, you normally have 20 days to pay without further interest charges applying. If you are going to have to pay anyway, you may as well take advantage of this "interest-free" period and pay the balance on the 20th day.

Taxpayers sometimes think they should not pay an amount in dispute because "that would be an admission of guilt", or because Revenue Canada would then have no incentive to settle the case. Such reasoning is misplaced. You cannot prejudice your case by paying the tax. The determination as to your legal rights is not affected by whether or not the tax has been paid.

The only circumstance where you are better not to have paid your account is where you are applying for a waiver of interest and penalty, at Revenue Canada's discretion, on the grounds of "inability to pay". Once you have paid, it is difficult to argue that you cannot find the money to pay your tax bill and require a waiver of interest to be able to meet the requested payments.

14.6 References

The following publications can be obtained (in person or by telephone request) from your nearest Revenue Canada District Taxation Office. Forms and guides may also be available from Revenue Canada's Internet site at www.revcan.ca.

Interpretation Bulletin IT-241, "Reassessments made after the four-year limit"

Information Circular 75-7R3, "Reassessment of a return of income"

Information Circular 92-2, "Guidelines for cancellation and waiver of interest and penalties"

Information Circular 92-3, "Guidelines for refunds beyond the normal three-year period"

Form T1, "General individual income tax return"

Form T1-DD, "Direct deposit request form for individuals"

Form T183, "Information return for electronic filing"

Form T400A, "Notice of objection"

Form T1013, "Consent Form"

Form T2029, "Waiver in respect of the normal reassessment period"

Brochure, "Electronic Filing (EFILE)—Questions and Answers"

Brochure, "Now That You Have Used EFILE..."

Brochure, "Your Appeal Rights: Under the *Income Tax Act*"

If you live in Québec

- Be aware of differences between the tax systems (15.2)
- Claim a refundable credit if you adopt a child (15.2.4)
- Claim the credit for housing "direct ascendants" (15.2.7)
- Withdraw your RHOSP funds to buy a home or furniture or for another qualifying purpose before the year 2000 (15.2.15)
- Foreign researchers and trainers, sailors and international financial centre employees—take a tax holiday in Québec (15.2.24)
- Boost your Québec business entertainment expense deduction by subscribing to eligible Québec cultural performances (15.2.25)
- Invest in the FSTQ or the Fondaction and transfer the shares to your RRSP (15.3.5)

Québec is different from all other provinces in that it does not piggy-back on the federal system of personal taxation. Québec residents must file a separate tax return. The Québec *Taxation Act (Loi sur les impôts)* is largely modelled on the federal *Income Tax Act*, but there are a number of differences. We review those in 15.2. In 15.3 we discuss the incentive plans that are unique to Québec. These plans—QSSP, QBIC (or SPEQ), CIP (or RIC), FSTQ and others—form a veritable alphabet soup of incentives to investment in various kinds of Québec activities.

15.1 Québec income tax rates

Québec's 1997 budget announced major reforms to the province's personal tax system that will take effect in 1998. These changes include paring down the number of tax brackets, eliminating the province's surtaxes, increasing the rate of refundable tax credits, and introducing an optional, simplified method of calculating your Québec tax. The rules in effect for 1997 are discussed in 15.1.1. Changes resulting from Québec's personal tax reform are discussed in 15.1.2 and 15.1.3.

15.1.1 1997 Québec tax rates

Québec's 1997 provincial income tax rates are listed in Appendix III. For 1997, there is an **income tax reduction** for low and middle-income taxpayers. This is the reverse of a surtax (discussed in 2.1.2). If tax payable after deducting the non-refundable tax credits is less than $10,000, Québec tax is reduced by an amount equal to 2% of the difference. Thus, for someone whose basic Québec tax is $1,000, the reduction is

2% of $9,000, or $180, while for someone with basic Québec tax of $10,000 or more there is no reduction.

Federal tax is reduced by 16.5% of basic federal tax for Québec residents, with the result that the top *federal* marginal tax rate for Québec residents is 26.5% rather than 31.3% (including surtaxes). The combined effect of federal tax, federal surtax and Québec tax rates is provided in Appendix III.

15.1.2 Québec 1998 tax and non-refundable tax credit rates

As a result of Québec's personal tax reform initiative (see 15.1), as of 1998 the province will only have three tax brackets, instead of the current five. Both of Québec's 5% surtaxes and the 2% income tax reduction are also being eliminated. The current and the new tax brackets are:

Taxable Income	1997*	1998 and later years
$0 – $7,000	16%	20%
$7,000 – $14,000	19%	20%
$14,000 – $23,000	21%	20%
$23,000 – $25,000	23%	20%
$25,000 – $50,000	23%	23%
over $50,000	24%	26%

* As discussed above, for 1997, a 5% surtax applies to Quebec tax over $5,000 plus an additional surtax of 5% on Quebec tax over $10,000. However, a tax reduction is available equal to 2% of the difference between $10,000 and Quebec tax payable after deducting non-refundable tax credits.

All of Québec's non-refundable tax credits will be worth 23% of the related amounts in 1998, instead of the 20% rate for 1997 and earlier years.

15.1.3 Québec's new optional simplified tax filing system

When you file your 1998 Québec tax return, if you are a Québec resident on December 31 of that year, you will be able to choose between the province's general tax filing system and a new simplified system. Obviously, your choice will depend on which system will give you the greater tax savings, so you will need to estimate your taxes payable under both systems.

Although the province has not released detailed legislation, based on information available at the time of writing, the main features of the simplified system will be as follows:

■ A series of Québec deductions and non-refundable tax credits will be replaced by a single, lump-sum tax credit of $2,350 per person. Refundable credits will be treated the same way under both systems. You will be able to transfer the lump-sum credit to your spouse, which may be advantageous in many cases since most of the deductions and credits being replaced are not currently transferable. (See 2.1.3 for some planning ideas involving the transfer of credits.)

▪ If you and your spouse both opt to use the simplified system, the two of you can elect to file a joint Québec tax return.

▪ You will also be able to transfer to your spouse other non-refundable credits that are not replaced by the lump-sum amount whether you file jointly or separately under the simplified system. These credits, which are also transferable under the general system, include the basic personal amount of $5,900, the credits for dependants, the age and retirement income credits and the charitable donations credit.

Whether you stand to benefit under the simplified system will depend on whether the lump-sum amount under the new system is greater than the sum of the replaced deductions and non-refundable credits. Québec's 1998 tax return package will include a workchart for figuring out your taxes under both systems. If you choose to file your return using the general system, the Québec government says it will calculate your taxes payable under both systems and return any additional tax savings that you would have obtained by following the simplified system.

15.2 Differences from federal tax

In this section we highlight the principal differences between Québec and federal tax law that affect personal tax. We present the topics in approximately the same order as the relevant material appears in the rest of the book.

Be aware of differences between the federal and Québec tax systems.

You should review the differences between the federal and the Québec income tax systems, as highlighted below. Be cautious of the possible Québec tax implications of any step you take for federal tax purposes.

15.2.1 If you live alone or alone with children

In addition to credits for oneself and various types of dependants, analogous to those discussed in 2.2, Québec allows a non-refundable tax credit of $210 for a "person living alone". To qualify, you must be living by yourself for the entire calendar year in a self-contained home (i.e., not with a spouse or other domestic partner, roommate, housemate, etc.), or with no one other than dependent children whom you claim for tax purposes, and you must attach to your tax return a real estate tax certificate (Relevé 4), a copy of your property tax bills, or Form TP-752.0.1.h-V ("Declaration concerning the Maintenance of a Self-Contained Domestic Establishment"). If you are separated but you support your spouse, you cannot claim this credit;

however, if you pay only alimony which you deduct on your tax return, you and your spouse can both claim the credit.

Eligibility for this credit is subject to an income test. For 1997 and later years, the credit is reduced by 15% (up from 7.5% in 1996) of Québec net income over $26,000, so that the credit is fully eliminated if your net income is $33,000 or more in that year.

Starting in 1998, the credit will be based on the combined income of you and your spouse, or "family net income." Also, the $26,000 income test will be used to reduce the tax credit for persons living alone, the Québec age credit, and the Québec retirement income credit (see 15.2.6). Your amounts eligible for claiming all three of these credits will be totalled and then reduced by $26,000 (before 1998, the $26,000 income test reduced each credit separately). The tax credit's rate will increase to 23% in 1998, so the maximum credit for persons living alone will be worth $242 (up from $210 in 1997).

15.2.2 Child care expenses

There are a number of differences between the federal rules discussed in 2.3.2 and the Québec rules. First, receipts for the child care expenses must be attached to the Québec tax return. For federal tax purposes, Revenue Canada's administrative policy is that they need only be kept on file.

Second, child care expenses give rise to a refundable **credit** in Québec instead of a deduction. (See 2.1.2 for discussion of refundable credits and the difference between a deduction and a credit.) The credit is on a sliding scale, worth 75% of the expenses for the poorest families, down to 26.4% for families with adjusted family incomes of about $48,000 or more. Thus, instead of being more valuable to higher-income families as is the federal deduction, the Québec credit for child care expenses is more valuable to lower-income families, such as where both parents are attending school full-time.

Third, in addition to the other special circumstances where the lower-income spouse is not expected to care for the children (see 2.3.2), you do not have to take into account the lower-income spouse's "earned income" for periods in which he or she is operating a business that generates a loss or low profits. As with the other situations, the amount of child care expenses that the higher-income spouse can claim is limited to $150 per week for each child under 7 or for each child of any age suffering from an impairment, and $90 per week for each child aged 7 to 16.

Finally, unlike the federal rules, Québec disregards any income earned by the child in determining whether child care expenses are eligible.

Example:

Nicole and Daniel have two pre-school children. In 1997 Daniel earns $70,000, and Nicole earns $8,000 working part-time. They pay $5,500 in day care, required to enable them both to work.

For federal purposes, Nicole can claim the least of (a) the amount paid—$5,500; (b) $5,000 per child—$10,000; and (c) two-thirds of her earned income—$5,333. She can thus deduct $5,333 from income.

For Québec purposes, Nicole's credit will be based on the least of (a) the amount paid—$5,500; (b) $5,000 per child—$10,000; and (c) 100% of Nicole's earned income—$8,000. Since Nicole's and Daniel's combined work income is more than $48,000, the credit is thus 26.4% of $5,500, or $1,452.

Child care expenses eligible for the Québec credit will not include the $5 per day contribution that has to be paid by parents of children attending the province's new early childhood centres.

15.2.3 Allowances for children

The federal Child Tax Benefit described in 2.3.1 replaced the former dependent child credit and family allowance payments, as well as the former federal Child Tax Credit. Québec continues to offer a non-refundable credit for dependent children of $520 ($598 in 1998) for your first child and $480 ($552 in 1998) for each other child.

Before September 1997, Québec also provided a provincial family allowance payment, a supplementary allowance for children under six, as well as an allowance for newborn children. As of September 1, 1997, Québec proposes to replace these allowances with a new Québec integrated family allowance which varies depending on family situation and income. Québec residents may receive the new allowance in addition to the federal Child Tax Benefit.

The allowance for newborns remains available for children born before October 1, 1997. This allowance provides $500 for the first child born or adopted, $1,000 for the second child in the family, and $8,000 for the third and each subsequent child. The $500 is paid shortly after birth. The $1,000 is paid in two instalments: one when the child is born and one on the child's first birthday. The $8,000 is paid over five years, in 20 quarterly instalments of $400 each following the child's birth.

As well, Québec's "Maternity Benefit Program" will pay a $360 supplement to a woman who leaves work temporarily to have a child, as long as her gross family income is less than $55,000. This supplement is taxable for both federal and Québec purposes.

15.2.4 Adoption expenses

Claim a refundable tax credit if you adopt a child.

Québec offers a refundable credit for **adoption expenses** to help finance the expenses associated with adopting children from overseas, but is available even for local adoptions. The credit is 20% of up to $10,000 in expenses paid by you, or by you and your spouse, to a maximum $2,000 credit per child. Qualifying expenses include court fees, legal fees, travelling and translation expenses (for adoptions from other countries), and fees charged by approved agencies.

Since the credit is refundable, it is available even if you have no tax to pay for the year. You will have to keep records of your expenses and claim only those that qualify.

15.2.5 **Tuition fees**

Tuition fees, which generate non-refundable credits under the federal system (see 2.4), were a *deduction* for the student for Québec tax purposes until 1996. Starting in 1997, the deduction is converted to a 20% non-refundable credit (23% in 1998).

Unlike the federal government, Québec does not allow the transfer of undeducted tuition fees to the parent. The province has decided to follow the federal lead in allowing unused tuition fees to be carried forward indefinitely as of 1997 and applied against income in later years.

Québec does not have a credit to parallel the federal education amount. Instead, Québec increases the non-refundable credit for dependent children or other dependants (see 15.2.3) by $330 per semester (for up to two semesters) if the dependant is a full-time student at a post-secondary institution. Starting in 1998, the credit will increase to $380 per semester.

15.2.6 **Seniors**

Québec offers a 20% non-refundable tax credit (23% in 1998) similar to the federal credit for persons who are 65 and older (see 2.5.1). The Québec credit is worth up to $440 ($506 in 1998). Like the federal credit, the Québec credit is reduced or eliminated for higher-income taxpayers. If you are 65 or older and your net income is $26,000 or more, the age credit is reduced by 15% for each dollar over $26,000. The same rules apply to the amount allowed for Québec's pension income tax credit.

Starting in 1998, both of these credits will be reduced if your Québec family income (the combined income of both spouses) is more than $26,000. The amounts available for claiming each of these credits and the credit for persons living alone will be added together and then reduced by 15% of your family income over that amount (before 1998, the amount is applied to reduce each credit individually).

In 1994, Québec announced that a new refundable tax credit would be available for seniors who hire domestic employees. The province appears to have abandoned this idea in favour of a financial assistance program for domestic help services. This program, to be administered by the ministère de la Santé et des Services sociaux du Québec, will not be restricted to seniors only. To help seniors with the paperwork involved in hiring and remunerating domestic help, Québec also expects to establish a "service employment paycheque" system, although details of this system have not been announced at the time of writing.

Adults housing "direct ascendants"

Claim the credit for housing "direct ascendants".

Québec provides a refundable tax credit of $550 for an adult taxpayer who lives with his or her parent, grandparent or great-grandparent (including in-laws). Since the credit is refundable, it is available even if you have no tax to pay for the year.

To claim the credit, your "ascendant" must be 70 or older (or 60 or older and disabled), but there is no requirement that the "ascendant" be financially dependent on the taxpayer or be in a low-income bracket. (In fact, the "ascendant" could be financially supporting the taxpayer who makes the claim. However, the taxpayer making the claim must own or rent the home.) This measure is designed to encourage family support for the elderly.

15.2.8 Legal fees for establishing support payments

Under the federal system, legal fees to enforce payment of taxable amounts of alimony or maintenance (support) owing are deductible, but not fees paid to establish a right to alimony or maintenance (see 2.9.2). Nor are fees deductible where they are paid in connection with a court application to increase or decrease such payments. Québec taxation is different, in that fees paid in connection with a court application to increase or decrease the level of support are deductible.

15.2.9 Charitable donations

Québec provides a 20% credit for charitable donations, in addition to the 17%/29% federal credit discussed in 2.8.1. Québec has decided not to follow the federal government's lead in raising the charitable donations limits, so the amount of donations you can claim in a year on your Québec return may not be over 20% of your Québec net income. The province has also decided not to reduce the income inclusion rate for capital gains arising from gifts of publicly traded securities and other appreciable property (see 13.7).

For Québec purposes there is a special restriction on the credit for gifts of **works of art** made after May 9, 1995. The valuation of the gift is limited to the price the charity receives when it sells the art. Furthermore, the credit can only be claimed (by the donor) if the charity sells the art within the next five years of accepting the donation. This rule does not apply to donations to certain museums and galleries, recognized artistic organizations, governments or municipalities.

This restriction was designed to curb ongoing abuses where individuals would obtain appraisals entitling them to value their donations at far higher amounts than can actually be obtained by the charity to whom the art is donated. (Typically, the charity in such cases sells the art at an auction, and the entire valuation, donation and auction process is organized for the charity by an art dealer or auctioneer.)

15.2.10   Medical expenses

As of 1997, the Québec credit for medical expenses is substantially different—and much less generous— than it was in past years. Before 1997, the credit was the same as the federal credit but calculated at the rate of 20% instead of the federal rate of 17%.

Similar to the federal credit (see 2.8.2), allowable medical expenses are reduced by 3% of Québec net income, but, as of 1997, the maximum reduction is no longer capped at $1,614. Further, the net income amount is now based on the combined income of *both* spouses. As a result, many Québec residents will no longer be eligible for the credit.

Québec has also introduced a refundable tax credit for medical expenses similar to the new-federal medical expense supplement for low-income workers discussed in 2.8.2. For Québec purposes, the credit is reduced by 5% of your net family income over $17,500 (instead of the $16,069 threshold for claiming the federal supplement).

The list of allowable expenses is generally identical to the federal list. In addition, however, if you (or a dependant) require long-term care that can only be provided in a Québec health establishment located 250 km or more from your residence, your moving expenses will be allowed as medical expenses by Québec. For this purpose, "moving expenses" are those listed in 2.9.1.

Also, as noted in 15.2.18 below, the taxable benefit for employer-paid private health insurance premiums also qualifies as a medical expense for Québec purposes.

15.2.11   Credit for disabled persons

Québec offers a non-refundable tax credit for persons with severe and prolonged physical or mental impairment. The Québec credit is similar to the federal credit discussed at 2.6.1 and you must meet essentially the same criteria to be eligible. To claim the Québec credit for the first time, you must file form TP-752.0.14-V with your Québec tax return for that year. The maximum amount available for the credit is $2,200, which means it may be worth up to $440 to you (rising to $506 in 1998). If you have a dependent child who suffers from an impairment, your child's unused disability credit can be transferred to your Québec return.

15.2.12   Political contributions

As noted in 2.8.3, many provinces provide credits for contributions to provincial political parties, riding associations and election candidates. In Québec's case, the credit is 75% of the first $200 of such contributions and 50% of the next $200, as a credit against Québec tax. The maximum credit is $250.

15.2.13   Québec Sales Tax Credit

Québec offers a sales tax refund similar to the GST Credit available to low-income families (see 2.10.3). The refund is $104 for you and $104 for your spouse, plus an extra $53 if you live alone or with only dependants. If you have dependants, an additional $21 ($31 in 1996) is available for each dependant plus an additional $12 ($18 in 1996) for the first child of a single-parent family. The additional amounts for dependants are being phased out and will be incorporated with the province's new integrated child allowance (see 15.2.3) as of 1998. The basic refund for adults will rise to $154 in 1998 and the additional amount for persons living alone will rise to $103.

The total credit is reduced by 3% of you and your spouse's combined net income. For 1997, the family net income amount is then subject to various adjustments; for 1998 and later years, the reduction will apply to family net income in excess of $26,000. The credit is refundable and is claimed on your Québec tax return.

Québec also offers a sales tax rebate that parallels the GST rebate for employees (see 7.11) and partners (see 8.3.7).

15.2.14   Real estate tax refund

You may be entitled to a refund of a portion of the property taxes that apply on your dwelling. If you own the property, taxes eligible for the refund include school, water and municipal taxes. If you rent, the eligible amount is indicated on the Relevé 4 supplied to you by your landlord each year. The credit is claimed on your Québec tax return.

The eligible property tax is reduced by $430 for each spouse. The refund is 40% of this amount, to a maximum of $514, minus 3% of you and your spouse's combined net income, subject to various adjustments. Since it is refundable, the real estate tax refund is paid to you even if you have no Québec tax to pay for the year.

15.2.15   Registered Home Ownership Savings Plans ("RHOSPs")

RHOSPs were a popular savings plan until 1985, when they were abolished under the federal tax system. Before 1985, contributions to an RHOSP could be deducted (subject to certain dollar limits), and the withdrawals were not taxed at all provided the funds were used to purchase a first home. In its 1996 budget, Québec announced that the province will be eliminating RHOSPs by the year 2000.

When RHOSPs were abolished federally, the federal rules were changed to allow withdrawals from all existing plans without paying any federal tax, so most Canadians simply withdrew their RHOSP funds. However, since Québec did not follow this federal change at the time, it is possible that you may still have funds in an RHOSP—if so, you have until December 31, 1999 to use the funds or the value of the funds will be taxable at that time.

In order to withdraw funds without paying Québec tax, the funds withdrawn must be spent on the purchase of a home or new household furnishings (residential furniture and major appliances). As of May 10, 1996, Québec also allows you to withdraw RHOSP funds for eligible renovation work to a home you own and occupy as long as the work is carried out by a Québec licensed contractor.

Withdraw your RHOSP funds for a qualifying purpose before the year 2000.

If you still have an RHOSP, you should consider using up the funds on your next home purchase, on qualifying renovations to your current home, or on a shopping spree for new furniture and appliances before the end of 1999. Otherwise, the remaining balance will be taxable in Québec at that time.

No matter when in the year you withdraw the funds, you have until 60 days after the end of the year to take delivery of the goods or have the renovation work completed and paid for without triggering tax on the RHOSP withdrawal.

If you withdraw funds from an RHOSP account to make an eligible purchase, you should file Form TP-955-V ("Statement of the use of funds from a Registered Home Ownership Savings Plan") with your income tax return for the year of the withdrawal to ensure that the amount withdrawn is not included in your income for Québec tax purposes.

15.2.16   "First Home" refundable tax credit

If you purchased a new or used home in Québec between December 20, 1994 and January 1, 1996, you may be eligible for the "Premier Toit" ("First Home") refundable tax credit. This credit is worth up to 20% of the first two years of mortgage interest on your new home to a maximum credit of $2,000 per year, or 10% of the renovation costs of your resale home to a maximum credit of $3,000.

Although the credit is no longer available for purchases in 1996 or later (except for condominium units acquired by June 30, 1996 if the offer to purchase was accepted by December 31, 1995), the tax benefits of this program may still be available if you made a qualifying purchase within the above-noted timeframe. Because renovation work must be completed within one year of the home's acquisition, the tax credit for renovation work will not be available after 1996. However, in some cases, availability of the credit for mortgage interest could extend beyond 1997.

To be eligible for the credit, you had to be a "first-time" buyer, a term which is given the same meaning as under the Home Buyers' Plan (see 3.3.6). In general, you must not have owned a home in the year prior to the purchase or during the four previous calendar years. The home also had to meet a number of criteria, including the requirement that the home be used as a principal residence within six months of its acquisition.

15.2.17 Cumulative net investment loss

As we saw in 5.4.3, investment expenses and tax shelter write-offs create a cumulative net investment loss ("CNIL"), which reduces your ability to claim the $500,000 capital gains exemption.

For Québec tax purposes, the special investment incentives, which we will discuss in 15.3, are *not* included in your CNIL calculation. That is, they will not affect your ability to claim the capital gains exemption on your Québec tax return.

The incentives in question are the deductions you claim under the Québec Stock Savings Plan, the Cooperative Investment Plan, Québec Business Investment Companies, certain scientific research and development expenses, certified Québec film and television productions, and resource exploration expenses incurred in Québec. These collectively form the "strategic economic investment account", or "compte d'investissements stratégiques pour l'économie" ("CISE").

15.2.18 Employer-paid private health insurance

As we saw in 7.1.1, employer contributions to a private health services plan are non-taxable employee benefits for federal purposes. These contributions are, however, taxable for Québec tax purposes. Thus, if your employer pays for your group sickness, drug or dental plan, the value of the benefit will be included in your employment income on your Relevé 1 and must be reported on your Québec tax return, even though it does not appear on your T4 for federal income tax purposes. As a result, employer health plan contributions will normally make your employment income for Québec tax purposes higher than it is for federal purposes. You (or your spouse) can claim the taxable benefit as a medical expense on your Québec tax return.

15.2.19 Moving allowances

Moving allowances are generally taxable for federal purposes while employer reimbursements of moving expenses are generally not taxable (see 7.1). The Québec government has decided that these amounts should not be treated differently since the distinction is often merely in the method of compensation. As a result, starting in 1997, if you are relocated by your employer and receive a moving allowance, you do not have to include in your Québec income an amount equal to two weeks' worth of your salary (based on your new salary after your relocation).

15.2.20 Union and professional dues

Starting in 1997, union and professional dues (excluding professional insurance), which are deductible for federal tax purposes (see 7.10.5), are no longer deductible on your Québec tax return. Instead, these and similar payments will entitle you to a 20% tax credit (23% in 1998). This rule applies to employees and self-employed individuals alike. If you are self-employed and you are used to deducting your professional dues in calculating your Québec self-employment income, as of 1997, you will have to add the dues back to your self-employment income and claim the corresponding credit instead.

15.2.21 Safety deposit box rental fees

Starting in 1998, safety deposit box rental fees will no longer be deductible from business or property income for Québec purposes.

15.2.22 Artists' deduction from copyright income

If you are a painter, writer, performer or other artist, a special deduction is available that effectively exempts from Québec tax a portion of your income from your original copyrights. The deduction is limited to $15,000 a year, and is reduced by 1.5 times the amount of the eligible copyright income over $20,000. Thus, it is effectively eliminated for artists who earn over $30,000 in copyright income. To be eligible for this credit, you must be eligible for membership in one of several recognized associations of artists.

15.2.23 Overseas employment tax deduction

We discussed the federal overseas employment tax credit in 7.9. The Québec rules accomplish essentially the same goals of not taxing certain income earned while working on projects outside Canada, but do so rather differently.

First, the Québec system allows the overseas income as a deduction, rather than allowing a tax credit for a percentage of it. For each consecutive 30-day period that the employee works outside Canada on a qualified project, 1/12 of the income earned abroad in the year can be deducted.

Second, foreign living allowances are completely tax exempt, provided they do not exceed one-half of the income earned abroad.

Third, the recognized activities for purposes of the deduction are broader than under the federal system. As well as the projects that qualify for federal purposes, the installation of computer or office automation systems or data communications systems, and the provision of scientific and technical services, entitle you to the deduction for Québec purposes.

15.2.24 Tax holidays for researchers, trainers, sailors and International Financial Centre ("IFC") employees

Québec offers "**tax holidays**", or exemptions from Québec income tax for certain individuals, to promote employment and business activity in selected industries.

Foreign researchers and trainers , sailors and IFC employees—take a tax holiday in Québec.

If you are a **foreign researcher** who works in Québec on an eligible research and development project and certain other conditions are met, you may be able to deduct, for Québec tax purposes, all of your employment income for your first two years on the project. In 1997, Québec announced that a similar credit will be available to **foreign trainers** employed by corporations carrying on business in Information Technology Development Centres.

A similar two-year Québec tax holiday may be available in some cases if you are a non-resident of Québec who is a **specialist in international financial transactions** and you work in Québec for an IFC. After your first two years, one-third of your employment income from the IFC may be exempt from Québec tax.

Some Québec **sailors** who are assigned to qualifying international freighters for at least 30 consecutive days do not have to pay Québec income tax on their employment income earned after August 31, 1996. To be eligible for this tax holiday, the shipowner must be a Canadian-resident company (or a subsidiary of one), the ministère des Transports must issue an eligibility certificate to be filed with the sailor's tax return and certain other conditions must be met.

15.2.25 Meals and entertainment expenses

As we saw in 8.2.10, if you are self-employed and you take a client or business contact out for a meal or to an entertainment event, your deduction for your costs as a business expense is limited to 50% of the amount paid for federal tax purposes. In 1996, Québec announced that the deduction for business meals and entertainment expenses would be further capped at 1% of your gross business income for the year. This restriction is currently on hold pending further government study.

Boost your Québec business entertainment expense deduction by subscribing to eligible Québec cultural performances.

Some business entertainment expenses for cultural events held in Québec are still 100% deductible for Québec tax purposes. These include the cost of a subscription to a symphony orchestra, classical or jazz ensemble, and opera, dance, theatre, and vocal performances. To qualify for this special deduction, the subscription must be for at least three performances in eligible artistic disciplines.

15.2.26 Home office expenses

The federal tax rules governing deductions for home office expenses are discussed in 7.10.4 and 8.2.11. In the past, the same rules applied for Québec tax purposes but for tax years starting after May 9, 1996, the deduction for self-employed individuals is limited to 50% of eligible home office expenses. The home office expense claims of employees are not subject to this restriction.

15.2.27 Rental expenses—documentation

If you report rental income (or loss), and you claim any expenses for renovation, improvement, maintenance or repair of the property, you must include with your Québec income tax return Form TP-1086.R.23.12-V ("Statement of Labour Costs Incurred with Respect to an Immovable") with the contractor's name, address, social insurance number (if an individual) and QST registration number (if available) as well as the amount paid for the work carried out. This measure is designed to combat tax evasion in the contracting and renovation sectors.

15.2.28 Minimum tax

The Québec alternative minimum tax ("AMT") differs from the federal AMT (see Chapter 12) in three ways. First, the minimum tax rate is 20% (23% in 1998), while the federal rate is 17%.

Second, certain tax benefits, such as deductions for resource exploration in Québec and investment tax credits for research and development, are not considered tax preferences for minimum tax purposes. Starting in 1997, a retiring allowance or severance pay transferred to your RRSP (see 3.3.2) is no longer added back as an adjustment for Québec AMT purposes.

Third, the basic exemption of $40,000 is reduced for Québec AMT purposes to $25,000 as of 1997, thereby increasing the risk of Québec AMT exposure for many Québec residents. The lower exemption could also delay the recovery of Québec AMT that has already been paid.

15.2.29 Instalments

Québec instalment requirements are parallel to those for federal tax described in 14.2.2, with some minor differences.

The penalty for late or insufficient instalments is an extra 10% in addition to the normal interest rate. This penalty is substantially higher than the federal penalty, so if you can only pay part of your instalments, you are better off to pay your Québec instalments on time.

The determination of who has to pay instalments is the same as under the federal system, as outlined in 14.2.2. Instalments are required where your balance of Québec tax owing at the end of the year exceeds $1,200 for both the current year and either of the previous two years.

For Québec residents, quarterly *federal* tax instalments are payable if you have federal taxes owing of $1,200 owing in the current year and either of the previous two years. Since Québec tax can be higher or lower than federal tax for any individual (depending on many factors including those outlined throughout 15.2 above), there can be cases where you must remit federal instalments but not Québec instalments, or vice versa.

15.2.30 Health Services Fund contribution

Your income from all sources (other than employment income) is subject to a "contribution" to the Health Services Fund (i.e., another tax). The income taxed is generally the total shown on your income tax return including business income, investment income, pension or retirement income and taxable capital gains, but not employment income, Old Age Security or alimony. Certain specific deductions are permitted to arrive at the base amount for the contribution, and a further $5,000 exemption is allowed.

The Health Services Fund contribution is calculated on a graduated scale, which tops out at $1,000 once your income exceeds $125,000. In the top bracket, the contribution is $150 plus 1% of the excess of your income over $40,000 (but not over $125,000). Your contribution is then offset by a non-refundable tax credit of 20% (23% in 1998).

If you are required to pay income tax instalments (see 15.2.29), you must also pay quarterly instalments on your Health Services Fund contribution.

15.3 Special Québec incentives

15.3.1 Québec Stock Savings Plans ("QSSP")

A QSSP (also know as a "Régime d'épargne action", or "REA") is a Québec tax incentive available to Québec residents that is designed to encourage investments in certain companies that have assets under $250 million and that operate mainly in Québec. Essentially, if you buy a qualifying investment as part of a public issue and you reside in Québec on December 31, you will be entitled to a Québec tax deduction of 50%, 75%, or 100% of the cost of your investment, depending on the type of investment you purchase. Generally, your total deduction cannot exceed 10% of your net income for the year.

If you are an employee of the corporation in which you are investing, you may be able to deduct an additional 25% of your investment. To qualify for the additional deduction, you must buy the shares through a stock ownership plan that offers financing and that is only available to employees who (together with their families) each own less than 5% of the corporation's shares. Your total deduction will still be capped at 10% of your net income.

A further deduction is available where the qualifying corporation is a "regional venture capital corporation" that finances businesses outside the Hull-Montréal-Québec City triangle. Although this deduction is not limited by 10% of your net income, the total deduction cannot exceed 200% of your investment.

If you deduct an amount for your QSSP investment, you cannot sell the investment until the third year after the year of purchase. Otherwise, you will have to include the amount of your previous deduction in your income for Québec tax purposes in the year of sale. You can avoid the income inclusion by purchasing sufficient qualifying shares in the year of sale to make up for the value of your previous deduction.

Because the deduction for your QSSP investment only applies for Québec tax purposes, if your income is over $50,000, the maximum value of the deduction is about 26.4% of the amount you deduct, depending on the amounts of any other tax credits that you claim.

The QSSP rules have undergone a number of changes over the past few years and have become quite complex. However, if a share issue qualifies as a QSSP investment, your investment broker should be able to help you to determine how the rules apply in respect of your particular QSSP investments.

15.3.2 Investment clubs and investment funds

Québec permits taxpayers to form groups, known as investment clubs, which pool their members' assets for investing in shares, thus reducing the risk. The deductions are granted to the investment club, and then allocated to the individual members.

QSSP investment funds ("QIFs"), which are similar to mutual funds, can also be formed for the purposes of investing in QSSP shares. When a QIF undertakes to invest at least 50% of its funds in common shares of QSSP growth corporations, you can claim a tax deduction for the year you invest in the QIF, even though the QIF might not invest in the QSSP shares until the following year. By investing in a QIF, you can receive the tax benefits of a QSSP while diversifying your investments.

15.3.3 Québec Business Investment Companies ("QBIC")

The QSSP, as we have seen, encourages investment by Québec residents in *publicly-traded* corporations. The QBIC, on the other hand, is a vehicle for investing capital in *private* corporations, typically ones that are newly formed and not yet ready to go public.

A QBIC is more commonly referred to as a "SPEQ" (Société de placements dans l'entreprise québécoise). It is a private investment corporation whose purpose is to invest in new shares of "eligible corporations" (see below). It must be registered with the Société de développement industriel.

When you invest in a QBIC, you receive a basic deduction for 125% of the QBIC's eligible investments, in proportion to your interest in the QBIC. However, your deduction may not exceed 30% of your net income.

Example:
Jean and four of his friends get together and invest $20,000 each in a QBIC. The QBIC invests $60,000 (60% of its funds) in eligible corporations in 1997.

Jean's deduction for 1997 will be limited to $15,000, which is 125% of 60% of his investment. If Jean's net income is less than $50,000, his deduction will be reduced to 30% of his net income.

A QBIC deduction that cannot be used because of the net income limitation can be carried forward and used in any of the next five years, subject to the same limitation.

Additional deductions

Beyond the basic 125% of the investment, two additional deductions are available for incentive purposes, although the total deduction cannot exceed 200% of the investment. First, where the investor is an employee of an eligible corporation, an additional 25% deduction is available for investments of the QBIC in that corporation or a subsidiary of it. Second, an additional 25% deduction is available for investments in a "regional QBIC", or a QBIC which invests exclusively in "regional corporations". ("Regional" refers to the remoter areas of Québec, and covers most of the province outside the Hull-Montréal-Sherbrooke-Québec City triangle.)

In these cases, the additional deduction is available to you as an investor in the QBIC. However, the 30%-of-net-income limitation continues to apply.

15.3.4 Cooperative Investment Plans ("CIP")

Cooperative Investment Plans, or Régimes d'investissement coopératif ("RIC"), are parallel to QBICs. They provide incentives to investment by members and workers in units issued by co-operatives governed by the *Cooperatives Act*—typically producing, processing, agricultural or workers' co-operatives. Various conditions and requirements must be met for the units to qualify.

15.3.5 Labour-sponsored venture capital corporations ("LSVCCs")

Unlike the plans we have looked at so far, the Fondaction and FSTQ (Fonds de solidarité des travailleurs du Québec) are labour-sponsored venture capital corporations that entitle you to tax benefits from both the federal and the Québec tax systems. The Québec rules are similar to the federal rules discussed at 6.3.8.

In 1996, Québec followed the federal government's lead in reducing the rate of the credit to 15% (down from 20%) and in reducing the maximum allowable investment to $3,500 (down from $5,000).

Invest in the FSTQ or the Fondaction and transfer the shares to your RRSP

Consider investing in the FSTQ or the Fondaction, along with a simultaneous transfer of the shares to an RRSP (see Chapter 3). The investment will generate a combined federal and Québec credit of 30%. A contribution of $3,500 worth of shares to an RRSP will give you a $3,500 deduction, worth about $1,855 if you are in the top combined federal/Québec tax bracket. The maximum net cost of the shares to you will only be about 17% of their original cost (see 6.3.8).

This strategy will be particularly useful if you are not otherwise contributing the maximum to an RRSP, and, therefore, still have room to contribute. It may also be very attractive if you are nearing age 55 and close to retiring.

15.3.6 Worker gain sharing plans

Québec offers a credit and deduction for qualifying "worker gain sharing plans" (profit-sharing plans). Companies wanting these benefits must have obtained a certificate from the ministère de l'Industrie, du Commerce et de la Technologie and must have registered their plan with the ministère du Revenu before January 1, 1996. The company must be a Canadian-controlled private corporation with less than $25 million in assets or no more than $10 million in shareholders' equity.

To qualify, a gain sharing plan must allow employees to receive cash compensation based on the results of the business as a whole. The formula must have been proposed to all employees and agreed to by a majority of them. As well, the business must have progressed through some of the stages of a "total quality approach" aimed at improving productivity.

Employees can deduct amounts received from the employer under the gain sharing plan, up to $3,000 per year, with a limit of $6,000 over five years. The **employer** can receive a 15% credit against Québec tax for the amounts paid to the employee, provided it has less than $25 million in assets or less than $10 million in net shareholder's equity. The credit for employers is also limited to a five-year period. Employees who own more than 5% of the shares of the employer do not qualify for the tax benefits.

15.3.7 Resource exploration expenses

If you invest in flow-through shares of a mining or oil and gas company, you can deduct certain expenses which the company "renounces" in your favour. Essentially, the company incurs the expense, but instead of deducting the amount, the company passes the deduction on to its shareholders so they can deduct it on their own return.

To encourage resource exploration in Québec, the province allows you to deduct 125% of the amount of resource exploration costs incurred in Québec which are renounced in your favour. The deduction rate jumps to 175% if the expenses are for certain surface mining explorations incurred in Québec, and for certain Québec oil and gas exploration expenses incurred after May 9, 1996. These enhanced deductions are available until the end of 2000.

There is also a special exemption from Québec tax on capital gains resulting from certain flow-through share expenses in the resource sector. Where flow-through shares are sold, any amount received normally gives rise to a capital gain. The details of the exemption are complex, and you should get professional advice if you are selling flow-through shares acquired between May 14, 1992 and the end of 2000.

15.4 References

Revenu Québec has offices in Hull, Jonquière, Montréal, Québec, Rimouski, Rouyn-Noranda, Sainte-Foy, Sept-Iles, Sherbrooke, Sorel, Trois-Rivières and Toronto.

Revenu Québec produces a number of publications to assist taxpayers, the most notable of which is the *Guide and General Information* book that accompanies the provincial income tax return. Québec tax forms and guides are also available in French and English from the government of Québec's Internet site at www.revenu.gouv.qc.ca.

U.S. citizens in Canada

■ If you're married, file a joint return where appropriate (16.7.1)

■ Claim the foreign earned income exclusion if beneficial (16.2.1)

■ Aim for maximum foreign tax credit (16.2.2)

■ Keep records of expenses deductible on your U.S. return (16.3.1)

■ Beware of differences between Canadian and U.S. rules governing retirement income (16.3.4)

■ Elect to defer U.S. taxation of income accruing in your RRSP and other Canadian retirement plans (16.3.4)

■ Watch out for ownership of Canadian mutual funds, and other Canadian corporations earning passive income (16.3.6)

■ Be cautious of using the $500,000 capital gains exemption (16.4.3)

■ Elect out of "instalment sale" rules where appropriate (16.4.4)

■ Seek professional tax advice before moving to Canada (16.4.8)

■ Watch out for U.S. alternate minimum tax liability (16.5)

■ Review income splitting arrangements to prevent double taxation (16.6.2)

■ Plan to minimize U.S. estate and gift taxes (16.8)

■ Beware of the new U.S. gift and foreign trust reporting rules (16.8.3)

In this chapter we address the difficult and complicated tax problems of the United States citizen who lives in Canada. We can only scratch the surface, due to the interaction of two highly complex tax systems which are both subject to continual change.

The discussion in this chapter is based on current law. At the time of writing, the U.S. Congress is considering a number of amendments to the U.S. tax laws, including changes to the tax treatment of capital gains. Whether any of these proposals will become law is uncertain. You should seek professional advice if you are a U.S. citizen living in Canada.

16.1 Two systems of taxation

The income tax systems of the United States and Canada are similar in some general ways, but very different in their details. A U.S. citizen resident in Canada must deal with both systems.

The United States is one of the few countries in the world that taxes its **citizens** on their worldwide income, whether or not they are physically in the United States. Canada taxes only

Canadian **residents** on their world income; non-residents (including Canadian citizens) are taxed by Canada only on certain income from Canadian sources.

The result is that U.S. citizens living in Canada must file returns under both systems, and often must pay tax to both governments. Safeguards exist to prevent double taxation: clearly, you could not afford to pay a large percentage of your income to each country. But the safeguards, which are outlined in 16.2 below, are not perfect. Much of this chapter deals with the double taxation problems that arise due to differences between the two systems' ways of calculating income and tax.

In general, you will find that U.S. taxation is lower than Canadian. U.S. federal tax currently reaches a maximum rate of 39.6%. Canadian federal tax reaches 31.32% (including surtaxes), but as a resident of Canada you also have a provincial tax liability, which raises the top rate to 50% or more, depending on your province of residence. As a U.S. citizen not resident or domiciled in any state, you have no liability for any U.S. state tax except, perhaps, to the extent you have income arising in a state.

The 1997 U.S. income tax rates for single people with no dependants and for married couples filing joint returns (see 16.7.1) are:

Single (see 16.7.1) Taxable Income	Federal tax
$0 – $24,650	15%
$24,650 – $59,750	$3,697.50 plus 28% of excess over $24,650
$59,750 – $124,650	$13,525.50 plus 31% of excess over $59,750
$124,650 – $271,050	$33,644.50 plus 36% of excess over $124,650
$271,050 and up	$86,348.50 plus 39.6% of excess over $271,050

Married filing joint income returns (see 16.7.1) Taxable Income	Federal tax
$0 – $41,200	15%
$41,200 – $99,600	$6,180 plus 28% of excess over $41,200
$99,600 – $151,750	$22,532 plus 31% of excess over $99,600
$151,750 – $271,050	$38,698.50 plus 36% of excess over $151,750
$271,050 and up	$81,646.50 plus 39.6% of excess over $271,050

(The rates for other types of taxpayers are different; see 16.7.1 for a discussion of the types of filers.)

The highest effective marginal rate is thus 39.6% for most taxpayers. Due to certain adjustments such as a phaseout of personal exemptions and a limitation on itemized deductions for high-income taxpayers, the effective marginal rate can be higher still in some cases.

The 39.6% marginal rate applies to taxable income over $271,050 regardless of filing status. However, married individuals filing separately (see 16.7.1) become subject to the surtax at taxable income in excess of $135,525.

16.2 Basic mechanisms for avoiding double taxation

There are three mechanisms in place to help you avoid paying tax twice on the same income.

16.2.1 Foreign earned income exclusion (U.S. tax law)

The simplest way to avoid double taxation is the U.S. "foreign earned income exclusion". You may exclude from your income, on your U.S. tax return, up to US$70,000 of "earned income" (employment or services income) earned from services provided outside the United States.

If you do not have any income other than your employment or professional services income, and your annual income is under US$70,000, this exclusion will be all you need to escape U.S. tax entirely. You must still file a U.S. return (see 16.7.2 below) and claim the exclusion.

> Example:
> Gordon is a citizen of the United States who lives in Vancouver. He works as an accountant and earns Cdn$80,000 in 1997. (Assume the Canadian dollar is worth an average of US72¢ through 1997.) He has no other income.
>
> On his U.S. tax return, Gordon will report his income of approximately US$57,600. He will then elect to use the foreign earned income exclusion, and will deduct the same $57,600, to show a total income of $0. As a result he will pay no tax to the United States. His Canadian tax return will not be affected by his U.S. citizenship.

Note that if you file as "married filing jointly" (see 16.7.1 below), you and your spouse can each claim up to US$70,000 for purposes of the exclusion against your respective earned incomes. This can be done even if your spouse is not a U.S. citizen.

Claim the foreign earned income exclusion if beneficial.

The regulations make it possible to elect the foreign earned income exclusion on late-filed returns in a number of cases. If you are eligible for the foreign earned income exclusion, you should normally claim it. However, there are some unusual circumstances (mostly involving carryovers of foreign tax credits—see16.2.2) where claiming a foreign tax credit can be more beneficial than claiming the exclusion. If you claim the exclusion and then, in a later year, elect not to claim it, you cannot normally claim it again for five years. Because of this restriction, and on the off-chance that the foreign tax credit might be more valuable in some future year, many accountants will calculate tax both ways and not claim the exclusion if no tax is payable in either case.

16.2.2   **Foreign tax credit (both U.S. and Canadian law)**

The foreign tax credit is a unilateral mechanism provided by many countries to prevent double taxation. Both the U.S. and Canada provide foreign tax credits. While the details differ, the concept is basically the same for both.

Consider the U.S. foreign tax credit as an example. If you are subject to U.S. taxation (because you are a citizen), but you have paid tax to Canada on **Canadian-source income**, you can, in general, claim a foreign tax credit to offset your U.S. tax on that income. Your credit cannot be greater than the Canadian tax you paid.

Example:

Ron is a U.S. citizen who lives and works in Winnipeg. He earns Cdn$1,389 (equivalent to US$1,000) in interest on his Winnipeg bank account in 1997. He also receives a salary in Canada and income from investments in the United States.

Ron will be required to include the US$1,000 in his income for U.S. tax purposes. (Because it is investment income and not earned income, it is not eligible for the foreign earned income exclusion.) Assume that he is in the 31% bracket (i.e., his taxable income is less than $124,650 and he is single), so his additional U.S. tax is US$310. If he is in a 50% tax bracket in Canada, so that he has paid the equivalent of US$500 to Canada (and Manitoba) on the income, he can receive a foreign tax credit for the full US$310 on his U.S. return. On the other hand, if his Canadian tax rate were lower and he paid only US$270 to Canada (and Manitoba), he could only claim US$270 as his foreign tax credit.

The above example is highly simplified, but it demonstrates the basic effect of the credit. When you total up the tax to both countries (including provincial and state tax) and the foreign tax credits of each, you should end up paying a total that is equal to the higher of the two countries' rates of tax.

The Canadian foreign tax credit follows essentially the same principles. Since Canada taxes Canadian residents on their worldwide income, Ron in our example will have to report his U.S.-source investment income on his Canadian tax return. He will then be eligible for a foreign tax credit for U.S. taxes paid on his U.S.-source investment income to offset the Canadian tax that applies. (Note that each country's foreign tax credit applies only to foreign taxes on income from sources outside that country.)

The details of the foreign tax credit rules are very complicated. For U.S. foreign tax credit purposes, your non-U.S. income is grouped into several different "baskets", or pools, and a separate foreign tax credit is available for each. Expenses, deductions and Canadian taxes must be allocated to each basket using prescribed allocation rules. Canadian tax you have paid on your employment income, for example, generally cannot be used to create a foreign tax credit for tax on investment income or capital gains.

For U.S. foreign tax credit purposes, excess (non-creditable) foreign tax can be carried back two years and forward five years. For Canadian foreign tax credit purposes, excess foreign tax can be deducted from income in the current year. If the excess foreign tax relates to business income, the excess generally can be carried back three years and forward seven years.

Aim for maximum foreign tax credit.

Over the course of the year, you may be able to structure your income from various sources—U.S. and Canadian, employment and investment income, etc.—in such a way as to maximize your "pools" of foreign tax paid on foreign-source income for purposes of the foreign tax credits of both the U.S. and Canada.

While normally you cannot receive credit for all Canadian tax paid because Canadian taxes are higher than U.S. taxes, you may be able to take particular advantage of the credit if you are resident in Canada for a relatively short time before another foreign posting. That is because you may apply your excess Canadian taxes when determining the foreign tax credit on income earned in other foreign countries.

If you receive income for personal services performed in both the U.S. and Canada, it is a good idea to keep a diary to record U.S. and Canadian work days.

If you have various sources of income and need to claim a foreign tax credit under one or both systems, you should consult a professional advisor.

16.2.3 Canada-U.S. tax treaty

The third safeguard against double taxation is the Canada-U.S. **tax treaty** (also known as a tax convention). Both Canada and the U.S. have such treaties with many countries. The purpose of a tax treaty is twofold: to prevent double taxation, and to reduce tax evasion by allowing exchange of taxpayer information between the two governments.

The Canada-U.S. treaty, for the most part, does not apply to United States citizens resident in Canada except in specific circumstances.

For example, the treaty allows a U.S. citizen resident in Canada to defer U.S. taxation of funds accruing in an **RRSP**. Were it not for this provision, U.S.

tax could apply to the accruing funds, which are specifically exempt from Canadian tax under the RRSP rules (see 3.1.5 and 16.3.4). A Protocol (amendment) to the Canada-U.S. treaty ratified on November 9, 1995 extended the deferral election to RPPs, RRIFs and other retirement arrangements. The Protocol is effective for 1996 and later years.

Another treaty provision clarifies how to calculate the foreign tax credit (see 16.2.2) where you are claiming credits on both returns, and each one depends on the tax paid to the other country (which in turn depends on the credit available, leading to circularity). The rule is that you compute your U.S. tax first, without taking your U.S. foreign tax credit into account. Then you calculate your Canadian tax, and base the Canadian foreign tax credit on that U.S. tax figure. Finally, you go back to your U.S. return, and claim your U.S. foreign tax credit based on the Canadian tax actually paid. If you have U.S.-source interest, dividend or royalty income, this treaty provision may even result in a U.S. foreign tax credit for a portion of the Canadian and provincial taxes paid on your U.S.-source income.

Yet another provision in the treaty deals with **child support** paid by a U.S. resident to a resident of Canada. For U.S. tax purposes, such support (as distinct from alimony or maintenance that goes to support the spouse) is not included in income. As a result, the treaty provides that child support will not be included in income for Canadian tax purposes either. This applies whether or not you are a U.S. citizen.

If you are using the treaty to reduce your U.S. tax liability, you are generally required to disclose the specific details on your U.S. tax return. If you do not, the treaty benefits can be denied.

16.3 Differences in calculating income

In theory, the foreign tax credit mechanism prevents you from paying tax twice. However, there are many differences between U.S. and Canadian calculations of income for tax purposes. These differences can lead to unexpected tax liabilities.

16.3.1 Deductions on U.S. return that are not available in Canada

Home mortgage interest may normally be deducted on your U.S. tax return, while it is not deductible in Canada, except to the extent you can claim an office in your home (see 6.2.3 and 8.2.11). The same applies to **property taxes.**

State taxes, which may be imposed to the extent you reside in or have income arising in a U.S. state, are generally deductible for U.S. income tax purposes, while provincial income taxes are not deductible in Canada.

Keep records of expenses deductible on your U.S. return.

Certain employment-related expenses not available in Canada can also be deducted on your U.S. return. If you are claiming deductions on your U.S. return that are not allowable in Canada, make sure to keep additional records sufficient to establish your claim.

16.3.2 **Deductions on Canadian return that are not available in the U.S.**

As we saw in 6.2.3, **interest paid** may be deducted for Canadian tax purposes where the funds were borrowed for the purposes of earning income from investments. There is no strict requirement that you actually earn more income from your investments than you spend in interest.

For U.S. tax purposes, your investment expense deduction is limited to your investment income. You cannot write off interest expense against other income such as employment or business income. This principle extends, under a separate set of complex rules, beyond interest expenses to all deductions relating to "passive" activities, including limited partnership write-offs and most rental losses.

Certain other expenses and deductions permitted for Canadian purposes will not be allowed on your U.S. return.

16.3.3 **Limitations on U.S. deductions for high-income taxpayers**

Two limitations apply to high-income taxpayers.

First, **personal exemptions** ($2,650 for you, your spouse and each dependant) are phased out once adjusted gross income ("AGI") exceeds a threshold. (Adjusted gross income is gross income minus certain deductions such as foreign earned income exclusion, alimony, and IRA [Individual Retirement Account] or Keogh plan contributions.) For married persons filing jointly, the threshold is $181,800; for single taxpayers it is $121,200; for married filing separately, it is $90,900. For each $1,250 ($2,500 for married individuals filing separately) or part thereof by which AGI exceeds the threshold, *each* exemption is reduced by 2% (not to exceed 100%).

Second, **itemized deductions** are reduced once AGI exceeds a threshold, which is $121,200 for single taxpayers and married filing jointly, and $60,600 for married filing separately. For each dollar over the threshold, itemized deductions that could otherwise be claimed are reduced by 3% (other than medical expenses, investment interest, casualty or theft losses and gambling losses). However, even for very high-income taxpayers, a base amount of 20% of itemized deductions can always be claimed (i.e., the reduction cannot go beyond 80% of the deductions).

Example:

George is married and earns $211,800. His wife Linda has no income and the couple is able to file jointly. George will claim two personal exemptions worth $5,300. He has itemized deductions of $20,000 consisting of home mortgage interest and property taxes.

George's income is $30,000 (12 × $2,500) over the $181,800 threshold. Each of George's $2,650 personal exemptions is thus reduced by 12 times 2%, or 24%. His total claim for exemptions is therefore $4,028 (that is, $5,300 − (5,300 × 24%)).

George's itemized deductions are reduced by 3% of $90,600 (which is the excess of his adjusted gross income over the $121,200 threshold), or $2,718. So George may deduct only $17,282 of his $20,000 in itemized deductions in determining his taxable income. (Note that the reduction can never exceed 80% of the itemized deductions, so no matter how high George's income was, he would always be able to deduct $4,000 of his $20,000 of itemized deductions.)

16.3.4 Retirement and profit-sharing plans

RRSPs, RPPs and DPSPs (see Chapter 3) can cause problems for U.S. citizens, because they are not given any special status in the U.S. Internal Revenue Code.

Beware of differences in rules governing retirement income.

Employer contributions to a registered pension plan or a deferred profit sharing plan are exempt from immediate Canadian tax (see 7.1.1). As we saw in 3.4.1, you are taxed on the funds only when you receive them (usually on retirement).

For U.S. tax purposes, there is no such exemption. The amount contributed by your employer is treated as an employment benefit and is taxed, once the contributions have vested in you (that is, you are entitled to them even if you leave your employment). Furthermore, these amounts are explicitly excluded from the definition of "foreign earned income" under U.S. tax law, so you cannot make use of the foreign earned income exclusion (see 16.2.1). You may have to pay U.S. tax on these contributions, depending on the circumstances and the amount of your unused foreign tax credit carryover.

Your own contributions to an RRSP or RPP, which are deductible on your Canadian return, are not deductible for U.S. tax purposes.

Elect to defer U.S. taxation of income accruing in your RRSP and other Canadian retirement plans.

Income accruing in your RRSP, RRIF and other Canadian retirement plans (see Chapter 3) would normally be taxable in the U.S. As noted in 16.2.3, the Canada-U.S. tax treaty allows you to elect each year to defer the taxation of the accruing income until you actually receive the funds from the plan. This allows you to report the income in the same year for Canadian and U.S. purposes. But since your RRSP is technically a foreign trust for U.S. purposes, it may be subject to new U.S. reporting rules — see 16.8.3.

If you contribute to an IRA (U.S. Individual Retirement Account) while resident in Canada, your contributions are deductible for U.S. tax purposes but not for Canadian tax purposes. Income accruing in an IRA is not taxed by Canada. When you withdraw funds from an IRA, Canada will tax the same amount that you would have had to include in your income under U.S. laws if you were a resident of the U.S. at the time of withdrawal. While you may be able to transfer lump sum payments received from an IRA into an RRSP free of Canadian tax, the amount transferred would be subject to U.S. tax. Foreign tax credits may alleviate double taxation.

Contributions to a U.S. deferred income plan by a U.S. employer may be taxable in Canada as an employment benefit or "retirement compensation arrangement" (see 7.6).

16.3.5 Dividends

As we saw in 6.1.2, Canada taxes dividends from Canadian corporations using the "gross-up and credit" system, which results in less tax being levied than on other kinds of income. For U.S. purposes, dividends are taxed at the same rate as other income. The actual amount that you receive, rather than the grossed-up amount, is included in income for U.S. purposes.

Since Canadian tax rates (when provincial tax is counted) are normally higher than U.S. federal rates, the effect of the dividend tax credit roughly equalizes the tax rates of the two countries on dividends. The maximum U.S. rate is 39.6%; the maximum Canadian rate on dividends received is about 35%, depending on your province of residence.

16.3.6 Canadian mutual funds or other Canadian corporations earning passive income

Watch out for ownership of Canadian mutual funds.

Investing in Canadian mutual funds and similar corporations can result in unexpected U.S. tax liability. Under U.S. law, if you invest in a non-U.S.

corporation that earns a substantial part of its income from investments (a "passive foreign investment corporation"), and then sell the stock or receive an "excess" distribution, there may be a theoretical deferral of U.S. tax (which would have applied if you had earned the investment income directly). In such a case, interest charged on this "deferred tax" may be imposed under U.S. tax law.

There is no minimum U.S. ownership required in a Canadian corporation to be subject to these rules. There are ways to avoid the interest charge, however; one way is to elect to include your *pro rata* share of the fund's earnings in your income on a current basis each year (which may result in a mismatching of income for Canadian and U.S. purposes).

16.3.7 Charitable donations

As discussed in 2.8.1, charitable donations of up to 75% of your net income entitle you to a credit for federal Canadian tax purposes (20% of net income for Québec purposes).

For Canadian tax purposes, charitable donations must normally be made to a Canadian charity to qualify (subject to certain specific exceptions). The Canada-U.S. tax treaty, however, provides that donations to U.S. charities will qualify, up to a limit of 50% of U.S.-source net income. You will need to obtain receipts from the U.S. charities and file them with your Canadian return.

Similarly, charitable donations are normally deductible in the U.S., subject to a limit of 50% of income for most charities. However, donations to Canadian charities may only be deducted for U.S. tax purposes to the extent of 50% of your *Canadian-source* "adjusted gross income". If you are excluding much or all of your Canadian-source income due to the foreign earned income exclusion (see 16.2.1), this limitation can cause problems.

16.3.8 Moving expenses

Moving expenses can present particular difficulties when dealing with the two tax systems. If you are posted to Canada and move to Canada, reimbursement by your employer of your moving expenses will normally be considered Canadian-source income for purposes of the U.S. foreign earned income exclusion and foreign tax credit. You may be able to claim certain moving expenses as a separate deduction on your U.S. tax return, but not if you have used the foreign earned income exclusion so that you have no Canadian-source employment income for tax purposes. Numerous special rules and restrictions apply to moving expenses claimed on a "foreign move" (a move *to* a non-U.S. home).

The deduction for moving expenses is limited to the costs of moving household goods and personal effects to the new residence and travel and lodging costs during the move. No deduction is allowed for meal expenses, expenses incurred while searching for a new home after obtaining employment, costs of selling the old residence or temporary lodging after obtaining employment. Reimbursement of moving costs by your employer is taxable income to you.

On a move back to the United States, a portion of your moving expenses may not be deductible, if the associated employer reimbursements are allocable to income eligible for the foreign earned income exclusion.

Under Canadian law, reimbursements of actual moving expenses are simply not taxed. A non-recoverable allowance for moving expenses is taxable if it exceeds $650, but the moving expenses themselves are deductible.

16.4 Differences in taxation of capital gains

16.4.1 Basic calculation

It is in the field of capital gains that one finds the most glaring differences between the Canadian and U.S. tax systems. Not only are many details different, but the basic scheme of taxation of capital gains is itself fundamentally different, which creates a large number of problems for U.S. citizens resident in Canada.

For Canadian tax purposes, only three-quarters of capital gains are taxed (see 5.2).

For U.S. tax purposes, capital gains are normally taxed like other income, at your marginal rate of 15%, 28%, 36% or 39.6% (see table in 16.1 above). However, the rate on *long-term* capital gains (generally from property held more than one year) is limited to 28%.

16.4.2 Use of capital losses

For Canadian purposes, allowable capital losses (three-quarters of your capital losses) can only be used to offset taxable capital gains, though they can be carried back three years and forward indefinitely against such gains (see 5.3.1). An exception exists for allowable business investment losses (on shares or debt of small business corporations), which can be used against any income (5.3.2).

For U.S. purposes, capital losses can be used against capital gains. In addition, US$3,000 of capital losses can be written off against other income ($1,500 for a married person filing separately). Unused capital losses can be carried forward, to be applied against capital gains or against $3,000 per year of other income in any future year.

16.4.3 The Canadian capital gains exemption

A $500,000 capital gains exemption is available in Canada for certain small business shares and farm property (see 5.4.1 and 5.4.2). No such exemption exists for U.S. tax purposes.

Be cautious of using the $500,000 capital gains exemption.

The Canadian foreign tax credit is calculated so as not to apply to any portion of a gain on foreign property for which the capital gains exemption was claimed. In other words, if you sell U.S. property and pay U.S. tax on the sale, you cannot claim a Canadian foreign tax credit for the portion of the U.S. tax that relates to the gain on which you or your spouse previously claimed the capital gains exemption for Canadian purposes.

If you sell small business corporation shares or farm property, the $500,000 capital gains exemption won't protect you from U.S. tax on the gain, even if you are not subject to Canadian tax. Generally, you should steer clear of the planning ideas discussed in 9.1 to "crystallize" your gains and use up your exemption.

The U.S. does have a limited form of capital gains exemption. U.S. citizens who invest in the shares of certain active small U.S. corporations after August 10, 1993, and hold the shares for at least five years, may be entitled to exclude up to 50% of any gains from income when the shares are sold. Numerous restrictions apply, however, and half of any excluded gain is treated as a "tax preference item" under the alternative minimum tax rules (see 16.5).

16.4.4 Reserves vs. instalment sales

Problems can arise when you sell capital property but do not receive full payment in the year of sale. As we saw in 5.5.1, a **reserve** is allowed for Canadian tax purposes, if you claim it. The reserve is based on the proportion of gain that has not yet been received, but at least one-fifth of the gain must be recognized cumulatively each year, so the reserve cannot be claimed for more than four years after the year of sale.

Elect out of "instalment sale" rules where appropriate.

For U.S. tax purposes, **instalment sale** rules cover the same situation. However, the rules apply *unless* you elect to have them not apply. The basic concept is the same—a "gross profit ratio" will apply to include a portion of each payment into your income—but the five-year rule does not exist. This can lead to mismatching of Canadian and U.S. income, and thus foreign tax credits, in a given year. If you are not claiming a reserve for Canadian tax purposes on the sale of a particular capital property, consider electing out of the "instalment sale" rules on your U.S. return.

If you are claiming a reserve that can last only five years, but deferring a large portion of your proceeds beyond five years, the instalment sale rules will again lead to a mismatch of Canadian and U.S. income.

If the gain is taxed in the U.S. some years after it is taxed in Canada due to the instalment sale rules, Revenue Canada may allow you to reopen an earlier year's return (back to 1985) in order to claim a foreign tax credit.

There are further differences between Canadian reserves and U.S. instalment sale rules. In particular, the instalment sale method may not be available if the instalment obligation is pledged as security for a debt.

16.4.5 **Foreign exchange gains or losses**

When you sell Canadian property, your gain for U.S. tax purposes must be calculated using the U.S. dollar equivalent of your cost, as of the date you purchased the property. This can lead to a foreign exchange gain or loss that is independent of your (Canadian-dollar) gain or loss on the property.

Example:
You purchase 100 shares of XYZ Corporation on the Toronto Stock Exchange when the Canadian dollar is at US70¢. You pay $20 per share including commission, or Cdn$2,000 (US$1,400). You sell the shares several years later, when the Canadian dollar is at US78¢, for $19 each (after commission), or Cdn$1,900 (US$1,482).

For Canadian tax purposes, you have a $100 capital loss, three-quarters of which can be deducted against taxable capital gains. For U.S. tax purposes, however, you have an $82 capital gain, which is taxed. Since you do not pay any Canadian tax on the gain, no foreign tax credit is available to offset your tax (maximum 28%) on US$82.

A taxable foreign exchange gain can also arise on the sale of your principal residence, even though the entire gain is "rolled over" into a new principal residence within the required time frame (see 16.4.7). The problem is that the foreign exchange gain realized on the discharge of a mortgage denominated in Canadian dollars is not a gain to which the U.S. principal residence rollover rules (see 16.4.7) apply.

Similarly, when you sell U.S. property, your gain for Canadian purposes must be calculated in Canadian dollars. The first $200 of your gain or loss on foreign currency in each year is ignored.

16.4.6 **Pre-1972 holdings**

As noted in 5.5.5, Canada taxes only capital gains accrued since 1972. The U.S. does not have any such rule. If you are a U.S. citizen and have owned property since before 1972, your gain for U.S. tax purposes could be substantially higher than your gain for Canadian tax purposes.

16.4.7 Principal residence

As we saw in 5.5.2, a gain on a "principal residence" is normally completely exempt from tax in Canada. The U.S. has two rules to deal with sales of a principal residence, but they are very different from the Canadian rules, and more restrictive.

First, if you are at least 55 years old, you may claim an exclusion of US$125,000 of gain on a principal residence. Certain requirements must be met; for example, you must have actually occupied the home for three of the past five years, and you and your spouse must not have claimed this exclusion in the past.

Second, you may defer the taxation of a gain on your principal residence if you buy another home (which may be outside the U.S.), except to the extent your new home costs less than what you sell the old home for. Your old home's cost will be transferred for tax purposes to your new home, so the gain may eventually be taxed. The time limitation for buying the new home is fairly generous: you must buy it within two years (before or after) of selling the old home. As well, the two-year period may be extended by a further two years during which your "tax home" (generally your place of employment) is outside the U.S. This means that you have up to four years after selling your old home to buy a new, more expensive one, if you are living in Canada.

Be careful if you buy more than one home during the two-year period. You will have to pay tax on any gain arising on the "middle" home.

A further difference between Canadian and U.S. exemptions for a principal residence lies in the definition of the term. As we saw in 5.5.2, a vacation property such as a cottage will generally qualify for Canadian tax purposes, although you can only designate one principal residence for each year. For U.S. purposes, a home will only qualify if it is the place where you "regularly reside".

Proposals to change the taxation of gains arising on the disposition of a principal residence may become law in 1997. These changes would eliminate the above tax deferral and $125,000 exemption and replace them with a $500,000 lifetime exemption on capital gains on the sale of your principal residence.

16.4.8 Immigrating to Canada

Most property you own is deemed to be acquired by you at its fair market value as of the date you immigrate to Canada. This means that Canada will tax only the capital gain that accrues while you are resident in Canada. The U.S., on the other hand, will use your actual cost for capital gains calculation purposes, resulting in a much higher capital gain in many cases.

Seek professional tax advice before moving to Canada.

If you are a U.S. citizen moving to Canada, you should obtain professional advice regarding strategies for minimizing your tax burden. There may be steps you should take before you arrive in Canada.

If you have significant non-Canadian investments, it may be worthwhile to set up a foreign trust before you become resident in Canada. A foreign trust can be exempt from Canadian tax for up to five years after you become resident. This may be a useful strategy where your U.S. tax rate is lower than your Canadian rate.

If you own property that has gone down in value, you should consider selling it before becoming a Canadian resident. The current market value of the property at the time you become resident will be used as your cost base for Canadian capital gains calculation purposes.

If you are being relocated to Canada by your employer, you may wish to negotiate for a payment to cover the higher taxes imposed in Canada. See also 16.3.8 regarding moving expenses.

Under the Canada-U.S. Social Security Agreement, you can be exempted for up to five years from Canada/Québec Pension Plan contributions if you are a U.S. citizen temporarily transferred to Canada. You would continue to be covered under and pay contributions to the U.S. social security system. Your employer will need to obtain a certificate of coverage under the U.S. system for you to obtain this exemption.

16.4.9 Emigrating from Canada to the U.S.

When you emigrate from Canada (i.e., when you cease to be resident in Canada for Canadian tax purposes), you are generally deemed to have sold all of your property at its fair market value. This allows Canada to tax gains that accrued on your assets while you were resident in Canada. As we saw in 5.5.4, the Canadian government has proposed significant changes to these rules that will have effect as of October 2, 1996 if they are enacted. Under these proposals, the principal exceptions from the deemed disposition rules are:

- Canadian real estate
- property that you already owned when you became resident in Canada, if your residence in Canada totalled no more than five years out of the last ten
- pension entitlements, including an RRSP or RRIF
- property used in a business in Canada
- certain stock options

For other property, the deemed disposition will result in an immediate tax liability on the resulting income or gains, although Revenue Canada will allow you to defer paying the tax on gains as long as you post acceptable security. If you emigrate in 1996 or later and you own property worth more than CDN$25,000 in total, under the new proposals you must provide Revenue Canada with a list of all your property and its fair market value at the time of emigration. For further details on these proposals, see 5.5.4.

Under the treaty, you can elect for the deemed disposition rules to apply for U.S. as well as Canadian tax purposes, so that you can use the Canadian taxes arising as a foreign tax credit on your U.S. return to offset the resulting U.S. tax and give you a higher cost basis in the assets for U.S. tax purposes. But do not make this election without considering the state tax consequences.

16.4.10 **Other capital gains differences**

Canada and the U.S. have very different rules with respect to the transfer of capital property to corporations, corporation reorganizations, mergers, windups, recapitalization, debt forgiveness, etc. If you are involved in such transactions, professional advice is essential, especially since there have been many changes to both systems.

16.5 **Minimum tax**

Canada's minimum tax was discussed in Chapter 12. The U.S. alternative minimum tax ("AMT") has the same general structure, but there are a number of important differences.

Watch out for U.S. alternate minimum tax.

First, the U.S. AMT exemption is US$45,000 for married taxpayers filing jointly (or a surviving spouse) and US$33,750 for a single taxpayer. (The Canadian exemption is Cdn$40,000 for federal tax purposes and $25,000 for Québec tax purposes.) As well, the U.S. exemption is phased out for those with adjusted minimum taxable income over $150,000 if married filing jointly ($112,500 if filing as a single taxpayer).

Second, the U.S. AMT rate is calculated under a two-tier graduated rate schedule. A 26% rate applies to the first US$175,000 of alternative minimum taxable income over the AMT exemption amount, and a 28% rate applies to alternative minimum taxable income over US$175,000. The 28% rate comes into effect at an alternative minimum taxable income over US$87,500 for married individuals filing separate returns. (The Canadian rate, including provincial tax, is about 27%.)

Third, the list of "AMT adjustments"—items added back to income for AMT purposes—is, of course, different between the two countries. For U.S. tax purposes, the list includes the standard deduction, property and state taxes paid, oil and gas drilling costs, mining exploration and development costs, a portion of accelerated depreciation, and various other specific deductions.

Fourth, the U.S. foreign tax credit can only be used to offset 90% of your AMT payable. This means that if your income (not counting income eligible for the foreign earned income exclusion) is higher than the AMT exemption level, you will almost always end up paying at least some tax to the United States.

Example:
Pete is an unmarried U.S. citizen living and working in Canada. In 1997, his employment income is Cdn$65,000, and he makes Cdn$100,000 (US$72,000) in gains on the stock market.

Pete will pay Canadian tax on his employment income and on 3/4 of his capital gain. For U.S. regular tax purposes, the employment income will be eligible for the foreign earned income exclusion, and the U.S. tax on the capital gain will be fully offset by a foreign tax credit for the Canadian tax he pays on the gain.

For U.S. AMT purposes, however, Pete's income will be US$72,000, minus his $33,750 AMT exemption. The AMT liability will therefore be 26% of $38,250, or $9,945. Only 90% of this amount can be offset by foreign tax credits, so Pete will have to pay $995 in U.S. tax. This will be in addition to his Canadian tax liability. No Canadian foreign tax credit will be available, since the gains are Canadian-source income even though they are being taxed by the U.S.

As you can see, if your income is high enough, you may have to pay a certain amount of U.S. alternative minimum tax even though your income is fully taxed by Canada. One way to reduce this liability is to earn additional U.S.-source income. Canada will give you a foreign tax credit for regular U.S. tax paid on the U.S.-source income, but not for U.S. AMT payable on Canadian-source income.

16.6 Income earned by children

16.6.1 Effects on dependant deduction

If you claim a deduction for a dependent child (US$2,650) on your U.S. return, that child may not claim the regular personal exemption on his or her own tax return. The effect is that any income the child earns is taxed.

In Canada, there is no longer a federal credit for dependent children (see 2.3). As a result, income earned by your children will not affect the tax you pay.

16.6.2 Attribution rules

We discussed the Canadian attribution rules with respect to minor children in 4.2.3. The basic rule is that if you give or lend funds to your child, the income from those funds will be taxed in your hands rather than the child's, until the child turns 18.

The U.S. tax system accomplishes the same general anti-income-splitting objective in a very different way. The income of the child is taxed in the child's hands, but may in part be taxed at the parent's marginal tax rate.

The first US$650 of **unearned income** (roughly equivalent in meaning to Canadian "income from property") of a child under 14 is not taxed. The next $650 is taxed as the child's income. Beyond US$1,300, if the child has no *earned* income (compensation for services rendered), any further unearned income will be taxed at the rate of the parent with the greater taxable income. So, beyond the $1,300 level, little is usually gained from a tax point of view by having a child under 14 earn investment income.

If certain requirements are met, the parent whose taxable income is used for calculating the child's tax rate may elect to include the child's income directly. This will eliminate the need to file a tax return for the child, and also lead to a better matching of incomes between the Canadian and U.S. tax systems.

Review income splitting arrangements to prevent double taxation.

Income splitting arrangements that are set up for Canadian income tax purposes can result in double taxation if you are not careful. For example, suppose you and your 13-year-old son are both U.S. citizens and your son has no income, and you lend funds to him with the intention of building up "secondary" income over time which will not be attributed back to you (see 4.3.5). The income on the funds you have loaned will be taxed in your hands under Canadian law, but in your son's hands (albeit at your marginal rate while the child is under 14) under U.S. law. Because different taxpayers are paying the tax, no foreign tax credit will be available and you may end up being taxed twice on the same income.

In this example, as long as your son is under 14, you can elect to include his unearned income on your return for U.S. tax purposes. That should solve the double taxation problem, since the income will be taxed in your hands under both systems.

16.7 U.S. filing requirements
16.7.1 Joint return or not?

For Canadian tax purposes, every taxpayer is distinct and must file separately. Combining the income of two spouses is only considered for certain specific purposes, such as eligibility for the Child Tax Benefit (2.3.1) and the GST Credit (2.10.3). For Québec purposes, spouses will have the option of filing joint returns in certain circumstances in 1998 and after.

File a joint return where appropriate.

For U.S. tax purposes, you have the option of filing a joint return with your spouse. If one spouse has little or no income, this will usually result in less tax than if you file as "married filing separately". For U.S. purposes, spouses must be legally married; in Canada, spouses include common-law spouses (see 2.2.1).

For U.S. purposes, a joint return is mandatory (if you are married) if you wish to claim certain deductions and credits. The child care credit is one example. Another is the $25,000 loss allowance for an owner who actively participates in rental real estate.

If you do not have a spouse, your filing status will be one of "single", "head of household" or "surviving spouse", all of which have different implications for your U.S. tax return.

If your spouse is a U.S. citizen, the decision as to whether to file jointly can be made annually. If your spouse is not a U.S. citizen, the decision to file jointly can only be made once.

If your spouse is not a U.S. citizen and has no U.S.-source income, and thus is not subject to U.S. tax, consider filing a "married filing separate" return. As a "non-resident alien", your spouse's Canadian income will not be relevant for U.S. tax purposes.

On the other hand, if your spouse has little income from any source but you are paying tax to the U.S., filing a joint return can be beneficial, as it will give you larger exclusions and wider tax brackets at the lower rates. The cost of doing this is that you bring your spouse's worldwide income within the U.S. tax system.

Note also that if you file jointly, you must always file jointly unless the election to file jointly is revoked; but once revoked, the decision can never be made again (unless you have a new spouse).

16.7.2 Time requirements for filing

The requirements for filing Canadian tax returns were discussed in 14.1.

U.S. tax returns must normally be postmarked by April 15 each year.

If you are a U.S. citizen whose "tax home" (place of employment) and "abode" (place of residence) are *both* outside the U.S., your filing deadline is automatically extended to June 15 each year. You must attach a statement to your return identifying that you are eligible for this extension. You mail your U.S. tax return to the IRS in Philadelphia.

If you are unable to meet your U.S. filing deadline, you may file for an extension of the deadline to August 15. The extension will be granted automatically.

Even though you are permitted to file your return in June or August, interest on any balance of taxes owing will run from April 15. If more than 10% of your tax for the year is owing, a late payment penalty applies as well.

16.7.3   **Estimated taxes**

We discussed the Canadian tax instalment requirements in 14.2.2. The U.S. has parallel requirements, which are called payments of "estimated taxes".

Estimated tax payments are due quarterly, on April 15, June 15, September 15 and the following January 15. As with the Canadian system, you can generally choose either last year's tax or this year's tax as the basis for your quarterly estimated tax payments.

If you are basing your payments on the current year's tax, you need only pay 90% of the year's tax liability (regular tax or AMT) in estimated tax payments—22.5% each quarter. If you are using last year's tax, you must normally pay 25% of that amount each quarter. However, if you are using last year's tax and last year's gross adjusted income exceeded US$150,000 (US$75,000 if married filing separately), you must pay 27.5% each quarter (i.e., 110% of last year's tax). In order to use last year's tax, you must have filed a return in the previous year and the year must have been a 12 month-period.

In either case, any balance still owing will be due with your tax return. No estimated tax payments are required if your total tax for the year is less than US$500.

If you do not make your estimated tax payments on time, non-deductible late payment penalties will apply.

16.7.4   **Disclosure requirements**

As well as filing a tax return, you must disclose a substantial amount of financial information under U.S. law.

First, you must disclose holdings in any non-U.S. corporations which you control directly or indirectly, or in which you have a substantial interest and which are controlled by other U.S. citizens or corporations. You are required to provide this information by filing a separate Form 5471 for each foreign corporation that you control.The IRS uses this information, among other things, to help determine your liability for tax on any undistributed income of closely-held non-U.S. corporations that earn passive income.

In some cases, a Canadian corporation's reporting year must be the calendar year for U.S. reporting purposes.

Second, you are required to file annually a "Report of Foreign Bank and Financial Accounts" form with the U.S. Department of the Treasury. This form is mailed separately from your tax return and is due by June 30. It is required if the total value of your foreign bank accounts, brokerage accounts, RRSPs, etc. exceeds US$10,000 at any time in the year.

New reporting rules are also in place for gifts and bequests over $10,000 in one year and transfers to and from foreign trusts which may include RRSPs — see 16.8.3.

Severe penalties apply under U.S. law for not complying with these disclosure requirements.

16.7.5 U.S. passport renewals

If you apply for a U.S. passport, or a renewal of your passport, while living outside the U.S., you will be required to provide your Social Security Number and file an IRS information return. If you have not been regularly filing U.S. tax returns, you will then likely receive a request to file from the Internal Revenue Service. Ignoring such requests can leave you liable to criminal penalties. In the future, the IRS hopes that legislation will be passed permitting the U.S. government to withhold renewal of your passport for non-filing of tax returns.

16.8 U.S. estate and gift taxes

16.8.1 Estate tax

The U.S. imposes estate tax on death of U.S. citizens, where the net value of the estate (when combined with certain taxable gifts) is over US$600,000. The tax applies at graduated rates, ranging from 18% for the value of an estate under US$10,000 to 55% of the value of an estate over US$3 million. See 17.4 for a more detailed discussion.

Plan to minimize U.S. estate tax.

A deduction is allowed for any amounts left to your spouse on death, if your spouse is a U.S. citizen. As a result, leaving all of your estate to your spouse will result in no estate tax applying on your death. This will result, however, in losing your $600,000 exemption, since on your spouse's death only one $600,000 exemption is available on your combined estate.

If your spouse is not a U.S. citizen, the deduction is not available. However, a "qualified domestic trust" can be set up to defer tax (see 17.4.1).

As noted in 5.5.3 and 13.1.2, Canada effectively taxes accrued capital gains on death by deeming capital property to have been disposed of at fair market value immediately before death.

Since the U.S. tax on death is an estate tax and the Canadian tax is an income tax, neither one would normally permit a foreign tax credit in respect of the other. This can result in double taxation. The Canada-U.S. treaty allows Canadian residents a credit against Canadian income tax payable on U.S.-source income on death for U.S. estate tax, and allows U.S. citizens or residents a credit against U.S. estate tax for Canadian income tax imposed on the property on death. These rules are subject to various restrictions. As well, a limited rollover to a spouse will be allowed even where the surviving spouse is not a U.S. citizen. These treaty provisions alleviate (but will not eliminate) the risk of double taxation. See 17.4.

These treaty provisions were amended by the Protocol ratified on November 9, 1995 and are retroactive to deaths occurring after November 10, 1988. A claim for a refund of Canadian or U.S. taxes paid on death needs to be filed within the domestic statute of limitations period (for U.S. returns, the period is usually three years from the later of the return's due date or the date it was filed; for Canadian returns, the period is generally three years from the return's assessment date).

Note that although U.S. estate tax will only apply to the extent the *net* value of the estate exceeds US$600,000, an estate tax return must be filed whenever the *gross* value of the estate exceeds that figure. Furthermore, to the extent you have made taxable gifts (see 16.8.2) during your lifetime, the $600,000 threshold is reduced.

16.8.2   Gift tax

Canada does not have a gift tax, although the giver of a gift (except to a spouse) is deemed to have sold the property at its current fair market value, possibly leading to income tax on a resulting taxable capital gain (see 5.5.5).

Watch out for U.S. gift tax.

The U.S. does have a gift tax, which applies only to those who make very substantial gifts. The *giver* is liable for the tax. Where the giver and recipient are spouses who are both U.S. citizens, no gift tax applies at all. Otherwise, if only the giver is a U.S. citizen, gift tax may apply.

Up to US$10,000 may be given tax-free each year to any one donee, and up to $100,000 to a spouse who is not a U.S. citizen. In addition, every U.S. citizen has a cumulative lifetime "unified credit" of $192,800 against gift and estate taxes; this can effectively exempt about $600,000 of gifts (over these $10,000 and $100,000 annual levels) over the course of your lifetime.

Beyond the $10,000 and $100,000 levels, gift tax applies at the same graduated rates as estate tax, ranging from 18% on taxable gifts under $10,000 to 55% on the portion of taxable gifts over $3 million.

The Canadian tax (if any) that applies on a gift is an income tax, while the U.S. tax is not. As a result, no foreign tax credit applies in either system for taxes of the other system. Caution must therefore be exercised if you are giving large gifts. One further problem with gifts is that, for U.S. purposes, your cost base of property will be carried through to the recipient of a gift, whereas on death, any property left to your beneficiaries is treated as acquired by them at its fair market value.

You must also watch out for the Canadian attribution rules, as outlined in Chapter 4.

The Canada-U.S. tax treaty does not provide any relief for U.S. gift tax, although you can elect to have a deemed disposition for U.S. purposes in order to match income recognition in the U.S. and Canada.

As discussed below in 16.8.3, U.S. recipients of gifts must also report gifts over $10,000.

16.8.3   New U.S. reporting rules for gifts and foreign trusts

If you are a U.S. citizen and you transfer money or property to a foreign trust, or you receive a distribution from one, you must report the transfer to the IRS. For transfers after August 20, 1996, the level of information that you must report has been greatly expanded and the penalties for not doing so are much higher. The penalty for not complying with these new reporting rules is 35% of the gross value of the money or property transferred, and additional penalties for continued failure can run up to 100% of the transferred amount.

Beware of new U.S. reporting rules for gifts and foreign trusts.

U.S. citizens must also report each gift or bequest received after August 20, 1996 to the IRS if the total of all gifts received in one taxation year is more than $10,000. Penalties for non-compliance are the same as those for transfers to and from foreign trusts.

Technically, Canadian RRSPs are trusts and it is currently unclear if they will be subject to the above proposals. At the time of writing, the treatment of RRSPs in the context of these reporting rules for foreign trusts has not been clarified. If you are a U.S. citizen with an RRSP or other foreign trust, you may wish to seek professional advice about these new reporting obligations.

16.9 References

The following publications can be obtained (in person or by telephone request) from your nearest Revenue Canada District Taxation Office. Forms and guides may also be available from Revenue Canada's Internet site at www.revcan.ca.

Interpretation Bulletin IT-122R2, "United States social security taxes and benefits"

Interpretation Bulletin IT-221R2, "Determination of an individual's residence status"

Interpretation Bulletin IT-270R2, "Foreign tax credit"

Interpretation Bulletin IT-395R, "Foreign tax credit—capital gains and capital losses on foreign property"

Interpretation Bulletin IT-506, "Foreign income taxes as a deduction from income"

Interpretation Bulletin IT-520, "Unused foreign tax credits—carryforward and carryback"

Form T2209, "Calculation of federal foreign tax credits"

Form T2036, "Calculation of provincial foreign tax credit"

Brochure, "Emigrants and Income Tax"

Brochure, "Newcomers to Canada"

The following may be obtained from any office of the Internal Revenue Service, and are generally available at U.S. embassy and consular offices, or from the IRS' Internet site at www.irs.ustreas.gov. Help is also available from the IRS office in Ottawa at (613) 563-1834, fax (613) 230-1376.

Publication 54, "Tax Guide For U.S. Citizens and Resident Aliens Abroad"

Publication 521, "Moving Expenses"

Publication 523, "Tax Information On Selling Your Home"

Publication 514, "Foreign Tax Credit For Individuals"

Form 1040, "U.S. Individual Income Tax Return"

Form 1116, "Computation of Foreign Tax Credit"

Form 2119, "Sale Of Your Home"

Form 2350, "Application For Extension Of Time to File U.S. Income Tax Return"

Form 2555, "Foreign Earned Income"

Form 3520, "Creation of or Transfers to Certain Foreign Trusts"

Form 3520A, "Annual Return of Foreign Trust With U.S. Beneficiaries"

Form 3903, "Moving Expenses"

Form 3903F, "Foreign Moving Expenses"

Form 4868, "Application for Automatic Extension of Time to File U.S. Individual Income Tax Return"

Form 5471, "Information Return With Respect To A Foreign Corporation"

Form 6251, "Alternative Minimum Tax—Individuals"

Form 8833, "Treaty-Based Return Position Disclosure under Section 6114 or 7701(b)"

Form TD F 90-22.1, "Report of Foreign Bank and Financial Accounts"

U.S. residency and ownership of U.S. property

- If you own rental real estate in the U.S., elect the net rental income method (17.1.1)
- Sell real estate to a buyer who will occupy it as a principal residence (17.2.1)
- Apply for a U.S. "withholding certificate" on sale of real estate (17.2.1)
- Avoid becoming a U.S. resident while visiting (17.3)
- Apply for Canadian income and U.S. estate tax refunds for individuals who died after November 10, 1988 (17.4)
- Be cautious when acquiring shares in U.S. corporations (17.4.1)
- Leave property to your spouse or a qualified domestic trust (17.4.1)
- Mortgage property (non-recourse) to reduce the value of your U.S. real estate (17.4.1)
- Acquire property jointly with your spouse or other person (17.4.1)
- Consider a split interest purchase with your child (17.4.1)
- Hold your U.S. property through a Canadian corporation (17.4.1)
- Acquire U.S. property through an irrevocable Canadian trust (17.4.1)
- Sell U.S. property before death (17.4.1)
- Be cautious about keeping artwork and other assets in the U.S. (17.4.3)
- Split your worldwide assets with your spouse (17.4.3)
- Keep the value of your worldwide estate below $1.2 million (17.4.5)
- Consider taking out life insurance to cover U.S. estate taxes (17.4.7)

In this chapter we discuss the United States taxes that apply to Canadian residents who are **not** U.S. citizens and who acquire U.S. investments such as stocks and real estate. (Taxation of U.S. citizens resident in Canada was covered in Chapter 16.) Such investments are taxed in three ways: on the income they generate; on their sale; and on death of the owner. We also discuss the "snowbird" rules that can make you resident in the U.S. for tax purposes.

In general, the interaction between the U.S. and Canadian tax systems can be highly complex. Transactions in U.S. real estate should not be undertaken without qualified professional tax advice.

17.1 Income from U.S. properties

Certain U.S.-source income is subject to U.S. tax even if you are not resident in the U.S.

17.1.1 Rent from real estate

A withholding tax of 30% normally applies to the gross amount of any rent paid to a resident of Canada on real estate located in the United States. (Unlike withholding taxes on interest and dividends, this tax is not reduced by the Canada-U.S. tax treaty.)

> Example:
> You live in Canada and own a condominium in Texas. You rent out the condominium for the entire year, receiving US$10,000 in rent. Your mortgage interest, maintenance costs, property taxes and depreciation total US$8,000.
>
> Over the course of the year, 30% of the rent paid to you, or US$3,000, should be withheld by your tenant and remitted to the IRS.

At the end of the year, you may elect to file a U.S. tax return and to pay U.S. tax on your net rental income. In the example above, your net rental income would be only US$2,000 rather than US$10,000. You can then receive a refund for the withholding tax, to the extent it exceeds the tax payable on your U.S. return. However, note that state tax (and possibly a small amount of city tax) will be payable on the rental income.

Elect the net rental income method.

If your expenses are significant (mortgage interest, maintenance, insurance, property management, property taxes, etc.), you will almost always want to elect the "net rental income" method. The amount subject to tax at your marginal rate will be substantially lower than the amount subject to 30% withholding.

Once you've elected to file on a net basis, the election is permanent and you will be taxed on the net basis in future years. If you make the election, it applies to all of your rental real estate. Make sure you take into account the fact that the election can only be revoked in limited circumstances.

If you make the election, you can provide Form 4224 (see 17.5) to your tenant, and 30% of the rent will not need to be withheld.

Depreciation must be claimed for U.S. income tax purposes. Unlike Canada's capital cost allowance system (see 8.2.7), depreciation is not a discretionary deduction in the U.S. Any allowable amount that you don't claim will reduce the property's cost base and increase the gain on its disposition.

If you wish to file on a net basis, the IRS sets a deadline by which you must file. For the 1997 year, your return must normally be filed by October 15, 1999, or you will not be able to claim any deductions and tax will be assessed on the gross income. This rule applies not only to real estate rent, but to any U.S.-source income against which you may wish to claim deductions, such as partnership income.

17.1.2 Dividends and interest from U.S. corporations

Like rental payments, payments of dividends and interest by U.S. corporations to residents of Canada are subject to U.S. withholding tax. The Canada-U.S. tax treaty limits the tax to **15%** for dividends and **10%** for interest in most cases. Certain interest may qualify for a "portfolio debt" exemption from U.S. tax.

You do not file a U.S. income tax return in respect of dividend and interest income on which the correct tax is withheld.

17.2 Sale of U.S. properties

17.2.1 Withholding tax ("FIRPTA") on sale of real estate

If you sell real estate located in the U.S., a withholding tax of **10%** of the sale price is normally payable under "**FIRPTA**" (the Foreign Investment in Real Property Tax Act of 1980). The tax withheld can be offset against the U.S. income tax payable on any gain you realize on the sale, and refunded if it exceeds your U.S. tax liability.

Sell real estate to a buyer who will occupy it as a principal residence.

If you are selling U.S. real estate for less than US$300,000, selling it to a buyer who intends to occupy it as a residence can be advantageous. Withholding under FIRPTA will not apply if the property is sold for less than US$300,000 and the purchaser intends to use it as a residence. For this exception to apply, the purchaser must have definite plans to reside at the property for at least half of the time that the property is in use during each of the two years following the sale. The purchaser does not have to be a U.S. citizen.

Bear in mind that the gain on the sale will still be taxable in the U.S. A U.S. tax return must be filed for every disposition of U.S. real property. Also make sure to take into account any state withholding tax rules.

Apply for a U.S. "withholding certificate" on the sale of real estate.

Another way of reducing the FIRPTA withholding is to apply to the IRS before the sale for a "withholding certificate" on the basis that your expected U.S. tax liability will be less than 10% of the sale price. The certificate will indicate what amount of tax should be withheld by the purchaser rather than the full 10%.

Be sure to apply for a "withholding certificate" if you are making an instalment sale—otherwise, the 10% withholding will be required on the entire sale price up front.

Some states have state withholding tax provisions that parallel FIRPTA.

17.2.2 Income tax on the sale of U.S. real estate

For income tax purposes, you must file a U.S. tax return to report the gain on the sale of U.S. real estate. You can then claim a credit for the FIRPTA tax withheld. Unlike Canada, the U.S. currently provides no reduced taxation for capital gains. However, the maximum U.S. tax rate on capital gains of 28% is lower than the effective high Canadian rate of about 37% (see 5.2). At the time of writing, the U.S. has proposed to reduce the capital gains tax rate to 50% of the rate otherwise payable. If enacted, the reduced rate will apply to gains recognized after May 7, 1997.

If you have owned the property and have been resident in Canada since before September 27, 1980 and used it only for personal use, you can likely take advantage of the Canada-U.S. tax treaty (see 16.2.3) to reduce your gain. In such a case, only your gain accruing since January 1, 1985 will be taxed.

Example:

You bought a cottage in the U.S. for personal use in 1976 for US$10,000. On January 1, 1985 it was worth US$30,000. In 1997, you sell the cottage for US$60,000.

The U.S. will tax only your gain of US$30,000, being the increase in value of the property since the beginning of 1985. State income tax may be based on a gain of either US$30,000 or US$50,000, depending on whether the state adheres to the Canada-U.S. tax treaty.

If you cannot establish a January 1, 1985 valuation, the gain accrued to that date is determined by assuming that the entire gain accrued equally over each month in the holding period.

The above rules also apply to certain rental properties. The Canadian tax will still be based on your entire gain.

To claim the benefit under the treaty, you will need to make the claim on your U.S. return and include a statement containing certain specific information about the transaction.

U.S. tax on the sale of U.S. property will generate a foreign tax credit that can be used to reduce the Canadian tax on the sale. (See 16.2.2 for an explanation of the operation of foreign tax credits.) However, if the amount of the gain taxed in Canada was reduced due to the capital gains exemption (see 5.4) or the principal residence exemption (see 5.5.2), the foreign tax credit available to you may be reduced.

17.2.3 Sales of U.S. stocks and bonds

As long as you are not a resident or citizen of the U.S., U.S. tax will normally not apply to sales of shares in U.S. corporations, whether public or private and no matter where they are traded.

However, if the majority of the corporation's assets are U.S. real estate, the corporation may be considered a "U.S. real property holding corporation" (unless it is a publicly traded company and you own less than 5% of the shares). In such a case, any gain on the sale of the shares of the corporation will be taxed by the U.S. in a manner similar to sales of real property.

17.3 Snowbirds—U.S. residency rules

Avoid becoming a U.S. resident while visiting.

If you spend a substantial portion of the year in the U.S., you may become a U.S. resident for tax purposes. If this happens you may be required to file U.S. tax returns and pay U.S. tax on your income from *all* sources, including Canada (except to the extent that you can claim foreign tax credits—see 17.2.2). If you accidentally become a U.S. resident for tax purposes, the tax cost can be substantial.

If you hold a "**green card**", you have the status of a U.S. permanent resident and will be considered resident in the U.S. for tax purposes.

If your "physical presence" in the U.S. totals **183 days** or more in the year, you will be deemed a U.S. resident. For this purpose, you must total up the number of days you spend in the U.S. in the current year, **1/3** of the days from the preceding year and **1/6** of the days from the second preceding year.

Example:
Simone spends the winter each year in Miami and the fall, spring and summer in Montréal. For 1995, 1996 and 1997, she is physically in the U.S. for 150, 90 and 140 days respectively.

For 1997, Simone's "physical presence" calculation is 140 + (1/3 × 90) + (1/6 × 150), or 195. Since this figure exceeds 183, she is considered resident in the U.S. for 1997 (subject to the "closer connection" rule described below).

If you are deemed a U.S. resident under the "physical presence" test but the number of days you spend in the U.S. in the *current* year is less than 183, you can be treated as non-resident for purposes of U.S. tax if you can establish that you have a **"closer connection"** to Canada than to the U.S. This information is reported on Form 8840 (see 17.5), which is due by June 15 of the following year.

If your current year's days in the U.S. are 183 or more, or if you hold a green card, you can gain a measure of protection from the Canada-U.S. tax treaty if you can establish that under the treaty you are resident in Canada rather than the U.S. (This protection is not as broad as being treated as non-resident under the "closer connection" rule above, however.) For this purpose you would need to show that you have a permanent home in Canada and not in the U.S.; or, if you have a permanent home in both countries or neither, that your personal and economic relations are closer to Canada. You will have to file information with the IRS within certain time limits to be entitled to this treaty "tie-breaker" protection.

17.4 U.S. estate taxes on death and the Canada-U.S. tax treaty

U.S. estate taxes can impose a very serious burden on the death of Canadians who own U.S. stocks and real estate. We shall discuss federal estate taxes only; many states also have estate taxes, and these must be considered as well.

The Protocol (amendment) to the Canada-U.S. tax treaty ratified on November 9, 1995 may reduce and, in some cases, eliminate the double tax exposure faced by Canadians who die owning U.S. property. However, if your net worth is high and your U.S. property has not increased significantly in value, you may be no better off than you were before the Protocol.

Apply for tax refunds for individuals who died after November 10, 1988.

The Protocol applies retroactively to deaths occurring after November 10, 1988. As a result, tax refunds are available for U.S. estate tax and Canadian taxes paid on deaths that have occurred since that date, as long as the claim is filed before the statute of limitations period has expired (for U.S. returns, the period is usually three years from the later of the return's due date or the date it was filed; for Canadian returns, the period is generally three years from the return's assessment date).

Determination of property subject to estate tax

U.S. estate tax applies to the deceased's "**property situated within the United States**". This includes:

- real property located in the U.S.
- certain tangible personal property located in the U.S.
- shares of U.S. corporations, regardless of the location of the share certificates and regardless of where the shares are traded
- debts of U.S. persons, including the U.S. government (such as U.S. Government Savings Bonds)
- interests in partnerships carrying on business in the U.S. (although this is not free from doubt).

Assets normally excluded from the definition include: shares of a non-U.S. corporation, regardless of where the corporation's assets are situated; U.S. bank deposits; certain U.S. corporate bonds that are publicly traded outside the U.S.; certain debt obligations that qualify for the "portfolio debt" exemption from U.S. tax; and life insurance proceeds payable on a non-resident alien's death.

Be cautious when acquiring shares in U.S. corporations.

Note that if you buy shares of U.S. corporations, whether in the U.S. or on a Canadian stock exchange, those shares form part of your taxable estate for U.S. estate tax purposes.

The "**taxable estate**" for estate tax purposes is the gross value of all of the deceased's property situated in the U.S., minus certain allowable deductions. The most significant deductions are:

- amounts left to the deceased's spouse if the spouse is a U.S. citizen (and will therefore be subject to U.S. estate tax on death)
- amounts transferred to a "qualified domestic trust" (a trust which meets certain requirements, as set out below)
- a deduction for a non-recourse mortgage (see below) encumbering U.S. property
- a deduction for an allocable share of the deceased's liabilities at time of death in respect of which the estate becomes liable—including Canadian income taxes payable.

To calculate and claim the allocable share of liabilities, the estate tax return must disclose the deceased's worldwide assets and liabilities.

Leave property to your spouse or a "qualified domestic trust".

Where property is left to a surviving spouse who is a U.S. citizen, or to a qualified domestic trust ("QDOT"), the estate tax can be deferred until the death of the surviving spouse.

To qualify as a QDOT, the trust instrument must provide that at least one trustee be a U.S. citizen or U.S. corporation, and that no distribution of capital may be made from the trust without the U.S. trustee being able to withhold U.S. estate tax. Any capital paid out of a QDOT will then become subject to estate tax. More stringent rules apply to QDOTs with assets exceeding US$2 million in value.

A QDOT will have the effect of capping the estate tax liability if appreciating assets are sold shortly after death and invested in U.S. fixed-income securities. The income may then be paid out to the surviving spouse and taxed on an ongoing basis, but the amount of estate tax pending will not increase beyond the fixed value of the QDOT's assets.

A properly structured QDOT may qualify as a "spousal trust" for Canadian tax purposes (see 13.3.2).

Mortgage property (non-recourse) to reduce the value of your U.S. real estate.

A "non-recourse" mortgage is one that entitles the lender to have recourse only against the property mortgaged. That is, if you default on payment, the mortgagee can seize the mortgaged property, but cannot come after you for the balance if the property is not worth enough to pay off the debt. A non-recourse mortgage outstanding on your U.S. real estate will reduce your equity in the property, and thus reduce the value of your taxable estate.

Consider taking out a substantial non-recourse mortgage on your U.S. property, even where it is already fully paid off.

Example:
You are not married and you own a condominium in Florida, now worth US$200,000 and clear of all mortgages. Your worldwide assets are substantial. If you die, the U.S. estate tax will come to US$41,800.

Assume you borrow US$100,000 against the property at 11%, on a non-recourse basis, and invest the funds in Canada at 10%. Subject to currency fluctuations, your annual cost will be approximately US$1,000. If you die after taking out this mortgage, your taxable estate will be only US$100,000, and the estate tax will be US$10,800—a US$31,000 saving.

The mortgage should be obtained from a lender resident in Canada (however, Canadian financial institutions generally are reluctant to lend on a non-recourse basis, so you will have to seek out other sources). Canadian withholding tax (usually 10%) will apply to the interest payments you make to a non-resident lender if you are deducting the interest paid for Canadian tax purposes. In Canada, your interest expense will normally be denied to the extent it exceeds the investment income you earn from investing the loan proceeds. This has the effect of reducing the hoped-for estate tax savings.

Over time, the property's value may increase and the mortgage amount will decrease. Because of this, the potential U.S. estate tax will increase as time goes by.

Acquire property jointly with your spouse or another person.

Another way you can reduce your estate tax exposure is by acquiring U.S. assets jointly with your spouse (or another person). For this to work, you and your spouse will each have to supply your own funds; you cannot simply give half of the interest in the property to your spouse, or give your spouse the funds to invest.

If you have each invested your own funds and you and your spouse jointly own a condominium worth US$200,000, for example, only US$100,000 of that value will form part of your estate on your death.

Consider a split interest purchase with your child.

In some situations, it may be beneficial for U.S. estate tax purposes for you to split your interest in an asset with your child. In this strategy, you would acquire a life interest in the property and your child would acquire a remainder interest with his or her own funds. The rules in this area are extremely complex—if you want to pursue this strategy, professional advice is a must.

Hold your U.S. property through a Canadian corporation.

An obvious solution to U.S. estate tax is to hold any U.S. stocks and real estate in a Canadian corporation rather than personally. When you die, your corporation does not, and no U.S. estate tax applies. You have effectively converted the "location" of your assets from the U.S. to Canada. While this solution is often useful, it is fraught with pitfalls, and qualified professional advice should be obtained. Revenue Canada is currently reviewing its administrative position in this area, so be sure to check on the status of this review before you adopt this technique. Some possible problems that should be addressed include:

- Beyond the initial setup costs, there are ongoing costs to maintaining a corporation, including legal and accounting fees, and capital taxes in some Canadian provinces.

- The acquisition of the U.S. assets by the corporation must be legally complete, and all corporate formalities must be observed. If it is determined that the corporation was only acting as an agent or mere title holder for you, estate tax can still apply to the property on your death.

- Any income earned by the corporation on its U.S. assets (such as interest, dividends, rent) will be subject to tax both when originally earned and when paid out to you in the form of dividends. The combined effect of the taxes may be higher than the tax you would pay if you held the assets directly.

- If the property is U.S. real estate that you already own personally, any accrued gain will normally be taxed by the U.S. when you transfer the property to the corporation. (As noted in 17.2.2, the tax can be reduced where you have owned the property since before September 27, 1980.) This suggests that the corporation route may only be useful for future acquisitions of U.S. real estate, and not for transfers of existing holdings.

- If the property is a personal use property, the accrued gains will generally be taxable in Canada at the time of its transfer to the corporation.

- If you or members of your family will be using the property for personal purposes (e.g., a vacation property which you occupy for a few weeks each year), you may be taxed in Canada as having received a shareholder benefit from the corporation.

Acquire U.S. property through an irrevocable Canadian trust.

It may be possible to acquire your U.S. property through a trust that is resident in Canada, thus removing the property from the ambit of U.S. estate tax. Extreme care must, however, be exercised in drafting the trust document, selecting the trustees, and setting out the powers of the trustees and the beneficiaries.

Sell U.S. property before death.

If you sell your U.S. assets (say, to a family member) before your death, and receive in exchange assets that are not "located in the U.S." (e.g., cash or a promissory note situated in Canada), you will have no U.S. assets left to form a taxable estate.

This step may be useful when death is anticipated within a short time period. For example, property could be sold to a child to whom you intend to leave the property anyway, in exchange for a bona fide promissory note. The note might then be left to your spouse or to another family member. If the note were left to the child, the sale may be treated as a gift and subject to U.S. gift tax.

On such a sale, U.S. and Canadian income tax will apply to any gain (the Canadian tax applying to three-quarters of the capital gain (see 5.2). A foreign tax credit will normally be available in Canada to offset part or all of the U.S. tax paid. The U.S. instalment sale rules (see 16.4.4) may apply where you take back a promissory note rather than cash.

Be aware of the possible application of the Canadian attribution rules (see Chapter 4) where you have transferred property to your spouse or to a family member who is under 18. Also, make sure you do not take back debt (such as a promissory note) from someone resident in the United States, since certain debts of U.S. residents are considered to be property located in the U.S. Before undertaking any transaction, be sure to compare the tax consequences that will arise on death to the tax consequences that will arise on a transfer before death.

17.4.2 U.S. federal estate tax rates

Once the "taxable estate" has been determined, U.S. federal estate tax applies at 16 graduated rates ranging from 18% on the first US$10,000 to 55% on any amount over $3 million. A "unified credit" will then reduce this tax, as we shall see below.

Some examples of the U.S. federal estate tax payable at the graduated rates (all figures in U.S. dollars) are shown below:

Taxable Estate	Tax (before credit)
$10,000	$1,800
$50,000	$10,600
$100,000	$23,800
$200,000	$54,800
$500,000	$155,800
$1,000,000	$345,800

17.4.3 Enhanced unified credit

Under U.S. domestic law, non-residents of the U.S. who are not U.S. citizens can apply a "unified credit" of US$13,000 against the estate tax. This credit effectively exempts US$60,000 of the estate from taxation. The estate will also be liable for state death taxes, but will receive a credit against federal estate tax for such state taxes. Most states limit their death taxes to the amount of this credit, so the total combined amount of tax is not increased by the application of state tax.

The Canada-U.S. tax treaty increases the U.S. unified credit for residents and citizens of Canada from the US$13,000 allowed under U.S. law to US$192,800. This credit must, however, be prorated by the value of the Canadian deceased's U.S. estate over the value of the deceased individual's worldwide estate (as determined under U.S. rules).

The proration of the credit means that Canadians will not be subject to U.S. estate tax unless the value of their worldwide gross estate exceeds **US$600,000**. It also means that wealthy Canadians who hold a relatively small proportion of their total estate in the United States may not be in a much better position than they were prior to the treaty Protocol. These Canadians may, therefore, choose to avail themselves of the planning techniques discussed earlier in this chapter.

Example:

Bertram, a Canadian citizen and resident, acquired undeveloped land in Washington state for US$180,000 in 1997. At the time of his death later that year, Bertram's worldwide assets had a fair market value of US$600,000 and the value of the land in Washington was still US$180,000.

If Bertram had died before the Protocol took effect, his U.S. estate tax would have been US$35,400 (U.S. estate tax of US$48,400 on his U.S. property, minus the regular US$13,000 unified credit). However, due to the Protocol's enhanced unified credit of up to US$192,800, Bertram's U.S. estate tax on the value of the Washington property would be zero.

But what if the value of Bertram's worldwide asset was US$1.2 million (instead of US$600,000) at the time of his death? Since the enhanced unified credit must be prorated by the value of Bertram's U.S. estate, his U.S. estate tax credit would be US$28,920 (US$180,000 ÷ US$1,200,000 × US$192,800), and Bertram's U.S. estate tax liability would be US$19,480 (US$48,400 − US$28,920).

Credits previously claimed against U.S. gift tax will also reduce the credit available on death. As well, all information necessary for the computation and verification of the credit must be provided to the U.S. authorities or the credit will be denied.

A deceased Canadian's worldwide estate for purposes of the calculation includes some surprising items that may erode the amount of the credit. The value of life insurance policies may be included if the deceased had the right to change beneficiaries at the time of death. This may be the case even though the deceased was not a named beneficiary under the policy. Similarly, the shares of a family holding corporation that are owned by a family trust (see 13.3.4) may be included if the deceased is the trustee (and regardless of whether the deceased is a beneficiary of the trust).

Be cautious about keeping artwork and other assets in the U.S.

U.S. estate tax could apply to any of your personal assets that are located in the U.S. at the time of your death. U.S. case law has established that the assets must be located in the U.S. with a degree of permanence, so the tax probably will not apply to jewellery or other items you might take with you on vacation. However, furniture and artwork in your condominium, for example, may be subject U.S. estate tax.

If you own U.S. real estate, the enhanced unified credit may not wipe out all of your estate tax. In such a case, any personal assets could be subject to estate tax. You may wish to limit the value of the personal assets such as artwork which you keep in the U.S.

Split your worldwide assets with your spouse.

If your spouse has no assets or assets of minor value, consider having your spouse acquire ownership of one or more of your U.S. assets, such as a vacation property, worth up to the US$600,000 exemption amount. Seek professional tax advice before doing so, however, since the transfer could trigger the attribution rules and/or liability for U.S. property purchase tax.

17.4.4 Marital credit

An additional "**marital credit**" will be available if an estate tax marital deduction would have been available had the surviving spouse been a U.S. citizen. However, this credit will be capped at the lesser of the unified credit allowed to the deceased's estate and the U.S. estate tax payable after other credits. This effectively allows a minimum $26,000 credit (i.e., 2 × $13,000) where U.S. property is transferred to a spouse on death. Since this provision was introduced in the Protocol (see 17.4), the estates of wealthy individuals who after died November 10, 1988 may be entitled to an estate tax refund if U.S. property was transferred to a spouse on death.

The executor of the estate must elect to take advantage of this provision and must irrevocably waive the benefit of any estate tax marital deduction which may have been allowable. The deadline for the election and waiver is the date on which a qualified domestic trust election (see 17.4.1) could be made under U.S. law (usually nine months after the date of death).

Special rules for smaller estates

Keep the value of your worldwide estate below $1.2 million.

If the value at death of the worldwide estate of a Canadian resident individual (other than a U.S. citizen) is less than US$1.2 million (determined under U.S. rules), the Protocol narrows the range of U.S. assets on which estate tax may be levied to properties the gain on the sale of which would have been subject to U.S. income tax under the treaty.

As we saw in 17.4.1, U.S. estate tax normally applies to the deceased's "property situated within the U.S.", including U.S. real estate, certain tangible personal property located in the U.S., shares of U.S. corporations (regardless of the location of the share certificates and of where the shares are traded), debts of U.S. persons, and interests in partnerships carrying on business in the U.S.

Under the treaty, the U.S. may only tax U.S. real estate (including U.S. real property holding corporations) and personal property constituting business property if your worldwide estate is less than US$1.2 million at the time of death. As a result, you'll want to exercise caution if the value of your worldwide estate is close to US$1.2 million.

17.4.6 ## Canadian credit for U.S. estate taxes

On death, Canada will normally tax the accrued capital gains in the deceased's estate (see 13.1.2). A foreign tax credit is available in Canada to offset foreign income taxes paid on foreign-source income. However, U.S. estate taxes are not income taxes. As a result, no foreign tax credit is available under Canadian domestic law to offset taxes on death.

Under the Protocol, Canada now permits U.S. estate tax to be deducted from a Canadian resident's Canadian tax otherwise payable for the year of death. The credit will, however, be limited to the Canadian tax attributable to the deceased's U.S.-source income for the year.

Example:

Emmet, an unmarried Canadian citizen and resident, died owning U.S. stocks with a fair market value of US$1 million. His other assets were all situated in Canada. If Emmet's worldwide estate was worth US$1,199,000 at the time of his death, Emmet's U.S. estate tax liability would be zero.

However, if Emmet's worldwide estate was worth US $1,201,000 at the time of his death, his U.S. estate tax credit would be US$160,533 (US$1,000,000 ÷ US$1,201,000 × US$192,800), which would reduce his U.S. estate tax liability of US$345,800 on his US$1 million U.S. estate to US$185,267.

In order for Emmet's estate to use the entire U.S. estate tax amount as a foreign tax credit for Canadian tax purposes, the deemed gain on the shares at Emmet's death would have to be at least US$494,045— the amount of capital gain that would attract US$185,267 of Canadian tax (US$514,631 × 3/4 × 50% rate of tax).

17.4.7   Life insurance

Consider taking out life insurance to cover U.S. estate taxes.

If you anticipate that substantial estate tax will apply on your death, consider taking out life insurance as a way of funding the payment of the tax without requiring the sale of your U.S. assets. Life insurance proceeds will not form part of your estate on death, even if provided by a U.S. insurer (although they will be included in your worldwide assets for purposes of determining the "unified credit" discussed in 17.4.3). Bear in mind that premiums paid on a life insurance policy are not deductible for either Canadian or U.S. income tax purposes. Also, if the policy is with a U.S. insurer, have your professional advisor review the Canadian income tax implications of holding the policy.

17.5   References

Revenue Canada publishes a booklet titled "Canadian Residents Going Down South", available (in person or by phone) from any District Taxation Office or via the Internet at www.revcan.ca. Written jointly with the IRS, it includes information on U.S. tax laws.

The following publications may be obtained by telephoning or writing to any office of the Internal Revenue Service (IRS). They may also be available at United States embassy and consular offices, or from the IRS' Internet site at www.irs.ustreas.gov.

Form 706NA, "United States Estate (and Generation Skipping Transfer) Tax Return: Estate of nonresident not a citizen of the United States"

Form 1040NR, "U.S. Nonresident Alien Income Tax Return"

Form 4224, "Exemption from Withholding of Tax on Income Effectively Connected with the Conduct of a Trade or Business in the United States"

Form 8288-B, "Application for Withholding Certificate for Dispositions by Foreign Persons of U.S. Real Property Interests"

Form 8840, "Closer Connection Statement"

Publication 515, "Withholding of Tax on Nonresident Aliens and Foreign Corporations"

Publication 519, "U.S. Tax Guide for Aliens"

Assistance and advice on completing U.S. tax returns can be obtained from the Internal Revenue Service in Ottawa at (613) 563-1834, fax (613) 230-1376.

Appendix I
1997 Personal Tax Credits — Federal

	Value of Credit
Credits expressed as amounts	
Basic	$1,098
Married/Equivalent-to-spouse	915[1,2]
Income limit	538
Dependent child 18 or over and infirm	400[1,3]
Income limit	4,103
Education amount	
For each month	26[4,5,6]
Maximum transfer (education and tuition)	850
Person 65 or over	592[4,7]
Disability	720[4,5]
Credits expressed as percentages	
Employment insurance	17%
Pension income (maximum)	17%[4,8]
Canada/Québec Pension Plan	17%
Tuition fees	17%[4,5,9]
Charitable donations	
On the first $200	17%[10]
On the remainder	29%
Medical expense	17%[11]

---

[1] The credit will be reduced by 17% of net income in excess of the income limit.

[2] Eligible dependants for the equivalent-to-spouse credit are dependants under age 18 related to the taxpayer, or the taxpayer's parents/grandparents, or any other person who is related to the taxpayer and is infirm.

[3] The credit is reduced by any amount claimed in respect of this person for the equivalent-to-spouse credit.

[4] This tax credit is transferable to a spouse. To determine the amount available for transfer, the credits claimed for age, disability, tuition, education and pension are totalled and then reduced by 17% of the transferor's taxable income for federal tax purposes in excess of $6,456.

[5] This tax credit is transferable to a supporting parent or grandparent. The credit available for transfer is reduced by 17% of the transferor's taxable income in excess of $6,456.

[6] Calculated as a percentage of $150 for every month a full-time student attends a designated educational institution.

[7] The federal age amount ($3,482) used to determine the credit is reduced by an amount equal to 15% of a taxpayer's net income in excess of $25,921.

[8] Calculated as a percentage of eligible pension income, to a maximum of $1,000 of pension income.

[9] Calculated as a percentage of tuition paid in the calendar year (a receipt for at least $100 is required).

[10] For 1997 and later years, the maximum amount of donations that you can claim in a year is limited to 75% of net income. In the year of death and the preceding year, the limit is 100% of net income.

[11] Rate applied to qualifying medical expenses in excess of the lesser of 3% of net income or $1,614.

1997 Personal Tax Credits — Québec

Credits expressed as amounts	Value of Credit
Basic	$1,180
Person living alone	210[1]
Spousal	1,180[2]
Dependent child	
18 or under	520[2,3]
18 or over and full-time student	520[2,3]
18 or over and infirm	1,180[2]
Other dependants	
18 and over	480[2]
18 or over and infirm	1,180[2]
Post-secondary student	660[2,4]
Person 65 or over	440[1,5,6]
Disability	440[6]

Credits expressed as percentages	
Employment insurance	20%
Pension income (maximum)	20%
Canada/Québec Pension Plan	20%
Tuition fees	20%[7]
Charitable donations	20%[8]
Medical expenses	20%[9]

---

[1] For 1997, the credit will be reduced by 15% of Québec net income in excess of $26,000.

[2] The tax credit is reduced by 20% of the individual's net income.

[3] For the second and each subsequent child, the tax credit is decreased to $480. For single-parent families an additional tax credit of $260 is allowed for the first child.

[4] The tax credit is $330 per term, limited to two terms per year, and can only be claimed by a supporting person.

[5] This tax credit will not be affected by the taxpayer's employment and business income.

[6] This tax credit is transferable to a spouse. The credit available for transfer is reduced by 20% of the transferor's taxable income for Québec tax purposes in excess of $5,900 .

[7] The new Québec credit for tuition fees may only be claimed by the student (before 1997, tuition fees were a deduction for Québec tax purposes).

[8] The maximum amount of donations that you can claim in a year is limited to 20% of Québec net income.

[9] For 1997 and later years, medical expenses that are allowable for purposes of the credit are reduced by 3% of the combined Québec net income of both spouses.

Appendix II
1997 Federal Income Tax Rates

If Taxable Income is:

Over—	But not over—	The tax is:	Of the amount over—
$ 0	$ 29,590	$ 0 + 17%	$ 0
29,590	59,180	5,030 + 26%	29,590
59,180	—	12,724 + 29%	59,180

Federal Surtax

A surtax of 3% of federal tax is levied after taking into account any applicable credits. Where basic federal tax, after deducting any applicable credits and before adding the 3% surtax, exceeds $12,500, an additional surtax of 5% of the basic federal tax in excess of $12,500 is applicable.

1997 Provincial Income Tax Rates

	Percentage of Federal Tax		Percentage of Federal Tax
British Columbia	51.0%[1]	New Brunswick	63.0%[7]
Alberta	45.5%[2]	Nova Scotia	58.5%[8]
Saskatchewan	50.0%[3]	Prince Edward Island	59.5%[9]
Manitoba	52.0%[4]	Northwest Territories	45.0%
Ontario	48.0%[5]	Yukon	50.0%[10]
Québec	N/A[6]	Non-resident	52.0%
Newfoundland	69.0%		

[1] A surtax of 30% applies to B.C. tax in excess of $5,300 plus an additional surtax of 24.5% applies to B.C. tax in excess of $8,745.

[2] A surtax of 8% of basic Alberta tax in excess of $3,500 and a flat tax rate of 0.5% of Alberta taxable income are also levied.

[3] There is a flat tax of 2% of net income and a surtax of 15% on Saskatchewan tax (including flat tax) in excess of $4,000. A 10% "Deficit Surtax" applies to basic Saskatchewan tax plus the flat tax.

[4] A surtax equal to 2% of net income in excess of $30,000 and a flat tax of 2% of net income are levied in Manitoba.

[5] A surtax (i.e., the Fair Share Health Care Levy) of 20% applies to basic Ontario tax in excess of $4,550 and at a rate of 26% of basic Ontario tax in excess of $6,180.

[6] For Québec tax rate schedule, see Appendix III.

[7] A surtax of 10% applies to New Brunswick tax in excess of $7,900.

[8] A surtax of 10% applies to Nova Scotia tax in excess of $10,000.

[9] A surtax of 10% applies to basic P.E.I. tax in excess of $5,200.

[10] A surtax of 5% applies to basic Yukon tax in excess of $6,000.

Appendix III

1997 Québec Provincial Income Tax Rates*

Taxable Income	Québec Tax	On Next	Marginal Rate
NIL	NIL	$ 7,000	16%
$ 7,000	$ 1,120	7,000	19%
14,000	2,450	9,000	21%
23,000	4,340	27,000	23%
50,000 and over	10,550	remainder	24%

* Tax payable in Québec may be reduced by personal tax credits, any dividend tax credit (11.09% of actual amount of taxable Canadian dividends), foreign tax credits, shares relating to the Fonds de solidarité des travailleurs du Québec or shares relating to the Fondaction and contributions to Québec provincial political parties.

Québec residents and persons carrying on business in Québec receive a reduction of federal taxes equal to 16.5% of basic federal tax.

A surtax of 5% applies to Québec tax in excess of $5,000 plus an additional surtax of 5% applies to Québec tax in excess of $10,000. Starting in 1997, there is a mandatory contribution to the "Fonds de lutte contre la pauvreté par la réinsertion au travail" equal to 0.3% of Québec tax payable.

A tax reduction is available in Québec which is equal to 2% of the excess of $10,000 over Québec taxes payable after deducting non-refundable tax credits. The reduction declines as tax increases, reaching zero at $10,000 of taxes payable.

1997 Combined Federal and Québec Tax Rates[1]

Taxable Income	Combined Federal/Québec Tax[2]
$ 0 – $ 6,456	NIL
6,457 – 8,350	NIL plus 14.8% on excess over $ 6,456
8,351 – 14,000	$ 280 plus 34.1% on excess over 8,350
14,001 – 23,000	2,206 plus 36.2% on excess over 14,000
23,001 – 29,590	5,464 plus 38.3% on excess over 23,000
29,591 – 31,000	7,985 plus 46.0% on excess over 29,590
31,001 – 50,000	8,634 plus 47.2% on excess over 31,000
50,001 – 52,625	17,597 plus 48.2% on excess over 50,000
52,626 – 59,180	18,863 plus 49.0% on excess over 52,625
59,181 – 62,195	22,073 plus 51.5% on excess over 59,180
62,196 and over	23,627 plus 53.1% on excess over 62,195

[1] Assumes a single tax filer.
[2] Assumes a single tax filer with ordinary income who is only entitled to the basic personal credit of $1,098 for federal purposes and to the basic personal credit of $1,180 for Québec purposes. Amounts do not include mandatory contributions to the Québec Health Services Fund.

Index

meals and entertainment
expenses, 241-42
minimum tax, 242
QST credit on income tax return, 237
real estate tax refund, 237
simplified filing system, 230-31
tax holidays, 241
tax rates, 229-30, Appendix III

REA, *see* Québec Stock Savings Plan

RESP, *see* Registered Education
Savings Plan

RHOSP, *see* Registered Home
Ownership Savings Plan (Québec)

RIC, *see* Cooperative Investment
Plan (Québec)

RPP, *see* Registered Pension Plan (RPP)

RRIF, *see* Registered Retirement
Income Fund (RRIF)

RRSP, *see* Registered Retirement
Savings Plan (RRSP)

Racehorses, *see* Farming

Rates of tax, Appendices II, III

Real estate
investments, as tax shelter, 118
U.S.
rent from, 276-77
sale of, 277-78

Reasonable expectation of profit,
159, 175-76

Reassessment, 224
opening up return for other
claims, 225-26
time limit, 224
waiver of time limit, 224-25

Rebates of GST, *see* Goods and Services
Tax (GST): rebates

Recreational facilities provided by
employer, 124

Recreational vehicle, capital cost
allowance restrictions, 117

Reference information, *see* end of
each chapter
Refund of tax
"Direct Deposit" of, 221
interest on, 221-22
real estate tax (Québec), 237
why not good planning, 126

Registered Education Savings Plan,
10-11, 67-68

Registered Home Ownership Savings
Plan (Québec), 237-38

Registered Pension Plan (RPP), 63-65
contributions by employer non-
taxable, 123
Individual Pension Plan (IPP), 65-66
small business owners, for, 172-73
transfer to RRIF, 64
U.S. taxation of, 256-57
vesting of benefits, 64-65

Registered Retirement Income Fund
(RRIF), 53-54

Registered Retirement Savings Plan
(RRSP)
age limit, 52-53
borrowing contribution funds, 16
closing out, 52-56
contribution limits, 44-47
death of planholder, 57-58
early withdrawals, 55-56
"earned income", 44-45
getting money out of, 52-56
Home Buyer's Plan, 13, 59-63
locked-in, 57
overcontribution to, 58-59
pension adjustment (PA), 45-46
pension adjustment reversal
(PAR), 46-47
planning tips, 51-52
retiring allowance, transfer to,
57, 134
savings from, 48
self-directed, 49-51
setting up, 44
spousal, 56-57

Shares
  capital gains exemption on, 91-93
  dividends on, *see* Dividends
  donation to charity, 209-10
  flow-through, 116-17, 246-47
  preferred, 107
  small business corporation,
    91-93, 164
Shelters, *see* Tax shelters
Shows, limitation on expense, 154,
  241-42
Simplified filing system (Québec),
  230-31
Singer, *see* Artist
Small business corporation
  allowable business investment loss
    on, 90-91, 93
  capital gains exemption on, 91-93
  Cumulative Net Investment Loss
    (CNIL), 93-94
  meaning of, 90
  pension plan for owners, 172
  qualified, 91-92
Snowbirds, 279-80
Source withholdings
  credited on tax return, 219
  RRSP withdrawal, 53, 55
  reduction of, 126
  where required, 219
Sports event, limitation on expense,
  154, 241
Spousal RRSP, 56-57, 80-81, 193-
  94, 199
Spouse
  attribution rules, 72-73
  consulting fees to, 77, 170
  common-law, 22-23
  credit for, 22-23
  gift to, 72-73
  joint return (U.S.), 267
  loan to, 72-73, 78
  marital credit (U.S.), 287
  partnership with, 77

paying taxes for, 76
qualified domestic trust (U.S.), 282
RRSP for, 56-57, 80-81, 193-94, 199
salary to, 77, 170
separation from, 29
transfer of property to, 101
transfer of dividends, 108
trust for, 195, 200
Stock dividend, 107
Stock option plans, 128-30
Stock purchase plan, 130
Straddles, 117
Streamlined accounting (GST), 150-51
Stub period business income for
  1995, 146, 187
Stripped bonds, 50, 110
Students
  child care expenses, 24
  credit for, 25-26
  moving expenses, 37
  Québec, 234
Succession of business, planning for, 212
Superficial loss, 101-102
Supplies
  payable by employee,
    deductible, 138
Support payments, 29-32
  child support from U.S. resident, 254
Supreme Court of Canada, appeal to, 227
Surtax, 20

Tax avoidance, *see* Anti-avoidance rules
Tax convention, *see* Canada-U.S. tax
  treaty
Tax Court of Canada, appeal to, 226
Tax credits, *see* Credits
Tax deferral plans, Chapter 3
Tax rates, Appendices II, III
Tax return
  filing deadline, 217-18
  tips, Chapter 2
  U.S., 267-68